WAR DEPARTMENT.

REPORT

OF A

RECONNAISSANCE

FROM

CARROLL, MONTANA TERRITORY, ON THE UPPER MISSOURI,

TO THE

YELLOWSTONE NATIONAL PARK, AND RETURN,

MADE IN

THE SUMMER OF 1875,

BY

WILLIAM LUDLOW,
CAPTAIN OF ENGINEERS, BREVET LIEUTENANT-COLONEL, U. S. ARMY,
CHIEF ENGINEER DEPARTMENT OF DAKOTA.

WASHINGTON:
GOVERNMENT PRINTING OFFICE.
1876.

CONTENTS.

	Page.
Letters of transmittal	5
General report	7
Orders	10
Composition of the party and instruments employed	10
Saint Paul to Carroll via Northern Pacific Railroad and Missouri River	10
Carroll to Camp Baker, Montana, via Carroll Road	13
Judith Basin	14
Camp Baker to Fort Ellis, Montana, via Bridger Pass	15
Fort Ellis to the National Park	17
Mammoth Hot Springs	18
Yellowstone Falls	21
Yellowstone Lake	24
The Geysers	25
Upper Geyser Basin	26
Return to Ellis	29
Ellis to Carroll	31
Trip to the Little Rocky Mountains	33
Return to Saint Paul	35
Remarks and recommendations with reference to the Yellowstone Park	35
Legal enactments establishing the park	37
Astronomical observations for time and latitude at Carroll, Camp Lewis, and Camp Baker	38
Summary table of daily instrumental observations, with deduced altitudes, latitude, and longitude of each camp, and of the Montana posts, distances traveled, &c	52
Table of Missouri River distances from Benton to Bismarck, from survey by Lieut. F. V. Greene, United States Engineers, under direction of Capt. William J. Twining, Corps of Engineers	53
Report of Lieut. R. E. Thompson, Sixth Infantry, United States Army	55
Trip to the Judith Basin	55
Trip from Carroll to Ellis, via Yellowstone River	56
Zoölogical report, by George Bird Grinnell	59
Chapter I—Mammals	63
Chapter II—Birds	72
Partial list of mammals and birds	90
Geological report, by Edward S. Dana and George Bird Grinnell	93
Preliminary remarks on the alluvial deposits of the Upper Missouri River	97
From Carroll to Box Elder Creek	99
Judith Mountains	103
From Box Elder to Camp Lewis	107
Camp Lewis to the Judith Gap	109
Snow Mountains	109
Little Belt Mountains	110
Judith Gap to the Musselshell Cañon	111
Musselshell Cañon to Camp Baker	113
Camp Baker	115
Camp Baker to Fort Ellis	117
Bridger Mountains	118
From the Bridger Mountains to the Forks of the Mussellshell	121
From Armells Creek to the mouth of the Judith	124
Little Rocky Mountains	127
The Geysers of the Yellowstone Park	130
General conclusions	132
Distribution of formations	132
Period of mountain-elevation	137
Description of new fossils, by R. P. Whitfield	139

MAPS AND ILLUSTRATIONS.

General map of the reconnaissance, scale 1 inch=12 miles; at end of volume.

Map of the Judith Basin, scale 1 inch=6 miles; to face	14
Map of the Upper Geyser Basin, scale 1 inch=500 feet; to face	26

Two plates of new species of fossils; at end of descriptions of new fossils.

LETTERS OF TRANSMITTAL.

OFFICE OF THE CHIEF OF ENGINEERS,
Washington, D. C., July 21, 1876.

SIR: Capt. William Ludlow, Corps of Engineers, Chief Engineer Department of Dakota, has submitted to this office a copy of the report of his reconnaissance from Carroll, Montana Territory, on the Upper Missouri, to the Yellowstone National Park, and return, made in the summer of 1875. It embraces the reports of reconnaissances by Lieut. R. E. Thompson, Sixth Infantry, and scientific reports by Messrs. George Bird Grinnell, Edward S. Dana, and R. P. Whitfield.

I have respectfully to recommend that the report be printed at the Government Printing-Office, and that 1,500 copies be furnished on the usual requisition.

Very respectfully, your obedient servant,

A. A. HUMPHREYS,
Brig. Gen. and Chief of Engineers.

Hon. J. D. CAMERON,
Secretary of War.

Approved by the Secretary of War:

H. T. CROSBY,
Chief Clerk.

WAR DEPARTMENT, *July* 21, 1876.

HEADQUARTERS DEPARTMENT OF DAKOTA,
OFFICE OF THE CHIEF ENGINEER,
Saint Paul, Minn., March 1, 1876.

SIR: I have the honor to forward herewith a copy of my report of the reconnaissance of last summer from Carroll, Mont., over the Carroll road, to Camp Baker, Mont., thence to Fort Ellis, Mont., including a brief tour through the Yellowstone National Park, and the return journey to Carroll. Accompanying my report, for incorporation therewith, are those of Messrs. Grinnell and Dana, which will be found both interesting and valuable.

A map of the reconnaissance is presented, which shows the authorities used, in addition to my own field-notes, which were made as complete as possible. Two sketches are added, one of the Judith Basin and the other of the Upper Geyser Basin, to be inserted in the proper places in the report.

A set of astronomical observations at Carroll, Camp Lewis, and Camp Baker, three principal points on the Carroll road, are furnished; also a tabular statement of latitudes, longitudes, distances, &c., and a list of distances on the Missouri River, from a survey by the United States Boundary Commission. The region included within the limits of the Yellowstone Park is, for its area, the most interesting in the world. It is situated at the very heart of the continent, where the hidden pulses can, as it were, be seen and felt to beat, and the closely-written geological pages constitute a book which, being interpreted, will expose many of the mysterious operations of nature. My own interest in this land of wonder is so keen as to lead me again to hope that it will be protected from the vandalism from which it has already suffered, and that the suggestion of an accurate topographical and geological survey, to complete the work so well inaugurated by Professor Hayden, may be made the subject of favorable consideration and recommendation by the Chief of Engineers.

Very respectfully, your obedient servant,

WILLIAM LUDLOW,
Captain of Engineers.

The CHIEF OF ENGINEERS, U. S. A.,
Washington, D. C.

RECONNAISSANCE FROM CARROLL, MONTANA, TO YELLOWSTONE NATIONAL PARK.

GENERAL REPORT.

GENERAL REPORT.

HEADQUARTERS DEPARTMENT OF DAKOTA,
OFFICE OF CHIEF ENGINEER,
Saint Paul, Minn., February 1, 1876.

SIR: I have the honor to submit herewith my report of the reconnaissance from Carroll, Mont., to Camp Baker, thence to Fort Ellis and the Yellowstone National Park, made during the months of July, August, and September, 1875, in accordance with the instructions given in Special Orders No. 110, dated Headquarters Department of Dakota, Saint Paul, Minn., June 14, 1875.

My report includes those of Mr. George Bird Grinnell on the paleontology and zoölogy and of Mr. Edward S. Dana on the geology of the region traversed. These reports will be found highly interesting and valuable. Drawings of fossils collected by Mr. Grinnell form a portion of his report.

Lieut. R. E. Thompson's report of the trip to the Judith Basin, and of the return from Carroll to Ellis, are also submitted; Lieutenant Thompson's topographical work having been incorporated in the general map.

A map of the route pursued is presented on a scale of six miles to the inch, and a tabular statement is appended to the report, giving the astronomically-determined positions of important points, tables of distance, instrumental observations, &c.

The determinations of Forts Shaw and Ellis are those of Lieut. F. V. Greene, Corps of Engineers, who was at those posts last summer on duty connected with the United States Boundary Commission. His labors obviated the necessity for my going to Fort Shaw (which would have consumed some valuable time), and also saved me additional delay at Fort Ellis, at which place, out of six days I spent there, rain fell continuously for five.

The position of Fort Benton and the map of the Missouri River below that post are from the survey of the same officer, under direction of Capt. William J. Twining, Corps of Engineers, chief astronomer of the Boundary Commission, who with his party descended the river from Benton to Bismarck in Mackinac boats, at the close of the season's operations in 1874, carefully mapping it, and establishing almost daily astronomical stations. The river distances determined by this survey show an enormous reduction from the crude and exaggerated estimates given in existing tables, and which have heretofore been accepted as fair approximations. Above Benton, the river is from the various published authorities collated, and as far as possible reconciled.

The topography adjoining the route is from the field-notes of the reconnaissance.

Sketches of the Judith and Upper Geyser Basins are given in the body of the report, also from field-notes.

The general topography of the Yellowstone Park is mainly taken from the published maps of Dr. Hayden and Captain Jones; using, however, my own latitudes wherever good observations were taken. This, however, was but seldom, since showers fell every day but one that we were in the park, and the nights were almost invariably cloudy.

Inasmuch as no one who has seen this interesting region can fail to be deeply solicitous for its care and preservation, I am impelled to express a hope for favorable consideration from the department commander of the remarks and suggestions in relation thereto.

I left Saint Paul on the evening of June 30, in obedience to Special Orders No. 110, series of 1875, from headquarters Department of Dakota, and proceeded, via the Northern Pacific Railroad, to Bismarck, its western terminus, on the Missouri River.

Departure from Saint Paul.

[Special Orders No. 110.]

HEADQUARTERS DEPARTMENT OF DAKOTA,
Saint Paul, Minn., June 14, 1875.

Orders.

Capt. William Ludlow, chief engineer of the department, will, on July 1 proximo, proceed, via the Northern Pacific Railroad and the Missouri River, to Carroll, Mont., and make a reconnaissance of the route from that place to Camp Baker. Having completed this duty, he will proceed to the several posts in the district of Montana, and determine their latitudes and longitudes. He will also, if time permits, make a reconnaissance from Fort Ellis to the Yellowstone Park. Captain Ludlow is authorized to take with him his assistant and the enlisted men of engineers under his command. He is also authorized to take with him a geologist and such other scientific gentlemen, not exceeding four in all, as may desire to accompany his party. The commanding officer of the District of Montana will furnish escorts to Captain Ludlow from point to point, wherever, in his judgment, it may be necessary, sending a party to Carroll for that purpose; the transportation being sufficient to furnish one wagon, one ambulance, and five saddle-horses for use of Captain Ludlow's party.

By command of Brigadier-General Terry:

O. D. GREENE,
Assistant Adjutant-General.

[Special Orders No. 127.]

HEADQUARTERS DEPARTMENT OF DAKOTA,
Saint Paul, Minn., July 7, 1875.

* * * * * * *

III. The Quartermaster's Department will employ one civilian guide and scout to accompany the reconnaissance under Capt. William Ludlow, United States Engineers, authorized in Department Special Orders No. 110, current series. He will be paid at the rate of $75 per month for the time he is actually employed, and will be furnished with transportation by steamboat for himself and horse from Bismarck to Carroll and return. The acting assistant quartermaster at Fort Abraham Lincoln will take him up on his "Report of persons and atricles."

IV. Second Lieut. R. E. Thompson, Sixth Infantry, will report to Capt. William Ludlow, Engineer Corps, for duty as topographer, with the reconnaissance under the latter-named officer, authorized by Special Orders No. 110, current series, from these headquarters.

By command of Brigadier-General Terry:

O. D. GREENE,
Assistant Adjutant-General.

Composition of the party.

My party consisted (beside my brother, Mr. Edwin Ludlow, of New York, and assistant, Mr. W. H. Wood) of Messrs. George Bird Grinnell and Edward S. Dana, both of Yale College, who had come out to Saint Paul upon my invitation for the purpose of joining me.

Messrs. Grinnell and Dana as special and uncompensated assistants.

These gentlemen traveled at their own expense, receiving no compensation for their services; and I cannot but consider myself extremely fortunate in having induced them to accompany me as special assistants. Mr. Grinnell would report upon the paleontology and zoölogy and Mr. Dana upon the geology of the country passed over.

The reports attest their zeal and industry, as well as the fullness of their qualifications for, and conscientious devotion to, their voluntarily-assumed tasks.

Special Orders No. 121 directed my detachment of engineer soldiers, consisting of Sergeants Becker and Wilson and five men, to report to me at Carroll for surveying purposes.

Lieutenant Thompson and Charles Reynolds added to the party.

At Bismarck, the party was increased by the addition to it of Lieut. R. E. Thompson, Sixth Infantry, who was to accompany it as topographer and general assistant, and of Charles Reynolds, a well-known frontiersman, who was to act as guide and hunter for the expedition.

Instruments used on the reconnaissance.

The instruments taken on the trip were a small Würdemann transit-theodolite, No. 94; a Spencer Browning & Co.'s sextant, No. 6536; a Gambay & Son reflecting-circle, No. 212; and two chronometers, a mean solar of Arnold & Dent, No. 1362, and a sidereal of Bond & Sons, No. 202. These instruments, with the exception of the circle, had been used on the reconnaissance to the Black Hills of the previous season, and were known to be good. In addition were four odometers, two thermometers, two aneroid barometers, and an odometer-cart, constructed for the purpose of measuring distances.

The party, after three days' detention at Bismarck, embarked on the steamer Josephine the evening of July 5, and sailed early on the morning of the 6th. Directions had been given Sergeant Becker to make a survey of the river while going up. This was continued during the day; but as night fell, and the boat continued to run, it was found impossible to take the necessary compass-bearings to points in advance.

Leave Bismarck on the Josephine.

Fort Stevenson, eighty-four miles from Bismarck, was reached at midnight. Here Lieutenant Thompson and Reynolds landed for the purpose of procuring some necessary articles, intending to join the boat again at Fort Berthold, which, although twenty-five miles above Stevenson by water, is only seven or eight miles by land.

Fort Stevenson, Dak.

July 7.—At 5 a. m., the boat reached Berthold, and stopped for two hours to land some freight, and Lieutenant Thompson and Reynolds again came on board. Berthold is the agency for the combined tribes of Rees, Gros Ventres, and Mandans, who occupy in common a village built on the north bank of the river, surrounding an old stockade of the Northwestern Fur Company, which had formerly a trading-post here. At that early hour, the village was still asleep, and a stroll through it resulted only in arousing the numerous Indian curs that with snarls and threatening aspect resented the intrusion.

Fort Berthold.

July 8.—Was hot and uneventful. Toward afternoon, the mosquitoes became more and more troublesome, and at night forbade sleep. About 11 p. m., the boat was stopped for the purpose of landing Reynolds (who had his horse with him), and dispatching him in advance to Fort Buford, with a note to the post-quartermaster for supplies and one to the post-surgeon. A member of the party had been severely attacked with a disorder brought on by the heat and the effect of the river-water, which it is injudicious for one unaccustomed to its use to indulge in freely.

July 9.—Arrived at Buford, three hundred miles above Bismarck, at 3 a. m. The surgeon, Dr. Middleton, kindly came down at once and announced that the invalid was suffering from a sharp attack, and that it would be in a high degree dangerous for him to proceed. I made preparations at once to go ashore and remain until the next succeeding boat, which would pass in a week or ten days, should enable me to continue the journey. Meanwhile Lieutenant Thompson would be in charge of the party, and instructions were given him to proceed to Carroll and examine thoroughly the neighboring country. A full opportunity would at the same time be afforded to determine the latitude and longitude of Carroll as a starting-point for the survey of the Carroll road, thence to Camp Baker, which might then be proceeded with immediately on my arrival.

Fort Buford, Dak.

Stop at Buford.

Lieutenant Thompson and party go on to Carroll.

July 15.—The Josephine returned to Buford from Carroll, having safely landed the party, and brought a note from Lieutenant Thompson to the effect that the Indians had been very troublesome on the Carroll road, had run off a drove of forty mules belonging to the Transportation Company, and had even boldly invaded Carroll and attempted to steal horses from the picket-rope.

News from Carroll received at Buford.

I received information also that three recruits of a large detachment which had recently gone up the river, destined for Fort Shaw, had been killed in the immediate vicinity of Camp Lewis, seventy-five miles out of Carroll.

Under the circumstances, and feeling some apprehension for the safety of the party, which had an escort of ten men only, it was weary waiting at Buford for the next boat up, the arrival of which was delayed from various causes, until I had nearly determined upon the overland trip of two hundred and seventy-five miles to Carroll, dangerous as this would have been, on account of the activity of the Indians and their large numbers in the vicinity of Fort Peck. However, the Key West at last arrived, on the morning of the 23d; and, hastily getting on board, the journey was resumed. Wolf Point, the Assiniboine agency, was reached at 10 p. m. of the 24th, and Fort Peck, the general up-river agency for the Sioux, on the evening of the 25th.

Start again on the Key West.

Peck, one hundred and eighty miles above Buford by water, stands on a narrow plateau of the north bank of the river, almost overhung by the hills in rear. The buildings are of logs, one story, and inclosed within a stockade. This agency is the most considerable on the Missouri River. I was informed that from 8,000 to 10,000 people were fed there.

Fort Peck.

The distance to the hostile camps of Sitting Bull on the Yellowstone is not much in excess of one hundred miles, and intercourse is easy and not infrequent. It seems more than probable that in order to make up the large number which it is claimed is furnished with food and clothing from this agency, the Indians of the Yellowstone must be included, the attitude of whom is one of vigilant and unvarying hostility to all white men.

July 26.—Left Fort Peck at 3 a. m. Up to this point, the character of the river and its valley appeared to be measurably unchanged, a broad, rapid, and turbid stream, about three feet deep in the channel, cutting into its banks at every turn, sand-bars frequently appearing in the muddy bed; the valley heavily timbered with cottonwood, and well defined by hills. Above Peck, the bed of the stream became more gravelly, the channel consequently more stable, and the water somewhat clearer. The river narrowed to a width of from 150 to 300 yards; the clay bluffs from 150 to 600 feet in height, more closely approached the banks, and became exceedingly barren and unattractive, of dark-gray hue and ashen texture, with thin alkaline streaks near the base. Small plates of selenite scattered over the surface glittered in the sun, and the grass was exceedingly poor and scanty. As we advanced, small cedars appeared on the higher elevations, and game became more abundant. Glimpses of deer half-concealed in the shrubbery were frequently caught; large bands of elk were seen in the timbered "points;" and the shore of the river was everywhere dotted with the footprints of wild animals.

<small>Character of the river.</small>

Three buffalo crossed the river in advance of the boat. One was killed and hoisted on deck; some Indians who had come on board at Wolf Point greedily appropriating the refuse portions. Just before sundown, a herd of seventy-five or eighty buffalo were seen dashing down the left bank in eager pursuit of three in advance, who had already entered the water and were half-way across the stream. The herd at once plunged in, and it was soon evident that the boat would intercept them. They kept on, however; the calves, of which there were several, swimming by the lower side of the cows, and all making strenuous efforts to overtake the leaders, who had meanwhile climbed the opposite bank. The stupid animals only turned back when the foremost actually struck the boat with their heads, and then, with bovine snorts and bellowings, they heaped together and climbed upon each other in desperate fright, within a few feet of us. It would have been butchery to kill them, especially as we did not need the beef, and they were allowed to escape unhurt.

<small>A herd of buffalo crossing the river.</small>

July 27.—Carroll was reached at 7 p. m. I found a note from Lieutenant Thompson to the effect that the vicinity of Carroll had been examined and the necessary observations taken; and, finding that forage and rations were becoming scarce, it had been determined to proceed on the road toward Camp Baker in order to save delay.

<small>Carroll, Mont.</small>

A courier was dispatched to Camp Lewis for escort and transportation by Lieutenant-Colonel Otis, assistant inspector-general of the department, who was *en route* to Helena, and we awaited the reply.

Carroll is a frontier " town" of perhaps twenty or twenty-five log buildings, on the south bank of the river, six hundred and forty miles above Bismarck and one hundred and sixty-five miles below Fort Benton, the limit of navigation on the Upper Missouri. The town is situated on a timbered plateau 15 or 20 feet above the level of the stream at low water, in the river-valley, which is some 800 to 900 feet in depth, with steep clay slopes covered with pine. It owes its existence to its being the terminus of the road recently opened from Helena, and the point at which freights are transferred to and from the boats.

Montana has long suffered from its isolation and from the want of an outlet for its productions. Until the opening of the Carroll road, the only regular communication with the outer world was by the road from Helena to Corinne, on the Union Pacific Railroad, a distance of over four hundred and fifty miles. The distance from Helena to Carroll is more than two hundred miles less than this, a difference which, to the heavy bull-trains averaging only twelve or thirteen miles per day, represents a saving of fifteen or sixteen days in time. The Missouri River as far up as Carroll is generally navigable for the flat-bottomed stern-wheel boats that ply upon it until some time in October; and it is evident that by the aid of a connection at Bismarck with the Northern Pacific an important and valuable outlet for the wealth of the Territory has been discovered, available from the opening of navigation in the spring until quite late in the fall, a period of over five months.

<small>The Carroll route from Helena.</small>

In addition to the encouragement to the industries of Montana, a large saving can be made by the Government in the cost of transporting its troops and supplies for the up-river and Montana posts by the use of this route. These considerations, supported by the necessity for maintaining troops to act as a check upon the lawlessness of the large number of Indians annually congregating in the vicinity of Fort Peck, constitute an appeal to the Government to protect the road against forays by the Indians, an obligation which is recognized in the distribution of troops along the line of the road. At Camp Baker, fifty-two miles east of Helena, is a permanent garrison of two companies of infantry; at the forks of the Musselshell, fifty-six miles farther east, is a summer camp of two companies of infantry and one of cavalry; at the Judith Gap, thirty miles farther, is a detachment of eighteen or twenty men; and at Camp Lewis, thirty miles farther and seventy-five miles out of Carroll, is another summer garrison of two companies of infantry, from which a small detachment guards the stage-station at Box Elder, forty miles out of Carroll. These posts can conveniently receive their supplies from Carroll. Military posts on the Carroll road.

If, in addition to the garrison at the forks of the Musselshell and Camp Lewis, a force of cavalry, sufficiently large to patrol the road and push reconnaissances south and east, could be established between Camp Lewis and the Judith Gap,—and in this range the requisites of wood, water, and grass are both excellent and abundant,—the route could be made as permanently safe as any other highway, and such loss of property and life as occurred last summer be prevented. The truth of the general proposition cannot, I think, be questioned that the settlements of Montana can best be protected by troops removed from their immediate vicinity and pushed out toward the sources whence hostile incursions are to be apprehended. Suggestions as to the use of cavalry on the Carroll road.
Suggestions as to the defense of the Montana settlements.

July 30.—The stage came in an early hour, bringing word from the commanding officer at Camp Lewis that, much as he desired to do so, he had no transportation or men that he could possibly send. Colonel Otis therefore hired such transportation as could be obtained in Carroll; and securing a few rifles and rounds of ammunition, we started soon after midday, our escort being half a dozen unarmed recruits, *en route* to Shaw. Start from Carroll.

The road out of Carroll leads up a long sharp ridge to the west, constantly ascending, with many turns, until an altitude of over nine hundred feet above the "town" is attained; the view thence was wide and varied. Up and down the river, the valley, sinuous and green, its steep slopes scored by deep ravines, could be traced for many miles. Bordering that, the tumbled Bad Lands on the south bank and the yellow prairie on the north, and in the distance the various ranges of mountains in detached groups—the Bear's Paw, seventy miles to the north and west; the Little Rockies, thirty miles north; the Judith Mountains, forty miles south and west; with the Great and Little Moccasins close by, and the Snowies beyond.

The road at first traversed a rolling, sterile prairie, gradually descending. Camp was made on Little Crooked Creek, thirteen miles from Carroll, and in what are called the Bad Lands, which extend out from Carroll for over thirty miles. The landscape is dreary to the last degree, with rolling and broken outlines. The soil throughout the region is a finely-ground clay of dark ashen hue and texture and irregularly striped by dirty alkaline streaks. In the absence of rain, it is dry and dusty; but thoroughly wetted, it becomes a greasy, slippery, fathomless mass of clinging mud, through which the straining animals can hardly drag the heavily-weighted wheels. Wood is almost entirely wanting; water is very scarce, and when found is alkaline and tepid. The vegetation is sage and cactus, with occasionally a little thin, poor grass. Near camp two trains were encountered going in to Carroll; they halted for the night two or three miles behind us. Mauvaises Terres.
Camp on Little Crooked Creek.

July 31.—Camp was broken early, and the journey resumed through the same enlivening scenery for twenty miles, crossing Crooked Creek, a sluggish alkaline stream, deeply cut into the dark-gray clay (where the sight of a party of mounted Indians some miles away disturbed our lunch and started us on the road), to where the bounds of the Bad Lands were reached, and the road ascended upon high rolling prairie, over which a push of seven miles led into the valley of Box Elder Creek. This is a stage-station, forty miles from Carroll, where a guard of four soldiers is maintained from Lewis. The halting-place is marked by a log cabin standing on the bank of the creek, a small stream of swift-flowing water, Box Elder Station, forty miles from Carroll.

which has its source in the slopes of the Judith Mountains. During the day, two or three single buffalo were seen, and antelope had appeared from time to time since leaving Carroll.

August 1.—The road led in a general southwest direction along the northern foot-hills of the mountains, which were eight to ten miles distant, rising steep and wooded to the height of some 2,000 feet. The road was good, although somewhat hilly, the grass fair, and the creeks, several of which we crossed, were all bright little streams of good water. As we advanced, the mountains began to define themselves. The Little and Greater Moccasins separated from the Judith and from each other, between them appearing the distant Highwoods, with patches of snow; the Snowies, to the south, also snow-crowned; and, separating them from the Little Belt, could be seen the depression which marks the Judith Gap. The road follows the western flank of the Judith, at the southwest extremity of which, on the banks of Big Spring Creek, finally appeared the garrison-flag and the white tents of Camp Lewis, thirty-five miles from Box Elder. The camp is situated in the level valley of the creek, the garrison consisting of two companies of the Seventh Infantry, Captain Browning commanding. The creek, the main affluent of the Judith River, rises a few miles above Lewis, in a huge spring, from which the stream emerges, full-grown, with a rapid, tumultuous current of ice-cold water, abounding with the black-speckled mountain-trout. The course is northwest in a gravelly bed 15 or 20 feet wide and 1 to 2 feet deep. Wood has in a great measure to be hauled by the garrison from the mountains, but the grass is rich and luxuriant.

<small>Camp Lewis, on Big Spring Creek, seventy-five miles from Carroll.</small>

August 2.—Lewis is the second stage-station on the Carroll road, seventy-five miles from the "town." We lay over one day to rest the animals.

August 3.—Took the road again at an early hour, ascending upon a partly level and rolling prairie fairly grassed over, where rapid progress, parallel to the Snowy Range, was made, crossing several fine creeks which rise in the Snowies and flow north and west into the Judith River.

The Judith Basin, a sketch of which is given, opened to the north and west, showing a fine, well-grassed, gently-rolling prairie, some fifty miles east and west and sixty miles north and south, of irregular diamond-shape, and inclosing about 1,500 square miles, from the borders of which rose, massive and detached, the encircling ranges, the Judith, Snowy, Little Belt, and Highwoods. Throughout this elevated region (and more especially later in the Yellowstone Park), we had daily occasion to observe the marked depth and clearness of the coloring, owing, I presume, to the utter purity of the atmosphere; the colors of objects comparatively near by seemed to possess an unsurpassable richness and reality, and even on distant mountains, seventy-five or eighty miles away, while the colors were necessarily blended and their details lost, they exhibited a wonderful transparency and distinctness, undimmed by the haze and vagueness which usually obscure such distant objects. It is this quality of the atmosphere that furnishes the chief beauty of the Judith Basin, which can hardly be termed a mountainous country, although the various ranges grouped about it, and separated from each other by broad intervals, form the principal feature of the landscape. Painted in a clear, transparent purple upon the sky, and seeming hardly to rest upon the yellow prairie which forms so fine a contrast, they look like massive islands in the tawny ocean that rolls against them.

<small>Judith Basin.</small>

<small>Judith Basin.</small>

The basin will some day be a great stock-raising, and, by the aid of irrigation, an agricultural region. It has always been considered a fine hunting country, where game of all kinds could be found, although we saw none, with the exception of a few antelope; the recent presence of the Crow camp having driven it off.

At Ross's Fork of the Judith, near the gap, and twenty-seven miles from Lewis, we met Lieutenant Thompson, who had come out from Baker with two spring-wagons to meet us. Camp was made, with good grass and fair water; wood scarce.

August 4.—Pulled out at 6 a. m. The road led directly through the gap. From the southeast extremity of the Little Belt Mountains rises a fine spring, flowing east at first, and then doubling back through the gap into Ross's Fork.

The gap is formed by a depression five or six miles in width between the timbered Snowy and Belt Ranges. It constitutes the head of the Judith Basin; to the south appearing a broad, level stretch of prairie, sloping down to the Musselshell, twenty or twenty-five miles distant. The Crow camp at the time we passed was said to be seven or eight miles to

<small>Judith Gap.</small>

the eastward, on the southern slope of the Snowies. We also heard that a fight had taken place two nights before between the Crows and a party of Sioux, and that a war-party of one hundred Sioux had passed subsequently through the gap, going northward.

Emerging from the gap, the road led west and south over a dry, sterile, and dusty prairie, in the teeth of a blistering southwest gale, across Hoppley's Hole and Haymaker's and Daisy Dean Creeks, into the valley of the Mussellshell, whose freshness and greenness and abundance of timber afforded the strongest contrast to the country behind us. The hired teams were mortally weary, and had been with the greatest difficulty urged all day against the strong, hot wind. Released from harness, they ran to the bank and leaped bodily into the stream, thrusting their muzzles deep into the cool water with great contentment. The river is twenty-five or thirty feet wide, and on the average seven or eight inches deep, of clear, rapid flow, over a gravelly bottom; the valley level, wide, fertile, and richly grassed, with heavy clumps of timber on the low banks of the stream. Camp on Mussel-shell River.

August 5.—Made an early start, and at two or three miles from camp came to the "forks" of the Mussellshell, where the north and south branches unite. Here a ranchman had established himself, raising cattle, and, by means of an irrigating-ditch, cultivating some seventy-five or eighty acres in oats and wheat. Throughout Montana, owing to the very thorough drainage, the general altitude above the sea, and the prevailing dryness of the atmosphere, irrigation is essential to successful agriculture. Forks of the Mussellshell.

A stage-station of the Carroll road is made at this ranch, sixty-five miles from Lewis and fifty-six miles from Baker.

The road followed west and north up the North Fork, passing through a rocky, wooded cañon of considerable beauty. Here the road, overlooking the stream, whose windings it followed, and deeply shaded by pines, made a very agreeable drive, the more so that we were now beyond any danger from Indians. Emerging from the cañon, the road led west and south over a high, rolling, and hilly prairie. At the foot of a long down-grade lay Copperopolis, which was found to consist of a mining-shaft and a deserted shanty. The North Fork of Deep Creek was reached at 4 p. m. and camp made. The creek abounded with trout, and the wood, water, and grass were plenty and good. North Fork of the Mussellshell. North Fork of Deep Creek.

August 6.—The road led down the valley of Deep Creek west and south to Brewer's Springs, where the luxuries of a hot bath, followed by a generous breakfast, were enjoyed. The waters well up freely, strongly impregnated with sulphur, from several springs, with temperatures varying from 105° to 115° Fahrenheit. They are taken up in wooden pipes, and introduced into the bathing-houses. The odor is at first unpleasant, but the water is soft and thoroughly delightful to the skin. The color is a milky, cloudy blue, and soft, delicate filaments of sulphur adhere to the sides of the bath and stream from the mouths of the supplying-tubes. A small hotel has been built for the accommodation of visitors. At this point unite the two forks of Deep Creek, which, bearing the name of Smith's River, flows here north and west past Camp Baker to join the Missouri. The Carroll road bifurcates, one branch going west over the mountains, the other following the rich and fertile river-valley, which supports thousands of cattle on its lush pasturage, until at sixteen and three-fourths miles from the springs the road reaches Camp Baker, where it deflects to the west, toward Helena. Brewer's Hot Sulphur Springs. Bifurcation of the Carroll road.

The post is an irregular-looking cluster of buildings planted in the midst of a level and stony plain, surrounded by mountains, upon which frequent patches of snow appear. An irrigating-ditch brings a current of water through the garrison, but hardly appears able to vivify the arid soil. The troops at Baker are two companies of the Seventh Infantry, Major Freeman commanding. I found here my party awaiting me, and without loss of time made preparations for the trip to Ellis. The transportation and escort which had hitherto accompanied the party had returned to Ellis, and as the road to that point was considered comparatively safe, a small force only was needed. Camp Baker, Mont.

August 7.—Pulled out at 8 a. m., with transportation consisting of two six-mule teams and a four-mule ambulance, with saddle-horses for the party, and a sergeant and two men for guard and camp duty. There are two routes from Baker to Ellis: one, called the Duck Creek route, via the Missouri and Gallatin Valleys, is perfectly safe, being within the set- Two routes from Baker to Fort Ellis.

tlements, but several miles longer than the other, called the "outer" route, which, returning nearly to Brewer's Springs, goes up the South Fork of Deep Creek almost direct to Ellis, passing between the Crazy and Big Belt Mountains. From the springs south, the valley is at first broad and level and heavily grassed, the creek flowing northward. Many antelope were seen grazing in the meadows. Camp was made at 3.30 p. m. near a fresh, cold spring issuing from the hillside on the east bank of the creek. The locality is the ordinary halting-place, twenty-seven miles out of Baker, and is called Moss Agate Springs. The grazing and water are excellent, but the supply of wood is small.

Moss Agate Springs.

August 8.—Course continued nearly south up the valley. The creek gradually became smaller and finally was dry. "Sixteen-mile Creek", a branch of the Missouri, flowing a strong current west and south, was crossed eleven miles from camp, and the road beyond lay over a dry, yellow, gently-undulating prairie, which farther on grew more hilly, and became an interminable waste of sagebrush. The antelope were numerous during the day. Cottonwood Creek, a small branch of Shield's River, was crossed thirteen and a half miles from Sixteen-mile Creek. The water is pure and plenty, and the valley well supplied with cotton-wood trees. Continuing, the sagebrush still occupied the ground, and camp was finally made on a small creek flowing east, the valley of which furnished an ample supply of excellent water and grass, and wood sufficient for camping purposes. Bridger Pass appeared seven or eight miles south of us, and Flathead Pass opened to the westward through the Big Belt Range.

Camp on branch of Shields' River.

August 9.—Pulled out at 6 a. m. The trail led into a broad valley, stretching eastward at the foot of the mountains, richly grassed, intersected by several small streams, and affording the finest pasturage for three or four herds of cattle which were browsing in the meadow. These had probably been driven over the mountains from the Gallatin Valley for the summer. Crossing the valley brought us to the foot-hills of Bridger Pass, which, though much lower than the neighboring mountains, still gave promise of an arduous climb for the heavy wagons. A creek flows out of the pass, up the valley of which a road of fair grade could be easily constructed. In the absence of this, the trail climbs several steep hills in succession, alternately ascending and descending, but constantly rising, though with more than double the necessary labor, until at the summit of a long, sloping hog-back, falling steeply on both sides, a preliminary divide was reached, whence descent was made, following a small branch, into the valley of Brackett's Creek. This is a tributary of Shield's River, flowing eastward and separating the group of mountains over which we had passed from the main range, the pass through which still lay before us. Crossing the creek, the second ascent was found to be more gradual and less severe than the former, although of about equal altitude. Reaching the second summit, the descent began down the left bank of Bridger Creek, flowing southward. The peaks to the west across the valley were lofty, varied in form, and from certain points of view exceedingly fine. Huge patches of snow rested in the more sheltered places on their summits, and one could begin to realize the altitude of 10,000 feet above the sea, which sufficed to maintain this wintry feature even under the clear, hot rays of the summer sun. The timber throughout the pass is pine, with various small woods in the creek bottoms. Grass is abundant, even among the timber, and the brooks are bright mountain-streams constantly fed from the snow-fields above, and abounding with trout. Elk and deer are numerous, though they are driven from the immediate vicinity of the trail by frequent travel and possibly by the flies, which in great numbers and varieties proved a serious annoyance to the cattle. Still following Bridger Creek, the road made a long bend to the south and west, around the base of Bridger Mountain, into the main valley, which turns west to join that of the Gallatin. Crossing the creek, the trail wound over a range of hills, and descended into the valley of the North Gallatin, upon the south bank of which, three or four miles farther west, Fort Ellis is situated. The Bozeman Pass road, leading east and south to the Yellowstone, climbs the hill-side opposite to where the road reaches the river.

Bridger Pass.

Brackett's Creek.

Bridger Mountains.

Fort Ellis, on the East Fork of Gallatin River.

Fort Ellis stands near the head of the Gallatin Valley, for the defense of which it was constructed. It appears as an assemblage of log houses, irregularly placed from frequent additions, of uninviting exterior, but comfortable within. The garrison, General Sweitzer commanding, includes four companies of the Second Cavalry and one of the Seventh Infantry; but during the summer the mounted troops are required to guard the passes and make frequent scouts, sometimes of considerable extent, and hence spend but little time in garrison. At the date of my arrival, two companies were absent, one scouting, the other acting as escort to the party of the Secretary of War in the Yellowstone Park, while a third was preparing for the field, and started early next morning.

August 10.—Employed the day in preparations for the trip to the park. The greater portion of the necessary pack-animals were then in the park, and my arrival was fortunately timed, since they were on the return, and expected back in two or three days. By advancing to meet them, double that time could be saved. Accordingly, the baggage was reduced to the smallest possible amount. All trunks and boxes were left behind, and the necessary articles put into canvas sacks, brought from Saint Paul for the purpose. Tents were discarded and only tent-flies carried. The instruments were carefully rolled in bundles of bedding, and the basket containing the chronometers strapped to the spring-seat of the odometer-cart. Riding-animals were obtained and a six-mule team secured to carry the baggage and stores until the pack-train should be met. Toward evening we went into camp about three miles southeast from Ellis, on Coal or Rocky Cañon Creek, a small affluent of the Gallatin, uniting with it near the fort. *_{Preparations for the trip into the Yellowstone Park.}* *_{Camp on Coal Creek.}*

August 11.—Broke camp at 6 a. m., and proceeded across the creek and up its valley. The trail followed the creek-bottom, crossing it several times, and over a rocky, hilly road, through a cañon of considerable grandeur, shaded by lofty, precipitous limestone pinnacles. The general course was south and east, up the east bank of the creek, gradually ascending and bending more to the southward. The road improved, the available space becoming greater and the hills less steep. Crossing a low divide extending across the valley, the head of Trail Creek, a tributary of the Yellowstone, was reached. Through both creek-valleys, the flies were very numerous and annoying. There are two ranches on Trail Creek, the second one twenty-five miles from Ellis, where the creek-valley widened and entered that of the Yellowstone, which presented the familiar features of a broad, dry, stony stretch of prairie, sloping down to a beautiful stream, with borders fringed with trees. The river has a stony and gravelly bed, an impetuous current of six or seven miles an hour, a depth of as many feet, and width of about 100 yards. The waters, constantly freshened by mountain springs and torrents, are cold and clear, and alive with trout of great size and variety. These range in weight from half a pound to two pounds and upward. Their favorite food is the grasshopper, great numbers of which fall into the stream, but they will also take the fly freely.

The Snow Mountains border the river on the south and east, their lofty pinnacles glittering with snow. Chief among the range is Emigrant Peak, rising 6,000 feet above the valley and attaining an altitude of 11,500 feet above the sea. It is a very handsome mountain, of fine outline and great richness of coloring. Débouching from Trail Creek, the road bends south and west up the left bank of the river. We here met the party of the Secretary of War, in two spring-wagons, going in to Ellis. The pack-train had been left behind at Gardner's River Springs, to follow more leisurely. Pushing on up the valley, crossing several small brooks flowing from the mountains, and passing two or three ranches, camp was made near Bottler's ranch, half-way to the Mammoth Springs and thirty-five miles from Ellis. Sufficient wood was readily attainable, and a swift-flowing brook was close at hand; but the grass, never luxuriant, had been thinned by frequent camping.

August 12.—Broke camp at 8 a. m. The road passed Bottler's ranch, where travelers can find fairly good food and lodging, and proceeded up the level valley to a rocky point coming down from the mountains to the river-bank. Surmounting this, we followed up the valley again, crossing two or three rude but sufficient bridges, at one of which was a toll-house. It appeared that a company in Bozeman had obtained a territorial charter for a toll road from that place to the Mammoth Springs. The road had been made practicable for wagons, and considerable work expended upon it up to the toll-bridge; but the main labor directed to the cañon above, which had hitherto been a serious obstacle and impassable to vehicles. Continuing, the road bent more to the south, and entered the cañon, following a hilly trail, blasted out of the rocks. The cañon is some three miles in length, and the view from the highest part of the road is very fine. The river, compressed to a width of 75 or 80 feet, is of a rich

3 w

green hue, splashed with white, and flows with great velocity; its surface breaking into great waves and swirls. The mountains on either side are 2,000 or 3,000 feet in height, rising precipitously from the brink, and exhibiting dark browns and grays, contrasting with the deep, somber hue of the pines and the more sparkling green of the river, flecked with foam.

Camp was made at the upper end of the cañon, on the bank. All the essentials for camping were present, and trout abounded in the swift and turbulent waters. The grayling, a long, slender fish, of less weight than the trout, but rivaling it in activity and game qualities, competed successfully for the fly with the larger fish.

Camp in Second Cañon.

August 13.—Started at 6.30 a. m., and soon afterward met Lieutenant Doane, with the pack-train. The six-mule team was exchanged for pack-mules, and, after some three hours' delay, the journey was resumed.

The pack-train met.

Cinnabar Mountain stands in the valley, on the right of the trail, and, as seen from any point of view, is a handsome peak. Looking from above it, on the river-bank, it stands out from the other elevations and makes a very striking picture. The strata are nearly vertical, with a perceptible overhang to the eastward, and strike nearly north and south. On the south front of the mountain is an immense "Devil's Slide", with smooth, dark, nearly vertical walls, some 150 or 200 feet in height (the intervening material having been removed), which curve to the right in ascending and reach the summit. Adjoining this are broad bands of red and yellow, which follow the same curve, and seize the eye at once from their brilliancy of color and vivid contrast.

Cinnabar Mountain.

The trail led us on up the valley, past two ranches, from which supplies were obtained, to within a few miles of Gardiner's River. At this point, it leaves the valley of the Yellowstone, and, over a hilly route, passes across the angle between the two streams, until, at the farther side of a level, well-grassed piece of prairie, it reaches the valley in which the Mammoth Hot Springs are situated. The rain had descended heavily all the afternoon and continued into the night.

Camp at Gardiner's River Hot Springs.

August 14.—The day opened wet, but cleared in a few hours. A thorough examination was made of the springs, which well repaid it.

They have been already described with great particularity and minuteness in the reports of Dr. Hayden and Captain Jones, and a few words of description from me will suffice.

This remark is not to be confined to the locality of the springs, but must be understood as applying, and in a still greater degree, to the whole park, of which I shall not even attempt a full description, but content myself with recording only a few of the more prominent and enduring impressions received in our hurried visit.

No full description of the park scenery will be attempted.

Pressed for time, with other work to do, our constant idea was one of eager haste, and we passed rapidly from place to place, thoroughly enjoying every hour, but always with some new wonder in advance, to divert our attention and to draw us on.

The park scenery, as a whole, is too grand, its scope too immense, its details too varied and minute, to admit of adequate description, save by some great writer, who, with mind and pen equally trained, could seize upon the salient points, and, with just discrimination, throw into proper relief the varied features of mingled grandeur, wonder, and beauty.

The Mammoth Hot Springs are the first point of interest in the park, the northern boundary of which was crossed yesterday some miles back. They occupy a small valley, discharging eastward into that of Gardiner's River, and which the spring-deposits have partly filled. Our camp was pleasantly situated in the valley below the springs, among trees growing out of these deposits, in which occasional pits and holes 15 to 20 feet in depth existed. Above the camp rose the extinct spring, called, from the shape of the mausoleum which it had itself constructed, the "Liberty Cap", or "Giant's Thumb", and beyond this again a succession of terraces, rising to a height of some 200 feet, dazzling white in the sun, indicated the presence of the active springs, which, indeed, had all along been evident enough from the vast clouds of vapor constantly arising. The terraces exhibited great variety and beauty of form, much enhanced by the quivering and sheeny effect of the thin, descending sheets of water.

Mammoth Hot Springs.

The material is a carbonate of lime, deposited by the cooling of the waters, of a nearly pure white, and, while wet, of a moderate hardness. Upon drying, the deposit becomes soft and friable, and a hunting-knife could be easily plunged into it to the hilt. The main springs occupy the upper portion of the terrace, and spread out into large limpid pools of a superb blue tint, boiling violently in places, and emitting clouds of steam. Overflowing the pools, the waters escape down the face of the terraces, and, in cooling, gradually part with the carbonate held in solution, making constant additions to the ornamentations of the surfaces, and constructing scalloped pools and "bath-tubs" of every form and temperature.

The whole vicinity of the springs returns a hollow echo to the tread, highly suggestive of pitfalls beneath. The party, however, overran the neighborhood, at first with tentative step, and afterward with all confidence, no accident occurring. Remains of extinct springs abound above and below the active ones, while still others in full flow exist near the river's edge.

The grass in the valley of the springs is poor, but on the small prairie above is excellent. Wood and cold water are sufficiently abundant and convenient.

There are two "ranches" near the springs, which do duty as "hotels", and are available for the use of travelers.

August 15.—Wagons can be taken as far as the springs without much difficulty; the road having been made entirely practicable, though of an occasionally undesirable steepness. At the springs, however, wheels must be abandoned, and everything carried upon pack-animals.

The odometer-cart was left behind, both on account of the difficulty of getting it along, and the danger of rendering it unfit for use on the return trip to Carroll. The mean solar chronometer was left with it, in charge of the "hotel"-keeper, and the sidereal was rolled in a bundle of bedding, and intrusted to the somewhat uncertain fortunes of the packs. All other reductions had been made at Ellis, and camp was broken at 8.15 a. m.; the "outfit" consisting, besides the party and the engineer soldiers, of three packers, a farrier, and a cook, in all twenty-two persons and thirty-three animals, of which eleven were pack-mules carrying about two hundred pounds. *The pack "outfit."*

The trail (a bridle-path only) leads up the valley of Gardiner's River (which is of considerable depth, and slopes steeply down to the water's edge) across the West Fork, and then the East, gradually climbing the eastern side of the valley to a plateau, whence on the right of the trail descend the waters of the river, and form a very pretty fall. The slopes of the river-valley are composed of loose basaltic *débris*, making a toilsome path, deeply gashed in places by washings from the foot of the great basaltic wall which towers above it on the east. Although not insecure, the ascent to the plateau is unnecessarily difficult, and a little labor expended upon it would serve to improve it greatly. *Gardiner's River Valley.*

The falls are some 20 feet in width, and make three plunges, estimated at about 45, 55, and 30 feet each; in all a descent of 130 feet. *Gardiner's River Falls.*

Leaving the river, the trail follows up in an easterly direction the shallow valley of a small brook called Black Tail Deer Creek, which traverses an open hilly prairie, and affords an excellent and easily-traveled road. Reaching the head of the creek, the trail bore to the right, through a dry cañony place to the edge of the valley of Meadow Brook, where, turning sharply to the left, it descends along a steep high slope, out of which the narrow trail is cut, to a fine open meadow, well grassed and watered, where camp was made, thirteen miles from the springs. Several of the party rode on a mile and a half farther to the Yellowstone River. It was found to be a foaming torrent, some 60 feet in width, with steep rocky banks. The water, a rich green in hue, was broken into pools and eddies by obstructing bowlders, and a strong odor of sulphur pervaded the air. Spanning the stream is a rough bridge some 80 feet in length, resting upon cribs at either extremity, and affording a passage to the east bank, where, at a short distance from the "bridge", is the "ranch" of Jack Baronet. *Divide between Gardiner's and Yellowstone Rivers.* *Yellowstone River near the falls.* *The bridge over the Yellowstone.*

Two or three miles below the "bridge", the two forks of the Yellowstone unite, and, to the traveler approaching it, the locality is marked by a large flat-topped butte, with steep escarpments, which stands in the angle, and from its shape is a noticeable object, contrasting with the pointed hills and peaks which surround it. The West Fork drains the lake, and the East, a mountainous district not yet thoroughly examined.

Rain fell again during the afternoon and night, and our experience of the weather in the park seemed to be similar to that of Captain Jones, as recorded in his report. On one day only of the two weeks passed in the park did we fail to have rain or shower, and night observations were in consequence greatly interfered with.

Rain in the park.

August 16.—Camp was broken at 8.30. The herd had wandered during the night, and a couple of hours were lost in getting them in and ready for the road. The pack-mules had been employed on similar duty just before, and heavily laden. The construction or adjustment of the army pack-saddle is doubtless capable of great improvement; at any rate, the backs and shoulders of the animals were in very bad condition, and one of them was found to be so unfit for a load that it was necessary to leave him at the bridge.

Army pack-mules.

While in the park, as there was no grain for the animals, they were allowed free range at night, and the grazing is so plentiful and nutritious that the majority of them held their own, although the work was occasionally severe. There need be little or no apprehension from Indians, and guards were not posted after leaving the Mammoth Springs.

The trail from Meadow Brook leads up the left bank of the Yellowstone, winding among some low hills, and at four and a half miles from camp makes a precipitous plunge into the valley of Tower Creek, crossing which it ascends the opposite bank by a more gradual incline. The stream is a strong rapid brook, 12 or 15 feet in width, and a foot or two in depth, with a stony bed, the waters fed from the snow-fields of the mountains. A short distance below the crossing are the falls, which leap down 150 feet into a narrow, dark cañon some 480 feet in depth. Basaltic-tufa cones and columns in the vicinity of the fall have suggested the name, and all the surroundings are picturesque in the highest degree. The finest view of the falls can be gained from a projecting spur on the south bank just below them, whence both the cañon and the creek-valley above can be seen. The stream discharges into the Yellowstone River near by, and at its mouth very fine fishing rewards the visitor.

Tower Creek.

Tower Falls.

There seem to be two varieties of trout here, the bulky ones of the Yellowstone, with bright-yellow bellies and stripings of red, and a smaller kind more silvery in appearance, and exhibiting much greater activity and game qualities. These latter seemed to come generally from the creek. The mouth of the creek may be called the lower end of the Grand Cañon, which extends up the river some sixteen miles to the foot of the Great Falls.

Trout.

Leaving the creek, the trail, alternately rising and falling, and curving to the right and left, gains the foot of a long, somewhat rolling ascent, which finally attains the western shoulder of Mount Washburne. The flanks of this incline fall steeply on both sides, displaying to the west an ocean of deep-green pine, surrounded by ragged, bare pinnacles, and to the east breaking into the foot-hills of Washburne. This incline is approximately located on Raynolds's map, and called the Elephant's Back, which name has on some later maps been transferred to a minor elevation near the Yellowstone Lake. The name is appropriate and descriptive, and, having been given by the first topographer of the region, should be allowed to have its original application.

Elephant's Back.

Over this the trail by a gradual ascent reaches a high point on Mount Washburne, passing between banks of snow, which had remained unmelted by the summer's sun. Here, leaving the trail, the party ascended to the summit of the mountain. The climb was made in less than an hour, and can almost be accomplished on horseback, so rounded is the mountain-top, although consideration for the saddle-horses would suggest making it on foot. In passing some stunted pines near the trail, it was observed that there were no branches or twigs on the northwest side of the tree, and that those which sprung from the northeast and southwest sides were twisted back and trailed away to the southeast. The explanation of this was not long in doubt. Reaching the summit, the whole panorama of the park sprung into view: the lake, with deeply sinuous shores and silver surface, interspersed with islands, with the Yellowstone River crooking away from it toward us, was set, as it were, in a vast expanse of green, rising and falling in huge billows, above which here and there jets of steam arose like spray; the encircling peaks, ragged and snow-clad, almost too numerous to count; Mount Humphreys, thirty or forty miles southeast, Sheridan and Hancock the same distance to the south, and beyond and above them,

Summit of Mount Washburne.

ninety miles away, looking almost mysterious from their distance and vast height, the Tetons, of a pale purple hue, with their piercing summits glittering like icebergs. Only to the southeast, looking toward the great Idaho Desert, did a space appear which showed no prominent peaks. We had scarcely time to more than glance at this superb landscape, while resting and eating lunch with the aid of a hatful of snow from a neighboring bank, when a ferocious squall of hail, rain, and snow burst upon us from the northwest, and swept us like dust from the bald summit of the mountain. We were instantly compelled to seek shelter on the lee side, where, cowering and half-frozen, we awaited the passing of the storm. Motion, however, was absolutely essential to warmth; so, without again trusting the untender mercies of the mountain, over which the wind still blew keen and cold, we plunged into a deep ravine leading steeply down its western flank, and regained the trail at the foot. The storm had wet the rich black mold, and made the path slippery and difficult through the densest timber of spruce and pine, where hardly sufficient cutting had been done to afford the narrowest of passage-ways. The projecting branches flapped back their freight of rain-drops into our faces and clothing, and many of the broken twigs bore trophies snatched from the packs. *Mount Washburne.*

There were several sharp pitches into and out of the valleys of small brooks, which could easily be avoided. At present, the trail is unnecessarily hilly and fatiguing, although delightful on account of the fine forest and the great number and variety of the flowers. The grass is everywhere luxuriant and sweet, the brooks are frequent, and flow in all directions, and camp could be made at almost any point. The trail, however, might be greatly improved by means of a little well-directed labor and the exercise of better judgment in selecting it. The work of a pack or saddle animal is vastly increased by unnecessary ascents and descents, which both their conformation and the position of the load render arduous, and the easiest road is one of even grade, though it be thrice the length of the more direct one.

Ascending to a low divide between two mountains, the valley of Cascade Creek was reached and followed to camp. The last three or four miles were over a meadow which in many places was wet and very boggy. The hail here had fallen in considerable quantity, and whitened all the ground; the sky was dark, and the air raw and wintry. Camp was made on the east bank of the creek, where it leaves the meadow and enters the narrow, steep valley through which it reaches the Yellowstone. A roaring camp-fire soon restored the warmth and cheerfulness of the party, which had been somewhat impaired by the shivering weather. We were only about a mile from the falls, and after everything had quieted down to silence their deep roar became vaguely audible. The evening was again cloudy and rainy. Distance traveled during the day estimated at eighteen miles. *Mount Washburne to camp on Cascade Creek.*

August 17.—Lay over in camp to visit the falls. The night had been cold, and by 8 a. m. the hail of yesterday had not disappeared. Waiting an hour longer for the sun to dry the heavy grass, we took on foot the trail which led us to the brink of the river-valley, half-way between the Upper and the Lower Fall, which are half a mile apart. Reserving the Lower Fall, whose deep thunder we could now plainly hear, we descended toward the Upper, and, after a short scramble over loose trachytic blocks, climbed out upon a point which, projecting into the cañon below the fall, furnished a fine view of it almost *en face*. The river makes a sharp bend to the eastward just above the fall, which in consequence fronts nearly at right angles to the general direction. From the sharp and narrow pinnacle on which we stood, or rather to which we clung, the cataract, some 150 feet distant, was exposed in its full height and beauty. It is a slanting one, having a base of perhaps one-half its altitude, which, as measured by a cord brought for the purpose and marked in ten-foot lengths, is 110 feet. The water leaps down its rocky slope between black, shining walls of trachyte, and its pure green is broken into foam and spray from the very summit. From the foot the currents of air drove the clouds of vapor up the steep sides of the cañon, which were clothed in vegetation of the freshest and most brilliant hue, while a double rainbow illumined the surface of the stream below. The picture was certainly a beautiful one, and we hung over it in delight for an hour, which, with the thunder of the Lower Fall still fresh in recollection, was all the time we could afford. Half an hour of rough climbing over bowlders and loose trachytic blocks, across Cascade Creek, and down the side of the main valley, brought us to a small plateau at the very crest of the main fall, *Yellowstone Falls. Upper Fall, 110 feet in height. Upper Fall.*

and almost at the water's edge, where the eye could plunge into the vast chasm below the fall, known as the Grand Cañon. I had not time to think of it then, but was afterward not a little amused to remember that we passed on the way one of the men who, seated on the bank, was pensively watching for a trout to seize his grasshopper. He had evidently wearied of too much bacon and scenery, and proposed a change at least of diet.

The view of the Grand Cañon from the point where we stood is perhaps the finest piece of scenery in the world. I can conceive of no combination of pictorial splendors which could unite more potently the two requisites of majesty and beauty.

Close at hand, the river narrowed in its bed to a width of some 70 feet and with a depth of 4 or 5 feet, through the pure deep green of which the hardly wavering outlines of the brown bowlders beneath are distinctly visible, springs to the crest with an intensity of motion that makes its clear depths fairly seem to quiver. Just before making the plunge, the stream is again contracted, and the waters are thrown in from both sides toward the center, so that two bold rounded prominences or buttresses, as it were, are formed where green and white commingle. Lying prostrate, and looking down into the depth, with the cold breath of the cañon fanning the face, one can see that these ribs continue downward, the whole mass of the fall gradually breaking into spray against the air, until lost in the vast cloud of vapor that hides its lowest third, and out of which comes up a mighty roar that shakes the hills and communicates a strange vibration to the nerves. From far below this cloud emerges a narrow, green ribbon, winding and twisting, in which the river is hardly recognizable, so dwarfed is it, and creeping with so oily and sluggish a current, as though its fall had stunned it. On either hand, the walls of the cañon curve back from the plunging torrent, and rise weltering with moisture to the level of the fall, again ascending 500 or 600 feet to the pine-fringed margin of the cañon; pinnacles and towers projecting far into the space between, and seeming to overhang their bases.

These details are comparatively easy to give, but how find words which shall suggest the marvelous picture as a whole! The sun had come out after a brief shower, and, shining nearly from the meridian straight into the cañon, flooded it with light, and illuminated it with a wealth and luxuriance of color almost supernatural.

The walls appeared to glow with a cold, inward radiance of their own, and gave back tints of orange, pink, yellow, red, white, and brown, of a vividness and massiveness hopeless to describe, and which would overtax the powers of the greatest artist to portray. The lower slopes, wet with spray, were decorated with the rich hue of vegetation, while through the midst the river, of a still more brilliant green, far below pursued its tortuous course, and the eye followed it down through this ocean of color until two or three miles away a curve in the cañon hid it from view and formed its own appropriate background.

The height of the fall, as ascertained by attaching a heavy weight to the measured cord, and lowering it down, is 310 feet. The first attempt to get the height was made from the little plateau by the side of the crest, but the spray soon hid the weight from view, and the water so tore at it that it was impossible to tell when the bottom had been reached. A point was found, however, to the left and in advance of the crest and some eighty feet above it, from which the weight fell nearly vertically, and by aid of the colored tags which marked the intervals of the cord could be followed with the eye until it reached the brink of the stream below. From this same point, a sort of perch upon the very border of the precipice, can be had a most comprehensive view at once of fall and cañon.

After making the measurement, we ascended the side of the cañon, and climbed out to one of the projecting pinnacles, half a mile farther down stream, whence a full view of the fall was obtained. It was remarkable to note how small a portion of the view was actually filled by the fall itself. Tremendous as it is, it seems but a minor incident in the picture constructed on the huge scale of the cañon.

From the projecting point, the width of the chasm across the top was estimated from the range of a carefully-sighted rifle at 700 yards. This, however, is greater than the average width, the cañon just below narrowing considerably and gaining at the same time in depth, which is about 300 yards. The corresponding cross-section would be similar to that in the accompanying sketch, which is intended to show the dimensions just below the fall, and another section farther down.

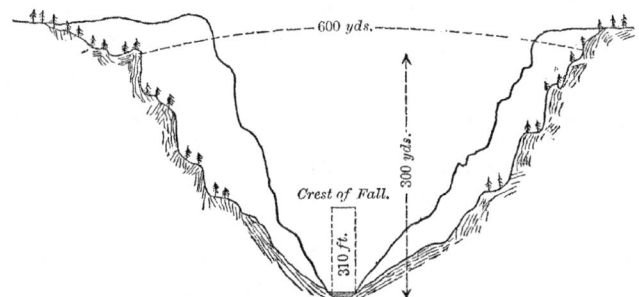

Sections of cañon just below the Lower Fall and farther down. Scale, 600 feet to 1 inch.

The descent to the bottom of the cañon from the east side is comparatively easy. From the west side it has also been accomplished, but it is toilsome and not unattended with danger, and the time necessary to descend and return would be considerable. Among other improvements that suggest themselves to the visitor as proper to be made in the future is the construction of facilities for making this descent, such as rude but strong ladders, which could readily be placed in position where their aid would obviate all danger and decrease the fatigue. One of the party made an attempt to get down, but lost time in looking for the most favorable place, and the afternoon waning, he was compelled to abandon the undertaking. *Descent to the bottom of the cañon difficult.*

August 18.—The morning opened cold and foggy. Camp was broken at 8. Took the trail which crosses Cascade Creek near the river by a steep pitch, and after a short ride over hilly ground and through timber reached comparatively open ground on the bank of the river, which was there 100 to 200 yards wide, and peaceful enough, flowing with smooth, gentle current, between low, grassy banks. The pack-train meanwhile had taken a trail somewhat farther to the westward, which avoided the steep descent into Cascade Creek and made an easier crossing of it. The two trails united at a small creek discharging into the river, crossed it, and through dense timber climbed around the shoulder of a mountain to again descend into the broad open valley of Alum Creek. This is a shallow, sluggish stream of tepid, undrinkable water, some 30 feet in width and an inch or two deep, with a general northeast course to the Yellowstone. Off to the right, across an open prairie, appeared the Sulphur Springs, or Soda Mountain, as it has been called, which we visited. Some forty or fifty acres are covered with extinct and active springs and their deposits. Pure sulphur in considerable quantity is distributed over the surface. Several springs were boiling violently, one of them to a height of 3 or 4 feet, and emitting large volumes of steam. Pursuing the course again toward the river, over a hilly prairie, and crossing one or two creeks and arms of the river, and a broad meadow, the borders of which were springy and boggy, the trail led to the edge of some timber, soon after entering which the Mud Geysers were found. We passed on to a small pine grove, favorably situated for camp near the river and twelve miles distant from Cascade Creek. Leaving the horses, we returned on foot to examine the geysers. The main one is a bubbling pool of muddy, hot water, some 50 or 60 feet across, with a sloping shore 4 or 5 feet high, and numerous small vents and springs within the perimeter. The water is thick with gray, unwholesome-looking mud, and exhales a fœtid odor. *Break camp for the lake.* *Alum Creek.* *Sulphur Springs.* *Mud Geysers.*

Another geyser, much more impressive in appearance, which however has not been seen to spout, at least of late years, has a crater some 50 feet in diameter and 25 feet deep, narrowing at the bottom to a mud pool of the consistence of boiling mush, about 15 feet across. From the northwest side of this a perpetual boiling takes place, with a threatening roar and huge clouds of steam. If the mud apparently splashed upon the trees in the vicinity would serve as an indication, when an explosion does take place the display must be a very fine one. The "Devil's Workshop" is a small steam spring issuing from a little cavern apparently 15 or 20 feet in depth horizontally, but constantly obscured by a great volume of vapor. Hollow, bubbling noises continually issue from it, which simulate, by aid of the cavern, the metrical clang and clash of great pieces of machinery, turning and splashing, accompanied by a recurring hiss of escaping steam. About 4 p. m., pistol-shots from the Mud Geyser summoned us to witness an explosion. The water had risen gradually until the smaller springs were submerged and the basin enlarged to its full dimensions. Near the center, the geyser was boiling and bubbling actively, and soon spurted to a height of 5 or 6 feet, falling and rising again, and after about three minutes of excitement subsided, the water lowered, being gradually swallowed down the several orifices, and the discharge was over. The geyser has a period of about $4\frac{1}{2}$ hours, and several of the subsequent eruptions were witnessed. None exceeded 10 or 15 feet in height. The force is evidently weakening, as indeed the large number of dead and dying thermal springs seen in other localities additionally testify. This geyser has been known in previous years to spout 50 and 75 feet. There is still, however, a wonderful amount of force at work, and in a marvelous variety of forms.

The fish taken from the river near camp were in appearance large and fine, weighing two pounds and upward; but out of the large number caught, all, with one exception, were affected by the worm mentioned by previous visitors and described by Professor Leidy. The appearance and health of the trout do not seem to be noticeably injured by them, but the presence of the worm in the flesh can almost invariably be detected from a slight protuberance or rounding-out on the sides. Laying this open, the worm is found, white, the size of a knitting-needle, and twisted in the flesh. We made no experiments to determine the flavor of these fish, although many of the men ate them heartily and pronounced them perfectly good. It is certainly most unfortunate that these fine fish should be so spoiled for the table. They abound in the lake and river, and, affording the finest sport, would be an immense attraction could they be used for food.

Wormy trout.

August 19.—Without moving camp, we rode seven or eight miles to a "ranch" in a grove on the west shore of the lake. From the Mud Geyser, the trail led through alternate forest and river side, with an occasional marsh, the landscape generally quiet and pastoral. Ascending upon a high prairie point, the lake lay before us, a beautiful sheet of water, with deeply-indented shores, and the wooded mountains closing it in on all sides. We chartered a small center-board cat-rigged sail-boat, cleverly constructed by the owner of pine cut out of the forest with a whip-saw, and crossed to the east shore. The water appeared filled with a round greenish seed, probably of some aquatic plant, and little windrows of the same seed lay upon the beach, thrown up by the waves. Some trout were taken with a spoon on the way over, all wormy, and a squall or two gave variety to the sail and tested the weatherly qualities of the boat.

Yellowstone Lake.

We passed the mouth of Pelican Creek, in the valley of which large numbers of thermal springs have been found, and landed near Steamboat Point, seven miles from the starting-point. Two or three steam-vents were seen, and one of them on the farther side of the point has suggested the name. From a small aperture, colorless superheated steam escapes with a hiss and roar that indicate an excessive tension, and imitating precisely the blowing-off from a full boiler. Multitudes of grasshoppers, unwittingly encountering the steam, had met instant death.

Steamboat Point.

From the projecting point, some 12 feet above the water, the finest fly-fishing was found. An arc of nearly 180° could be covered with the fly in from 6 to 10 feet of water, out into the lake as far as the skill of the fisherman would admit. The fish, though sometimes gorged with grasshoppers, would rise eagerly to the fly, and weighed from $1\frac{1}{2}$ to 4 pounds and upward. The largest measured 20 inches in length. None of them could be eaten.

August 20.—The trail to the Great Geyser Basin breaks away from the vicinity of the Mud Geyser to the west and north over an open sage-brush prairie, gradually becoming more hilly, crosses Alum Creek near its head, and following up a small *coulé* with flowing water at six miles from camp, climbs a hill and enters a heavy forest richly grassed. The ascent through this forest to the summit of the divide between the Yellowstone and Madison Basins is very gentle from the east. Two or three groups of sulphur springs were passed on the way. The descent from the divide into Madison Valley is precipitous, winding down a drop of a thousand feet through fallen and burned timber, and over a rocky, bare, and stony soil destitute

Divide between Yellowstone and Madison Rivers.

of grass. Reaching the border of the valley of the East Fork of Madison River, the trail winds along the foot-hills, to avoid an alkaline, boggy meadow, finally crosses the meadow and two or three alkaline brooks, in which the animals mired badly, and follows down the bank of the East Fork, which was forded two or three times. The stream is 10 to 20 feet wide and 2 or 3 feet deep; a clear, swift current and gravelly bottom, the water tepid and alkaline from the numerous hot springs which discharge into it. Camp was made in a grove of pine, after having traversed a pass between two hills which project into the Lower Geyser Basin. A small rill furnished a sufficient supply of good water, but the grazing was inferior. Several hot springs had been passed before reaching camp, and to the south the geysers appeared covering a large area. The distance traveled during the day was about twenty-six miles. *[margin: East Fork of Madison River. Camp in Lower Geyser Basin.]*

The upper valley of the Madison, including those of the forks, is quite barren and unattractive, owing probably to the action of the chemical hot springs which abound everywhere. The bordering hills are stony and bare, and at the time of our visit were covered with dead and burned timber. The landscape in consequence is uninviting, the grass poor, and good camping-places, such as can be made at almost any point in the Yellowstone Basin, are not to be found.

August 21.—The morning was devoted to the examination of the springs and geysers of the Lower Basin, which are very numerous, and cover a large extent of ground, the principal ones being about half a mile to the southward and eastward of camp. Minute descriptions of them have been published, and a detailed account is here unnecessary. Some are boiling, others spouting springs, the latter generally intermittent. On a high mound built by the geyser, we found a large pool about 25 by 15 feet, which was known to play, and the discharge of which we awaited. The water, of a deep azure hue and a surpassing clearness, was rising gradually but constantly to the level of its scalloped and ornamented rim, constantly becoming hotter, with bubbles of steam escaping more and more rapidly. Ebullition began near the middle, and the geyser finally commenced to spout, throwing the water about in all directions and to heights varying from 10 to 50 feet. The display continued for over an hour, and we left it playing, but with gradually-diminishing force. Meanwhile other smaller geysers in the vicinity played from time to time, all apparently independent of each other. The pools of all these, exhibiting every variety of form and ornamentation, possessed in common the beautiful azure tint and clearness of the water, contrasting finely with the light-gray hue of the silica deposited by them. The margins of all were incrusted with this in various forms of bead, coral, and sponge work, and wherever the geyser water flowed silicious shale was deposited. *[margin: Lower Geyser Basin.]*

Passing over a low ridge, a few hundred yards to the southeast, we came upon the "Paint Pots". This singular phenomenon consists of a "pool" some 60 by 40 feet, with a raised margin of dry and cracked mud, within which numerous mud puffs slowly rose and fell, some through the partially liquid mass, which again closed over them, others possessing a small crater of their own, to which additions were constantly making from the bursting of the sluggish bubbles. The pool displayed various colors, white, yellow, and red predominating, but shading into each other very beautifully through all the intermediate and combined tints. The clay was soft and smooth to the touch, with scarcely a trace of grit, and near where the bubbles emerged from below exceedingly hot. *[margin: The Paint Pots.]*

Leaving these, and passing by many other springs and small geysers, we went down to the Fire Hole River, crossed it, and pushed on up the west bank toward the Upper Basin, wherein are situated the Grand Geysers. After some two or three miles of travel over fallen timber and through marsh and bog, we came upon some immense springs and pools, boiling violently and discharging a great amount of water into the river. These exhibited many hues of red, yellow, and green, from the presence of iron and vegetable growths; the pure geyser blue appearing where the spring was deepest and clearest. From the pools, we continued, passing many curious springs and small geysers, and then, crossing to the east bank, pushed rapidly on through a sort of cañon on the river, until at about seven miles from camp, in the Lower Basin, we reached the lower end of the Upper, and were at once hurried across to the west bank again to examine the "Grotto", which began to play as we arrived. This geyser does not spout to any great height, 20 or 25 feet being the limit, but it is beautiful and interesting from the shape of its crater, which, some 12 or 14 feet in height, is curved and convoluted into massive *[margin: Between the two basins. The "Grotto" Geyser.]*

4 W

arches and exceedingly graceful forms. It played whenever we were by to see it, and evidently continues in operation for considerable periods, from the dimensions of the crater it has built. These craters are all constructed, by the geysers themselves, of the grayish-white silica, or geyserite, deposited by the cooling of the water; the process being very gradual and slow. The water in all is of the same pure clear blue, without a trace of any impurity. The taste, when cool, is the flat, insipid one of distilled water.

Close by the "Grotto" stands the picturesque crater of the "Giant", or "Broken Horn", a geyser of the first class. From the aperture of this, large volumes of steam were escaping, and the water was boiling violently 8 or 10 feet below the surface, occasionally rising in huge spurts and splashing over, symptoms which led us to watch it unavailingly for an hour in hope of a discharge.

Meanwhile the pack-train had been making its way along the regular trail up the east bank, and, reaching the Upper Basin, camp was established in the center of the basin on the west bank of Fire Hole River, in a small group of trees, with a fairly good marsh in front for the cattle. We found the waters of the river cool and palatable, and sufficient wood for camping purposes at hand. At short range from camp, and in full view of it, were the first-class geysers named "Old Faithful", the "Bee Hive", the "Giantess", the "Grand", and the "Castle"; while the "Giant" and "Grotto" were but a short distance farther down stream. Beside these, the "Pyramid" and "Punch Bowl", near the "Giant", could be easily seen. Almost as we reached camp, "Old Faithful", which stands at the head of the valley overlooking it, and which has earned its name from the regularity of its discharges, gave us his first display. The time was noted and the second discharge awaited. An hour after, we walked over to the elevation which marked his crater, 400 yards from camp. In a few minutes, after some preliminary spurts and splashes, the geyser, emitting a deep roar which shook the ground, shot up a clear, straight shaft of water, which, with two or three rapid impulses, gained an altitude of over 100 feet; clouds of steam towering far above and drifting with the wind. For full five minutes, the superb column maintained its height, and then, with some unavailing efforts to check its fall, sank down, and was swallowed up in the crater. An examination of this followed. An immense quantity of water had been ejected, which, after bathing the crater and refilling the adjacent pools, flowed down the slopes and discharged by various channels into the river. The crater of "Faithful" is one of the most beautiful of all. The lips are molded and rounded into many artistic forms, beaded and pearled with opal, while closely adjoining are little terraced pools of the clearest azure-hued water, with scalloped and highly-ornamented borders. The wetted margins and floors of these pools were tinted with the most delicate shades of white, cream, brown, and gray, so soft and velvety it seemed as though a touch would soil them. The material, however, is the constant silica, of which also are composed the pretty pebbles which furnish an additional charm to the pools.

The only blemishes on this artistic handiwork had been occasioned by the rude hand of man. The ornamental work about the crater and pools had been broken and defaced in the most prominent places by visitors, and the pebbles were inscribed in pencil with the names of great numbers of the most unimportant persons. Such practices should be stopped at once. The geysers are more than worthy of preservation. It is not only that they constitute a superb spectacle in themselves: they are likewise unique, both in performance and design. Nature, abandoning for the time all thoughts of utility, seems to have been amusing herself in this far-off and long-hidden corner of the world by devoting some of her grandest and most mysterious powers to the production of forms of majesty and beauty such as man may not hope to rival.

The geysers, in the slow process of centuries probably, have built up miracles of art, of an enduring though brittle material, that can be ruined in five minutes by a vandal armed with an ax, and nearly all the craters show signs of the hopeless and unrestrained barbarity of many of their visitors. It cannot fail to fill the mind with indignation to see the utter ruthlessness of these sacrilegious invaders of nature's sanctuary. To procure a specimen of perhaps a pound weight, a hundred pounds have been shattered and destroyed, and always in those places where the most cunning art has been displayed, and the ruin produced is correspondingly great. Upon our arrival in the basin, we found several persons already encamped, and a whisky-trader snugly ensconced beneath his 'paulin, spread in the shelter of a thick pine. The visitors prowled about with shovel and ax, chopping and hacking and prying up great pieces of the most ornamental work they could find; women and men alike joining in the barbarous pastime.

With regard to the play of the geysers, our visit was well-timed. Just at twilight, the "Bee Hive", 400 feet distant, on the opposite bank of the river, gave an exhibition of its power. The crater is a small, conical, gray mound of silica, severely simple and unpretentious in appearance, with an aperture of some 18 inches, from which steam gently escapes. Near by is a small vent, which is the herald and precursor of its greater neighbor. *The "Bee Hive".*

Before the "Bee Hive" plays, this vent commences to emit steam loudly, with occasional splashes of water. Soon the geyser begins to boil and steam, the water occasionally surging over. Suddenly comes a burst of 15 or 20 feet, and then almost instantly the slender shaft rises to a height of nearly 200 feet. So great is the impetus, and so slender the column, that the water, in its swift ascent, is nearly all dissolved into fine spray, which drifts off with the clouds of steam before the wind, to fall like rain. The play lasted about three minutes, and ceased as suddenly as it had commenced.

An hour and five minutes after his previous display, "Faithful" again reared his magnificent column, and during the night, whenever the roar was heard, we looked out from our tents at the grand sight, rendered more beautiful by moonlight. The intervals were exactly 65 minutes in every case.

August 22.—We were aroused at an early hour by the report that the "Bee Hive" was again about to play. This proved a false alarm, but sufficed to draw us across the river, which was some 25 feet wide and 1½ to 2 feet in depth, and while on the opposite bank we examined the huge pool of the "Giantess", which was known not to have played for some weeks, for symptoms of agitation. We found it full to the brim with beautifully clear water, of a deep blue, boiling gently, and giving out clouds of steam. It stands upon a hill of silica, 420 feet from the "Bee Hive" and 300 yards from camp. *Pool of the Giantess.*

While waiting for breakfast, attention was called to the Grand Geyser, half a mile below camp, on the east bank, which had begun to send out great volumes of steam. Hastily mounting the nearest horses, we hurried down to it. The Grand Geyser is double, the two orifices 15 or 20 feet apart. The down-stream one has a handsome crater, while the other has only an ornamental pool, several feet lower. It is from the pool, however, that the discharge takes place. Rising with rapidly-succeeding impulses, the column rushed to a height of some 80 feet, sustained itself for a few seconds, fell, rose again, and receded to its basin. In a minute or two, it again shot to the same height, again faltered, rose, and subsided. Still a third effort was made and exhausted, and the waters receded until the empty basin was exposed to view, and could be examined with impunity. Meanwhile the neighboring geyser was splashing its waters in all directions, and discharging clouds of steam, while a steam-vent close at hand kept up a most outrageous roar. Though not so lofty a play as some observed by previous visitors, the exhibition was very fine; the swiftly successive pulses of water and steam breaking into beads and spray at intervals up the full height of the column, accompanied by vast clouds of vapor, and the mighty roar combined to make an imposing and beautiful spectacle. *"The Grand."*

The surroundings of the "Grand" are the most ornate of all, and exhibit greater variety and beauty than any other.

The "Turban", which stands at the northern edge of the "pool", serves to distinguish the geyser. It is of singular form, highly ornamented, and I experienced almost a pang in becoming conscious of an apprehension that I should meet it again somewhere on exhibition. Some visitor, a little more enterprising than his predecessors, will be sure to detach it and carry it off. Shovel and ax had been busy with the geyser, and large quantities had been removed. *"Turk's Head", or "Turban".*

While returning to camp, the "Castle", on the west bank, was observed to be in agitation and giving out vast quantities of steam. A discharge soon took place, to a height of 10 or 15 feet only; but from the commanding position of the geyser and its handsome appearance, possessing, as it does, a high mound, richly decorated, and several apertures through which it plays at once, the sight is very fine. Several times during the morning it repeated its per- *The "Castle".*

formance, rarely exceeding, however, 20 or 25 feet. After breakfast we returned to the "Giantess", which was evidently becoming more excited, and, while awaiting its discharge, examined the surroundings more closely.

The basin is some 25 by 16 feet and 25 or 30 feet in depth, with scalloped margin; 70 feet north of this stands a handsome boiling spring, which has built itself a sarcophagus 2½ or 3 feet in height, like a huge bath-tub, with richly ornamental borders. This operates in sympathy with the "Giantess"; is excited, and boils violently with her; and we afterward found it empty and desolate, upon the dissipation of her power.

About 11 o'clock, this, the greatest geyser, gave its first spout, and we continued watching its subsequent action until nearly 3 p. m. The water was expelled by a succession of violent splashes to a height of 15 to 50 feet, but without at first reaching a great altitude. With occasional lulls, the performance went on, the water sometimes being thrown 100 feet in the air. Large stones and stumps were cast into the basin and hurled instantly to a height of 200 feet, the high wind which prevailed at the time preventing the water and steam from attaining a similar elevation. The water fell occasionally, leaving the basin empty; and by standing on the windward side we could look down into it and see the large triangular-shaped vent at the bottom, whence issued the transparent steam. Again and again the geyser renewed its strength, sending out vast volumes of steam with a deafening roar that shook the whole valley, and occasionally snatching hold of a new reservoir of water and instantly ejecting it; each fresh access of wrath or travail being heralded by deep, mighty thuds, as though some vast machinery were at work beneath. The exhibition of enormous power wasted in these prolonged spasms of blind rage was both fascinating and terrible, and the imagination, powerfully stimulated in the presence of such strength and fury, could not avoid imputing to the scene the attributes of gigantic passion and suffering. It seemed as though the geyser, maddened by some inexpressible and mysterious torment, were imprisoned beneath and gradually exhausting herself in unavailing struggles to escape it by bursting the bonds that held her, the paroxysms of efforts being alternated with intervals of stupor, again and again overcome by her still unabated rage.

The "Giantess".

During the afternoon, the "Bee Hive" again played, the high wind depressing its column below that of the previous discharge.

A party, about dark, came in from Virginia City. Following up the valley of the Madison River, they had brought two wagons without much difficulty through the Lower Basin, but were compelled to leave them a short distance above on account of the fallen timber and bog along the trail. The distance to the Upper Basin from Virginia City is one hundred and ten miles.

Virginia City to the geysers.

August 23.—All the first-class geysers had now been favorably seen, with the sole exception of the "Giant", toward whose picturesque crater we went, with the intention of devoting the day to it. The "Broken Horn" is a well-chosen and descriptive name, and worthy of being retained. The crater is a steeply conical mound of geyserite, 12 or 15 feet in height, tapering toward the summit, and having the west side broken down, or rather partly unconstructed. The geyser still boiled strongly, and we felt great hopes of seeing it play. Near by are the "Grotto", seen yesterday, and which played almost constantly during the day; the "Pyramid", a cone of silica 25 or 30 feet high, with steam slowly escaping from it, but its life now nearly extinct; the "Punch Bowl", and smaller ones. The last-named geyser played frequently during the day, some of its exhibitions being very fine. We waited the greater part of the day for the "Giant" to give us a display, but though evidently powerfully excited and from time to time arousing fresh hopes, to our great regret it failed to do so. Returning toward camp, the "Grand" again gave indications of strong disturbance, and we remained there for an hour, but without result.

The "Giant", or "Broken Horn".

While waiting, we had additional evidence of the brutality of the average visitors, several of whom, of both sexes, were busily chopping and prying out the most characteristic and conspicuous ornamental work. An earnest remonstrance was followed by a sulky suspension of hostilities, which were, however, no doubt renewed as soon as we were out of sight.

More vandalism.

The "Saw Mill", above the "Grand", is an interesting geyser. Its lively play, and its quick, energetic spouts of 25 or 30 feet in every direction, are very pleasing, and its borders abound in the pretty geyserite pebbles, some smooth, others ornamented, and others again resembling a rose-bud, with closely-folded leaves. *The "Saw Mill".*

Recrossing to the west side of the river, a close examination was made of the "Castle:" it has quite a lofty mound, broad, handsomely terraced, and profusely decorated with scalloped pools and little upright pinnacles and towers. It plays with great frequency, though not to a height exceeding perhaps 40 feet; still its very frequent flow and almost constant escape of large quantities of steam, with its striking-looking and highly-ornamented crater, constitute it properly a geyser of the first class. This, too, showed, and even in a greater degree than others, how greatly protection against vandalism is needed. From every part of the "Castle" pieces had been chopped, loosening quantities of the rock and threatening to ruin the construction. Two women, with tucked-up skirts and rubber shoes, armed, one with an ax, the other with a spade, were climbing about. Should this continue for another year or two, the beauty of form and outline of the geyser-craters would be destroyed. It should be remembered that these craters were constructed with the greatest slowness by almost imperceptible additions, which can only be made by a discharge from the geyser; while the material, though hard, is very brittle and easily knocked to pieces. We got back to camp just in time to prevent the fall of an uplifted ax, which a woman was evidently about to bring straight down on the summit of the "Bee Hive", whose modest crater forms so strong a contrast to the grandeur of its play. Our shouts fortunately reached her just in time, and subsequent remonstrance induced her at any rate to postpone the attack. *The "Castle".* *Geyser craters.*

Another party of four men came over in the afternoon from the lake. Including my party, there were now some thirty visitors in the basin.

August 24.—Broke camp for the return to Ellis. I should have liked to return by way of the Madison Valley for the purpose of examining that route, which at present is the only practicable one for wagons into the park; but I had reason to believe that the Missouri River navigation would probably close about September 20, and the long journey of three hundred and seventy-five miles back to Carroll had yet to be made, and a few days' delay at Ellis, in order to refit and procure fresh transportation, to be allowed for. We took the back trail to the Lower Basin, examining *en route* the Fan, Riverside, and Sentinel Geysers. The day was cold, dark, and wet, the air chill and raw. Below the Upper Basin we met three men going to the geysers, each of whom, I supposed, would carry off 20 pounds of specimens and destroy 500. The trail between the two basins is about the worst in the park, and stands in urgent need of improvement, which could readily be effected, and without the use of skilled labor. Timber, fallen and standing, could easily be chopped and thrown aside, and the marshy places in great part avoided by making the trail on higher ground along the foot-hills. Crossing the Lower Basin, which the rain had made miry, and passing our former camp, we continued up the valley of the East Fork, the principal features of which are alkaline marsh, dead timber, and little or no grass, the surrounding hills being equally uninteresting to the rapid traveler. *The return to Ellis.* *Trail from Upper to Lower Basin.*

I was desirous, on the score of time, to take the trail direct from the East Fork to Gardiner's River Springs, but a brief examination convinced me that nothing would be gained, as it was obstructed with fallen timber. The ascent out of the Madison Valley to the divide was laboriously made, the rise being fully 1,000 feet, and the back trail down the Yellowstone slope pursued. The Sulphur Springs, three in number, were briefly examined *en route*. They exhibit considerable activity, though evidently waning in force. The jets of vapor deposit small cones of nearly pure sulphur. *Trail back to the lake.*

Emerging from the timber, and soon after reaching the head of Alum Creek, we left the trail going on to the Mud Geyser, and inclining to the left crossed a range of prairie-hills, and followed down the left bank of Alum Creek until the main trail down the Yellowstone was reached. This was pursued for two or three miles farther, and camp made in a drenching rain on a small creek, which we named "Jay Creek," and near the point where the two trails from Cascade Creek had united coming up. We had traveled for eleven hours and made about thirty-six miles.

August 25.—Took the back trail over which the pack-train had traveled on the journey out, past our former camp of the 16th and 17th on Cascade Creek, and up the creek-valley. The day was very wet and cold, and desirous as I was of again looking at the Grand Cañon, I was unwilling to impair my vivid recollection of it by seeing it for the last time deprived of its marvelous wealth and brilliancy of color.

As we neared the belt of hills stretching nearly east and west across the trail, and commenced to ascend the shoulder of one of them, we were greeted with a sharp burst of hail, followed by successive gusty showers. The rain made the mountain-trail a hard one, turning the rich, black mold in the narrow bridle-path to a slippery mud, and making the up and down grades equally severe on the animals. The trail gradually ascends from the head of Cascade Creek to the divide between two mountains, thence following partly the valley of another creek, which rises nearly at the summit of the divide, descends a long winding slope, with many fatiguing and unnecessary rises and falls, until the west part of Mount Washburne is reached. Ascending this rapidly but laboriously to the shoulder, we were in a few minutes enveloped in a blinding snow-storm from the west and north, which forbade another ascent to the summit of the mountain, and continued until we were about to descend from the Elephant's Back. The thermometer fell below freezing, the wind blowing in furious gusts, and the snow occasionally turning to hail, with frequent splashes of rain. As we were about leaving the Elephant's Back, half-frozen and entirely discontented with the weather, a change took place. A rift suddenly opened in the clouds to the northward, and rapidly widening disclosed the mountain-tops brilliantly white with fresh-fallen snow, which reflected the clear rays of the sun; the dense strata of clouds drifting black and heavy beneath: the sun soon after reached us with grateful warmth.

Mount Washburne.

The trail winds rapidly down to Tower Creek, just before reaching which two deer were seen, the only game animals we encountered in the park. A number of trout were taken at the mouth of the creek, and we were much disappointed to find that out of twenty-five cooked for supper two certainly were affected by the worm previously mentioned. It has been hitherto stated, and generally believed, that the wormy trout were confined to the lake and river above the falls. It afterward appeared that one captured in Cottonwood Creek between Ellis and Baker, and several from Deep Creek east of Baker, were affected in the same way. Camp was made at the former place on Meadow Brook, and rain came on again in the evening.

August 26.—A visit was paid to Baronet's Ranch, across the bridge, in the forks. We found there a large collection of specimens from Amethyst Mountain, on the east side of the river, a locality which we had not time to visit. The specimens were mainly impure amethysts and forms of quartz chalcedony, &c.

Baronet's Ranch at the bridge.

The weather continued unpropitious as ever, and in a drenching rain the back trail up Meadow Brook was resumed. In such weather, the trail is difficult and in places not a little dangerous. It leads along and ascends slopes of clay which the rain makes exceedingly treacherous and slippery, where a misstep would precipitate a mule with its pack or a horse with its rider down several hundred feet. A great improvement could be made with comparatively little labor by widening the trail and placing rocks on its outer edge. Rain fell all day, with occasional intervals of sunshine; the trail over the broad rolling divide between the Yellowstone and Gardiner's River affording a good road, however, even in such weather. The Gardiner's River Falls were passed, and the long, sloping descent made into the valley, out of which we again climbed to the springs, just before reaching which camp was made. The rain lasted all night with great severity; the temperature steadily falling nearly to the freezing-point. Soon after our arrival, an ambulance from Ellis reached the springs, bringing Major Benham and his wife, who were about to make a tour of the park.

Trail from the "bridge" back to Gardiner River Springs.

August 27.—Leaving Lieutenant Thompson in charge of the party, I took the ambulance, and accompanied by Mr. Wood set out for Ellis, desiring to precede the party and gain time by having transportation ready to take us on to Carroll. The mountains and hills were covered with heavy snow but two or three hundred feet above us. The roads were exceedingly muddy and slippery; fresh rain falling at intervals during the day. At the toll-house, a certified memorandum of the Government transportation taken over the road was given to the proprietors. The tolls charged each way were $5.50 for a six-mule team, $4 for a four-mule team, and $1 for a single animal.

Bottler's Ranch was reached at 5 p. m., and very good meals and lodging obtained. We observed a small herd of cattle near by, with which three young buffalo were apparently entirely domesticated. *Bottler's Ranch.*

I was informed that the gold washings at Emigrant Gulch, adjoining the peak of the same name, were this year paying well; the owners taking out $10 to $25 per man, and the net profit on each laborer being $5 to $15 per day. *Washings at Emigrant Gulch.*

August 28.—Started at 7 a. m. The heavy rains had cleared up in a hard white frost. The Bottlers have about 90 acres under cultivation, irrigating from the mountains.

Under the bright sky, Emigrant Peak looked exceedingly handsome: the upper 2,000 feet covered with a broad mantle of new-fallen snow, and the air washed clean of all impurities, brought out with exceeding clearness the noble outlines and rich coloring. The road out of the Yellowstone Valley up Trail Creek needs additional work upon it, side-cutting and bridging. That down Coal and Rocky Cañon Creek is capable still of great improvement. Ellis was reached at 2.30 p. m. *Arrive at Ellis.*

August 29.—Rain fell all day. The Gallatin valley was a sea of mud.

August 30.—Rain continued throughout the day. At 2 p. m., Lieutenant Thompson, with the party and pack-train, arrived.

August 31.—Weather showed no signs of improving. The necessary transportation could not be procured at the post, and it became necessary to hire a citizen's team in Bozeman.

September 1.—Still raining. This prolonged continuance of wet was pronounced to be unparalleled in the valley. *Heavy rain.*

September 2.—Still raining. Despairing of any cessation of bad weather, I determined to make a start and try to get over the ground if only a few miles a day. Accordingly pulled out of Ellis in the afternoon with a train consisting of a four-mule ambulance, a six-mule team, and a citizen's team, consisting of six mules and a wheel-team of two broncos or Montana ponies, the eight hauling a wagon and a trail-wagon. This is the ordinary freight-wagon of the Territory. The trail is attached to the lead-wagon by a broad, short tongue, at the extremity of which an iron eye fits upon the pintle or trail-hook, projecting from the rear of the rear axle. Both wagons are provided with powerful brakes, which are set in descending hills. The two wagons can together carry over fair roads from 6,000 to 8,000 pounds. The escort consisted of two sergeants and eight men of the cavalry. *Transportation out of Ellis.*

By 9 p. m., the train, with the greatest difficulty, had made about six miles only, and camp was pitched in Bridger Creek Valley. The trail-wagon had to be left for the night some two or three miles back. Unfortunately, this wagon contained the greater part of our bedding and personal belongings, and, as the temperature was very low, water freezing in the buckets, the night was anything but a comfortable one.

September 3.—Sent back and brought up the trail, after which, with almost infinite labor, we made four miles and camped. Much of the difficulty of hauling over this Bridger Pass could be obviated by cutting and rough-bridging, with the labor of troops. *Bridger Pass.*

Three of the party came into camp late. They had been hunting in the pass; had seen a number of elk on Bridger Mountain, and killed two or three.

September 4.—Broke camp at 7, with the sun shining, and pulled up the long hill, the descent from which reaches Brackett's Creek. This hill is a plain illustration of the slight trouble required to avoid excessive labor. A road *around* this hill, nearly on a level grade, might easily be made. In fact, the road is there, except that in one place, for a hundred yards, the slope is so steep as to imperil the equilibrium of a heavily-loaded wagon. A half-day's work with fifty men would make it entirely practicable. From Brackett's Creek there is a road leading down it for a short distance; then north, up the valley of Shield's River, past the Three Peaks, to the headwater of the South Fork of Musselshell. It was represented, however, that this road was marshy in places, and, with the immense amount of rain which had fallen, would probably be impassable. I concluded, therefore, to take, in preference, the more hilly route over which we had come from Baker. About dark, after ten miles of very laborious pulling, camp was made on the north side of the mountains, at the intersection of two small streams flowing out of the pass.

September 5.—Pulled out at 6.30, and, after great difficulty, and with continual doubling of teams and dropping the trail-wagon, which had again to be brought up, we got clear of the foot-hills at the entrance of the pass. Crossing the creek, which flows from the westward out of Flathead Pass, and its broad meadow-valley, we continued past the camp of August 8, and over the rolling sage-brush prairie to Cottonwood Creek, where we camped, having made sixteen miles. During the day, three of the party ascended the mountains on the west of Bridger Pass, and obtained a superb view over the Gallatin Valley beyond.

September 6.—Broke camp at 7. Fair progress was made, but the effect of the wet weather was still evident in the lower places, and wherever a small creek crossed the road. Fourteen miles from Cottonwood Creek we passed Sixteen Mile Creek, and inclining eastward, and leaving the Baker road, made camp three miles farther on, at the head of the south fork of Deep Creek. There was but little wood in camp; the grass and water, however, being good.

<small>Camp on South Fork of Deep Creek.</small>

September 7.—Taking Reynolds, the guide, I started on in advance of the train for the forks of the Musselshell, with the double object in view of intercepting the Carroll mail-stage at that point, with probable advices for me, and of obtaining, if possible, some additional, or at least fresh, transportation, the animals having been greatly pulled down by the severity of the work since leaving Ellis.

Leaving the head of Deep Creek, the trail crosses a divide 200 or 300 feet high, and strikes the head of the South Fork of the Musselshell, which it follows to the junction with the North Fork.

The route for five or six miles is rough and broken, but finally follows the creek, which flows gently in a wide, fairly-grassed valley, surrounded by mountains. Many hundreds of cattle were grazing in this valley, which is an excellent stock-range. The "Forks" were reached at noon, thirty miles from camp. Captain Ball's company of the Second Cavalry and Rawn's of the Seventh Infantry were in camp on the broad, level tongue of land in the angle of the two streams. This camp is just on the border of the Indian range; is well supplied with all the principal requisites of wood, water, and forage; and would be an admirable location for a permanent post for the protection of the Carroll road and the thriving settlements to the westward. These districts are threatened almost every summer with forays by the Indians, from which garrisons far in their rear could scarcely avail to guard them. These hostile invasions are always sudden and generally unforeseen, and only the promptest movements of troops can be of effect. It is not difficult to see that such movements would be greatly expedited and their effect by so much increased by meeting the Indians at the very door, as it were, and punishing them there, rather than by trusting to the uncertain chance of overtaking them after the depredations had been committed. The garrison and post of Camp Baker, for example, moved forward and established anew at the forks of the Musselshell, would make almost secure the whole country behind, and, in addition, would afford a most favorable point from which to send out scouts and reconnaissances, or, on occasion, to initiate a campaign into the Indian country. Another consideration would be that the farther east such a post was established the cheaper and easier it would be to supply.

September 8.—The train came in at 9 a. m., having camped for the night five or six miles back. I was fortunate enough, through the kindness of Lieutenant English, Seventh Infantry, to obtain the loan for two days of an additional six-mule team, with which at noon we pulled out on the Carroll road, in company with Captain Browning and Lieutenant Woodruff, Seventh Infantry, made the twenty miles to Hoppley's Hole, and camped by a spring just north of the road. Wood was obtained from the eastern margin of this broad and deep *coulé*, in which, however, the grass was poor and thin.

September 9.—Started at 7 a. m., in advance of the train, with Captain Browning and a small party, for Camp Lewis. Near the spring, in Judith Gap, a small detachment of Eighteenth Infantry men was in camp. Scattered herds of buffalo could be seen grazing on the prairie south of Snowy Mountains. Deviating to the right of the Carroll road, we kept along the foot-hills of the mountains, crossing two or three small streams, and finding the grass of the hill-slopes rich and luxuriant. An hour's halt for rest was made on Little Trout Creek, and, resuming the journey, a heavy, recently-made Indian trail was crossed, leading northward. Lewis was reached at 5.15 p. m., after a rapid ride of forty-five miles.

September 10.—The train came in at 2 p. m., having camped on Buffalo Creek the night before.

September 11.—Pulled out at 8 a. m., and in a couple of hours met the Carroll stage at Warm Spring Creek. I was informed that the steamer Josephine would probably leave Carroll on the 18th or 19th, but was likely to make another trip, certainly if the stage of the river would admit. Camp was made on Arnell's Creek, twenty-five miles from Lewis, with excellent wood, water, and grass. Opposite camp, on the other side of the creek, was a plantation of wild hops in full bearing. Mr. Grinnell was exceedingly desirous of examining for fossils the lower extremity of the Judith Basin near the Musselshell River. As there was still a margin of seven or eight days, with the chance of a later trip of the boat, I determined to divide the party, sending a portion of it, under command of Lieutenant Thompson, to the mouth of the Judith River, while I should go on to Carroll, ascertain as exactly as possible the probabilities of a later boat, and send out word at what time the party should re-assemble. Mr. Dana concluded to accompany me to Carroll; his engagements at the East not admitting of any further delay on his part. The wagons were therefore reloaded with the view of sending one six-mule team and the greater part of the cavalry escort to the Judith.

<small>Camp on Arnell's Creek.</small>

September 12.—The six-mule team was loaded with fifteen days' rations; all superfluous baggage being loaded into the others. The supposed best route to the mouth of the Judith was to incline southwest from camp for a few miles, until the divide between Warm Spring and Arnell's Creeks was reached, thence west and north to the head of Dog River, and along the divide between that and Judith River, through a certain pass in the Bad Lands, of which we had general information only, to Claggett's Ranch or Camp Cooke, at the mouth of the Judith. At 8.30 the load was completed, and the two parties separated; Mr. Dana and myself, with a sergeant and one man of the cavalry escort and a sergeant and four men of the engineer detachment, proceeding on the road to Carroll, while all the others started for the Judith. We reached Box Elder Station nine miles from camp, the edge of the Bad Lands at sixteen miles, and Crooked Creek at thirty-two miles.

<small>The party divided.</small>

<small>Box Elder Creek.</small>

The day had been very hot and dusty, and we found no water between Box Elder and Crooked Creek. The bed of the creek was absolutely dry, and the single pool near the road had been trampled into a thick mud by the thirsty animals unhitched from two mule-trains and one bull-train, which had halted for the night on the creek. We had brought no water with us, and the prospects of a camp were wholly uninviting. About a mile farther down the creek-bed I observed two or three cottonwood-trees, and an examination of the locality resulted in the pleasing discovery of three small but undisturbed pools of water, tepid and alkaline, but much better than none. The grass in the vicinity too, though exceedingly poor and thin, had not been grazed by the freight-trains. Numbers of antelope had been seen all day, and from the high ground on the edge of the Bad Lands small herds of buffalo dotted the broken landscape toward the river.

<small>Camp in Bad Lands on Crooked Creek.</small>

September 13.—Pulled out at 8 a. m. Crossed Little Crooked Creek, and soon after ascended upon the high, rolling prairie, winding over which the road eventually leads out upon a high, narrow ridge near the river, where, turning to the eastward, the steep descent of 900 feet is made into the river-valley, where Carroll is situated. It was ascertained that the boat would probably reach Carroll on the 19th, and leave next day.

<small>Return to Carroll.</small>

There was a possibility that a later trip would be made; but, as this depended entirely upon the stage of water, which was very low and still falling, reliance could not be placed upon it. The week's heavy rains in the upper valleys had caused a rise of about six inches in the channel at Carroll, but this rise had been already exhausted, and more rain could hardly be looked for. I therefore dispatched a messenger to Lieutenant Thompson to be back in Carroll on the night of the 19th.

September 14.—Mr. Dana was desirous of examining the Little Rocky Mountains some thirty miles to the north and west, and we accordingly made preparations for a trip to them. The ambulance was placed in a Mackinac boat ready for transportation across the river in the morning.

September 15.—Crossed the river in the Mackinac, swimming the animals. The party consisted of Mr. Dana and myself and four men; one driving a pair of mules in the ambulance, which carried the rations and scanty allowance of bedding. Some of the Carroll

<small>Trip to the Little Rocky Mountains.</small>

5 W

hunters at first wished to accompany us, but were afterward deterred by reports of Indians near the mountains. I did not altogether regret this; for a small party entirely under control might be safer than a larger one without discipline. In order to get the ambulance out of the boat, we dropped down stream a mile and a half to the "point" below on the north bank, whence a hay-road led up the hill, climbing the 800 or 900 feet of ascent which was necessary to reach the prairie above, thence winding along narrow ridges formed by the deeply-penetrating *coulés* and ravines setting back from the river-valley. Reaching the prairie, the Little Rockies were in full view, and we traveled rapidly toward them over a dry, stony, nearly level road, with a brief halt for water at a pool in an unnamed creek-bed. Reaching the margin of the high prairie overlooking Little Rocky Creek, the descent appeared precipitous and the valley below difficult to travel. We therefore proceeded directly toward the mountains, and took our chance of finding water. Approaching within three or four miles, a very good camp for our small party was found near some springs. There was no wood, but we were fortunate enough to find a few pieces of drift brought down from the mountains during a freshet, and buffalo-chips were abundant. Two or three herds of buffalo were grazing within sight, gradually moving off as they became aware of our presence, and the antelope were more numerous than I had ever seen them. Soon after sunset, the harvest moon swung its broad disk above the eastern horizon, and flooded the yellow prairie with almost the light of day, shining brilliantly all night from a cloudless sky. The air was still, and the temperature mild and pleasant. About midnight, the snorting of the horses aroused me, and I found the men all up to keep the buffalo which surrounded the camp from coming so near as to stampede our cattle. They were approaching us to get water from the springs upon which we were encamped. The animals loomed up huge and black in contrast with the yellow prairie, and were evidently in great numbers, as their deep rattling snorts and snuffles could be heard in all directions.

In the gray light of early dawn, an antelope, attracted by the white cover of the ambulance, walked nearly into camp, and furnished an excellent breakfast. It was a barren doe, very fat and tender, with small horns, an inch or two in length.

September 16.—Mr. Dana spent the day exploring and examining the mountains. Camp was broken at 8 with the intention of finding another farther east in a sort of bay in the south side of the range, where wood would be more convenient, and which should offer better protection in case the Indians should discover us.

The presence of buffalo in such great numbers, and the known propinquity of a large Indian camp some twenty-five or thirty miles to the eastward, on Pouchette Creek, induced me to believe that a more concealed camp would be much safer. The party was so small that it would be just as well to remain undiscovered. Entering the valley, it was found full of buffalo and antelope. The adjacent *coulés* and ravines were thoroughly examined for water without success, and I finally concluded to return to last night's camp. This is ordinarily an injudicious thing to do; but the quiet demeanor of the buffalo induced me to believe that they had not recently been hunted. Sending the ambulance back to camp, I took one man, and entered a pass behind the prominent mountain, where a well-worn game-trail furnished a good path. The mountains are well wooded and some 1,200 or 1,500 feet in height, apparently destitute of running water at this season. At a narrow place in the trail, a buffalo was encountered, who, after an instant's halt, uttered a frightened snort, and whirling his huge bulk around with ludicrous suddenness, set off at full speed. A few deer were seen, but no elk or sign of any. The mountains, in fact, seem to be too destitute of water to abound in the ordinary game. Emerging from the pass directly north of and in view of camp, the bed of the stream which supplied the springs below was found to be dry and stony. High up on the mountain-slopes a herd of buffalo were grazing, and Mr. Dana was distinguished approaching them with his carbine. His shots killed one, and started the herd at headlong speed down the mountain. Hastily concealing ourselves in the bed of the stream, the herd swept past, losing two more of their number. I endeavored to overtake on horseback a calf, the mother of which had been killed, but my horse developed no great amount of speed, and the calf certainly did, skipping away from me with the utmost agility. We returned to camp and had a quiet night, though unpleasantly cold without tents, water freezing in the buckets.

September 17.—We had seen all that was necessary of the Little Rockies, and had more game than could be carried in; a prolonged stay might be attended with serious consequences, and camp was therefore broken at 8 for the return to Carroll. Steering by compass, we had proceeded for a couple of hours, when we saw half a mile ahead three men engaged in skinning a buffalo. Observing us, they mounted and started off, but soon halted and began to approach us. They proved to be Indians, a small hunting-party from the large camp, and got us to understand that they wanted to go in to Carroll with us as soon as they could dispose of the buffalo they were occupied with and another farther on. Though not anxious for their society, I assented, intending, in case of the appearance of a large party, and having any trouble with them, to hold the three as a sort of hostage. They worked with great earnestness and skill; and, having loaded three ponies with beef in a very short space of time, two of them joined us. The head-man pointed northeast, to where he said were forty-five lodges of his people. He denied being a Sioux, but spoke the language too well to be anything else. Approaching the river opposite Carroll, the two Indians wanted Mr. Dana and myself to go directly down the bluff to the river with them; but as my rifle had become disabled by an accident, and the pistol cartridges were exhausted, their offer was declined. One of them wished to assure me that he was unarmed, and throwing back his blanket showed an empty pistol-holster, and said he had lost it running buffalo. The same movement, however, exhibited the handle of a pistol on the other side. Apparently disgusted at our refusal, they plunged down the hill out of sight, and eventually reached town first.

<small>Indians encountered.</small>

<small>Return to Carroll.</small>

September 18.—Crossed the ambulance back to Carroll. The steamer Josephine was looked for hourly during the day.

September 19.—At 2 p. m., Lieutenant Thompson, Mr. Wood, and the wagon arrived, and a few hours later Messrs. Grinnell, Ludlow, and Reynolds reached town in a small Mackinac, with which they had descended the river from the Judith.

<small>Judith Basin party arrive.</small>

A march of forty-four miles in two days—September 12 and 13—had taken the party from the camp on Armell's Creek to the mouth of the Judith, where they remained two days, and returned to Carroll in four days. The lower portion of the Judith Basin is largely occupied by Mauvaises Terres, precipitous and forbidding, and very difficult to travel. A few interesting fossils were found; but the extent of the field and the limited time available prevented thorough search. A large camp of Gros Ventres was in the basin intending to winter there, and game was scarce. At 5 p. m., the Josephine reached Carroll and discharged.

September 20.—Boat took on 60 tons of freight, and left at 4.30 p. m. Lieutenant Thompson was instructed to take the cavalry escort and transportation to Ellis and to return to Saint Paul via the Union Pacific.

<small>Leave Carroll.</small>

The subsequent journey down the river was uneventful. The stream was very low, with only 18 inches of water on Buffalo Rapids, and we were frequently aground. When within fifteen or twenty miles of Buford, we met the Key West and exchanged freights; the Josephine returning to Carroll to make one more trip.

September 26.—We left Buford on the Key West at 8 a. m., reached Bismarck on the 29th, and Saint Paul October 2.

<small>Fort Buford.</small>

Thus terminated this most interesting trip, which had covered by rail, water, and on horseback thirty-three hundred miles of travel in ninety-three days through every variety of landscape, from the most forbidding to the grandest and most picturesque.

I beg leave to add the following suggestions relative to the National Park. The main points are such as would present themselves to any visitor capable of appreciating the wonders of the park, and have been in some cases anticipated in the remarks and recommendations of previous visitors. Nevertheless, a repetition of them can do no harm, and will at least show what the concurrent testimony on the subject is.

<small>Remarks and suggestions relative to National Park.</small>

Congress, by an act approved March 1, 1872 (sections 2474 and 2475, Revised Statutes, appended hereto), set aside the area therein defined (and which intended to include all the more remarkable objects and scenery) as a national domain, and consecrated it to the enjoyment and improvement of all mankind. For this purpose, the park was placed under the control of the Secretary of the Interior; but, unfortunately, the act provides no further practical measures for its improvement than authorizing the making of small temporary leases (the revenues from which should be devoted to the proper management and improvement of the park) and the promulgation of regulations mainly looking to the preservation of the game. I am not informed as to whether any such leases have been made; but it is certain that no expenditures have been made for the improvement of the park, nor even for its proper protection. Of the preservation of the game I will mention some facts further on. The park remains in the same wild, secluded condition in which it was discovered, a few squatters and hunters inhabiting it. The number of visitors is not great, but is yearly increasing, and is mainly made up from the inhabitants of the Montana towns. Until some railroad facilities shall make the journey less expensive and fatiguing, the people at large can hardly avail themselves of the "pleasuring ground" so provided. Meanwhile, however, those who from propinquity are able to do so are entering upon the possession of their privileges, and abusing them by the wanton destruction of what was intended to be for the edification of all.

Wanton destruction of curiosities in the Geyser Basin.

The treasures of art and beauty, cunningly contrived by the hand of nature, are in process of removal to territorial homesteads, and the proportion of material destroyed to that carried off is as ten to one. Hunters have for years devoted themselves to the slaughter of the game, until within the limits of the park it is hardly to be found. I was credibly informed by people on the spot, and personally cognizant of the facts, that during the winter of 1874 and 1875, at which season the heavy snows render the elk an easy prey, no less than from 1,500 to 2,000 of these, the largest and finest game animals in the country, were thus destroyed within a radius of fifteen miles of the Mammoth Springs. From this large number, representing an immense supply of the best food, the skins only were taken, netting to the hunter some $2.50 or $3 apiece; the frozen carcasses being left in the snow to feed the wolves or to decay in the spring. A continuance of this wholesale and wasteful butchery can have but one effect, viz, the extermination of the animal, and that, too, from the very region where he has a right to expect protection, and where his frequent inoffensive presence would give the greatest pleasure to the greatest number.

Slaughter of game.

The cure for these unlawful practices and undoubted evils can only be found in a thorough mounted police of the park. In the absence of any legislative provision for this, recourse can most readily be had to the already existing facilities afforded by the presence of troops in the vicinity and by the transfer of the park to the control of the War Department. Troops should be stationed to act as guards at the lake, the Mammoth Springs, and especially in the Geyser Basin. A couple of signal-sergeants might profitably be employed in keeping meteorological and geyser records, which would be of great interest and value.

Recommendation.

In time, with faithful supervision, the park could easily be made self-supporting. Franchises and leases will be valuable, and properly administered would furnish a revenue sufficient to proceed gradually with all the improvements required. But meanwhile, and before any improvements can be judiciously undertaken, an indispensable preliminary would be a thorough and accurate topographical survey, which, having been completed, would serve to indicate where roads and bridle-paths could best be opened or most improved. The boundaries of the park could at the same time be run and laid down upon the ground.

For this a small annual appropriation of from $8,000 to $10,000 should be made, and the survey might properly be under the charge of an engineer officer, who, while making his survey and map, might at the same time be turning his attention and devoting perhaps a certain sum to the selection and construction of better routes of travel. While it would not be possible at once to make the park practicable for vehicles, the pack-trails could be vastly improved at slight expense; the survey indicating the best routes. An observatory on Mount Washburne, with a wire to Bozeman, could be constructed cheaply, and furnish a starting-point whence all the higher peaks, and from them the intervening country, could be mapped. Rough bridges could be constructed where needed, and the worst portions of the trail corduroyed. This preliminary work accomplished, and about two seasons' work would be required for it, the yearly appropriation being continued, the roads could by degrees be made practicable for wagons and carriages. Lodging-places could be constructed at the Mammoth Springs, the bridge, the falls, the lake, and the geyser basins, for the accommodation of visitors; and these, after the construction by the engineer officer, should be under the charge of an officer detailed to make constant inspections of them and of the detachments doing guard and police duty in the park. Visitors should be forbidden to kill any game. The hunters should have their arms and spoils confiscated, besides being liable to prosecution.

For the accomplishment of these purposes, it would certainly be most convenient and expedient to take advantage of the presence and organization of the military, and to intrust the care of the park, at least temporarily, to the War Department; at least until such time as a civilian superintendent, living in the park, with a body of mounted police under his orders, should suffice for its protection.

The day will come, and it cannot be far distant, when this most interesting region, crowded with marvels and adorned with the most superb scenery, will be rendered accessible to all; and then, thronged with visitors from all over the world, it will be what nature and Congress, for once working together in unison, have declared it should be, a National Park.

Respectfully submitted.

WILLIAM LUDLOW,
Captain Corps of Engineers, U. S. A.,
Chief Engineer Department of Dakota.

The ASSISTANT ADJUTANT-GENERAL,
Department of Dakota, Saint Paul, Minn.

ACT APPROVED MARCH 1, 1872.

(*Revised Statutes of the United States, sections 2474 and 2475.*)

SEC. 2474. The tract of land in the Territories of Montana and Wyoming, lying near the headwaters of the Yellowstone River, and described as follows, to wit, commencing at the junction of Gardiner's River with the Yellowstone River, and running east to the meridian passing ten miles east of the most eastern point of the Yellowstone Lake; thence south along said meridian to the parallel of latitude passing ten miles south of the most southern point of Yellowstone Lake; thence west along said parallel to the meridian passing fifteen miles west of the most western point of Madison Lake; thence north along said meridian to the latitude of the junction of the Yellowstone and Gardiner's Rivers; thence east to the place of beginning, is reserved and withdrawn from settlement, occupancy, or sale under the laws of the United States, and dedicated and set apart as a public park or pleasuring ground for the benefit and enjoyment of the people; and all persons who locate or settle upon, or occupy any part of the land thus set apart as a public park, except as provided in the following section, shall be considered trespassers and removed therefrom.

Revised Statutes, sections 2474 and 2475.

SEC. 2475. Such public park shall be under the exclusive control of the Secretary of the Interior, whose duty it shall be, as soon as practicable, to make and publish such regulations as he may deem necessary or proper for the care and management of the same. Such regulations shall provide for the preservation from injury or spoliation of all timber, mineral deposits, natural curiosities, or wonders within the park, and their retention in their natural condition. The Secretary may, in his discretion, grant leases for building purposes, for terms not exceeding ten years, of small parcels of ground, at such places in the park as may require the erection of buildings for the accommodation of visitors; all of the proceeds of such leases, and all other revenues that may be derived from any source connected with the park to be expended under his direction in the management of the same, and the construction of roads and bridle-paths therein. He shall provide against the wanton destruction of the fish and game found within the park, and against their capture or destruction for the purpose of merchandise or profit. He shall also cause all persons trespassing upon the same to be removed therefrom, and generally is authorized to take all such measures as may be necessary or proper to fully carry out the objects and purposes of this section.

ASTRONOMICAL OBSERVATIONS FOR TIME AND LATITUDE AT CARROLL, CAMP LEWIS, AND CAMP BAKER.

Observation for time.

Station, Carroll, Montana.—Date, July 12, 1875.—Object observed, Arcturus.—Sextant, Spencer Browning, 6536.—Chronometer, Bond & Son, 202.—Index error, −60″.—Observer, Wood.—Computer, Wood.

Double altitudes observed.	Corresponding times.			
° ′ ″	h. m. s.		° ′ ″	
74 50 00	18 54 25.	Latitude = L	= 47 35 00
	54 55.5	N. polar dist. = Δ	= 70 10 00
	55 26.5	True altitude = A	= 37 08 20
	55 57.		
	56 26.5	2m = L + Δ + A	= 154 53 20
	56 58.5	m	= 77 26 40
73 50 00	18 57 29.	m − A	= 40 18 20
74 20 00	18 55 56.9	log cos m	= 9.3372319
		log sin (m − A)	= 9.8108128
		log cos m sin (m − A)	= 19.1480447
		log cos L sin Δ	= 9.8024365
		log sin² ½p	= 19.3456082
		log sin ½p	= 9.6728041

	° ′ ″
½p	= 28 05 02
p in arc	= 56 10 04
	h. m. s.
p in time	= 3 44 40.27
☆ Æ	= 14 09 59.5
Equation of time	=
True time	= 17 54 39.77
Time by chron.	= 18 55 56.87
Chron. fast	= 1 01 17.1

Right side:

	° ′ ″
Refraction = R	= 1 10
Parallax = P	=
Semi-diam. = Sd	=
R, P, and Sd	= 1 10
Observed 2 alt.	= 74 20 00
Index error	= − 1 00
2 alt. corrected	= 74 19 00
Altitude	= 37 09 30
R, P, and Sd	= − 1 10
True alt. = A	= 37 08 20
log cos L	= 9.8289930
log sin Δ	= 9.9734435
log cos L sin Δ	= 9.8024365

Determination of the latitude by observed double altitudes of Polaris off the meridian.

Station, Carroll, Montana.—Date, July 12, 1875.—Sextant, Spencer Browning.—Index error, −60″.—Chronometer, Bond & Son, 202.—Observer, Wood.—Computer, Wood.

Observed double altitudes.	Corresponding times.				
° ′ ″	h. m. s.				
94 32 00	19 19 43.	log cos p	= 9.3515862	log sin p	9.98875
32 20	20 36.	log Δ	= 3.6897527	log Δ	3.68975
33 00	21 20.				
33 10	22 07.	log Δ cos p	= 3.0413389	log Δ sin p	3.67850
33 50	22 42.5		= 1099″.9		
34 40	23 45.5		° ′ ″	log (Δ sin p)²	7.35700
94 35 20	19 24 45.5	1st term	= 18 19.9	log a	4.38454
94 33 29		Alt. = A	= 47 15 24.5	log tan A	0.03425
1 00	19 22 08.5	2d term	= 47 33 44.4	log 2d term	1.77579
94 32 29		Latitude	= 59.7	2d term	59″.7
			47 34 44.1		
47 16 14.5					
50.0					
47 15 24.5					

Refraction	−50″
Chron. correction	1ʰ 01ᵐ 17ˢ.1
Dec.	88° 38′ 25″
Δ	4895″

	h. m. s.
Æ Polaris	1 12 47.7
Sid. time at mean noon at this station	
Sid. interval from mean time of culmination	
Retardation of mean on sidereal time	
Mean time of culmination of star	
Error of chron. at time of observation	1 01 17.1
Time by chron. of culmination	2 14 04.8
Sid. time of observation	19 22 08.5
Hour-angle, p, in mean time	6 51 56.3
Sidereal equivalents in arc	102° 59′ 05″
p in arc	

Determination of latitude by circum-meridian altitudes.

Station, Carroll, Montana.—Date, September 20, 1875.—Object observed, ☉.—Sextant, Spencer Browning, 6536.—Index error, −1′ 15″.—Chronometer, Arnold & Dent, 1362.—Observer, Wood.—Computer, Wood.—Bar., 27^{in}. 61.—Ther., 61°.

Times of obs. by chron.	Mer. dist. $=p$.	$\dfrac{2\sin^2 \frac{1}{2}p}{\sin 1''} = k$	$\dfrac{\cos l \cos D}{\cos a}$	Red. to mer. in arc $=x$.	Obs'd 2 circum-meridian altitudes.	Obs'd altitudes, corrected for index error.	True altitudes $=a$.	True mer. alt's deduced $=a+x=A$.	Lat. deduced $=90°+D−A$.
h. m. s.	′ ″	″		″	° ′ ″	° ′ ″	° ′ ″	° ′ ″	° ′ ″
12 50 43.	4 42.	43		40	86 24 50	43 11 47	43 26 56	43 27 36	47 34 51
51 12.	4 13.	35		33	87 29 00	43 52	27 05	27 38	49
51 42.5	3 42.5	27		25	86 25 30	12 07	27 16	27 41	46
52 18.5	3 06.5	19		18	87 29 50	44 17	27 30	27 48	39
52 47.	2 38.	14		13	86 25 50	12 17	27 26	27 39	48
53 14.5	2 10.5	9	Constant multiplier, .93.	9	87 30 00	44 22	27 35	27 44	43
53 39.	1 46.	6		6	86 25 40	12 12	27 21	27 27	60
54 15.	1 10.	3		3	87 30 10	44 27	27 40	27 43	44
54 53.5	31.5	0		0	86 26 00	12 22	27 31	27 31	56
55 27.	02.	0		0	87 30 00	44 22	27 35	27 35	52
55 50.	25.	0		0	86 25 50	12 17	27 26	27 26	61
56 19.5	54.5	2		2	87 29 50	44 17	27 30	27 32	55
56 46.	1 21.	4		4	86 25 40	12 12	27 21	27 25	62
57 24.5	2 00.	8		8	87 29 50	44 17	27 30	27 38	49
57 57.5	2 32.5	13		12	86 25 30	12 07	27 16	27 28	59
58 25.5	3 00.5	18		17	87 29 30	44 07	27 20	27 37	50
58 46.5	3 21.5	22		21	86 25 20	12 02	27 11	27 32	55
59 20.	3 55.	30		28	87 29 20	44 02	27 15	27 43	44
12 59 49.	4 24.	38		35	86 25 00	43 11 52	43 27 01	43 27 36	47 34 51
Mean latitude...									47 34 51

		° ′ ″			h. m. s.		′ ″	′ ″
App. Lat. $=l$	$=$	47 35	cos 9.82899	Chron. correction	−1 02 04.16	Semi-diam.	+15 58.5	−15 58.5
Dec.	$=$	1 02 27.3	cos 9.99993	Equation of time	+ 6 38.92	Refraction	− 55.9	− 54.9
a	$=$	43 28 10.	cos 0.13922			Parallax	+ 6.3	+ 6.3
			9.96814		− 55 25.24		+15 09.	− 16 47.

Determination of the time by observed equal altitudes of the sun's limb.

TO CORRECT THE CHRONOMETER AT NOON.

Station, Carroll, Montana.—Date, September 20, 1875.—Sextant, Spencer Browning, 6536.—Chronometer, Arnold & Dent, 1362.—Observer, Wood.—Computer, Wood.

Observed double altitude.	Corresponding times.		$t−t'=$ elapsed time.	Equation of equal altitudes $=x$.	Chron. fast of mean time at appt. noon by each pair of equal altitudes.
	A. M. $=t$	P. M. $=t'$			
° ′ ″	h. m. s.	h. m. s.	h. m.	s.	h. m. s.
72 10 00	10 51 40.5	2 58 34.5			
	52 04.5	58 10.5			
	52 29.	57 47.			
	52 51.5	57 23.			
	53 14.5	57 00.			
	53 38.	56 37.			
	54 03.	56 14.5	4 2	+16.80	1 02 04.16
	54 27.	55 50.			
	54 50.5	55 27.5			
	55 14.5	55 04.			
	55 38.5	54 42.			
	56 02.	54 16.5			
73 10 00	10 56 26.5	2 53 53.			

							h. m. s.
T $=$	4^h 2^m	log A (page 164)	$= -9.4263$	log B	$= +9.3627$		10 54 03.08
δ $=$	−58″.33	log δ	$= -1.7659$	log δ	$= -1.7659$		14 56 13.81
L $=$	47° 35′	log tan	$= 0.0392$	log tan D	$= +8.2597$		25 50 16.89
1st term	$= +17^s.04$						12 55 08.44
2d term	$= -0^s.24$		$= +1.2314$		$= -9.3883$		16.80
	$= +16^s.8 =$ equation of equal altitudes.						12 55 25.24 = eq. of time.
							11 53 21.08
							1 02 04.16

Observation for time.

Station, Camp Lewis, Montana.—Date, July 25, 1875.—Object observed, Altair.—Ref. Circle, Gambay and Son, 212.—Chronometer, Bond & Son, 202.—Observer, Wood.—Computer, Wood.—Bar., $25^{in}.95$.—Ther., $58°$.

Double altitudes observed.	Corresponding times.							
° ′ ″	h. m. s.			° ′ ″			° ′ ″
	18 11 45.	Latitude = L	=	47 03 40	Refraction = R	=	63
	12 30.5	N. polar dist. = Δ	=	81 27 35	Parallax = P	=	
	13 32.	True altitude = A	=	39 22 52	Semi-diam. = Sd	=	
	14 28.5				R, P, and Sd	=	
	15 20.	$2m = L + Δ + A$	=	167 54 07	Observed 2 alt.	=	78 47 50
	15 55.5	m	=	83 57 03	Index error	=	
	16 34.5	$m - A$	=	44 34 11			
720 00 00	17 38.5				2 alt. corrected	=	78 47 50
67 58 20	18 31.5	log cos m	=	9.0227658			
	18 19 20.5	log sin $(m-A)$	=	9.8461989	Altitude	=	39 23 55
787 58 20					R, P, and Sd	=	1 03
	18 15 33.6	log cos m sin $(m-A)$	=	18.8689647			
78 47 50		log cos L sin Δ	=	9.8284436	True alt. = A	=	39 22 52
		log $\sin^2 \frac{1}{2} p$	=	19.0405211	log cos L	=	9.8332861
					log sin Δ	=	9.9951575
		log $\sin \frac{1}{2} p$	=	9.5202605			
				° ′ ″	log cos L sin Δ	=	9.8284436
		$\frac{1}{2} p$	=	19 20 58			
		p in arc	=	38 41 56			
				h. m. s.			
		p in time	=	2 34 47.7			
		✱ Æ	=	19 44 43.8			
		Equation of time	=				
		True time	=	17 09 56.1			
		Time by chron.	=	18 15 33.6			
		Chron. fast	=	1 05 37.5			

Observation for time.

Station, Camp Lewis, Montana.—Date, July 25, 1875.—Object observed, Arcturus.—Ref. Circle, Gambay & Son, 212.—Chronometer, Bond & Son, 202.—Observer, Wood.—Computer, Wood.—Bar., $25^{in}.95$.—Ther., $58°$.

Double altitudes observed.	Corresponding times.			° ′ ″			° ′ ″
° ′ ″	h. m. s.	Latitude = L	=	47 03 40	Refraction = R	=	50
	17 56 00.	N. polar dist. = Δ	=	70 10 00	Parallax = P	=	
	59 00.	True altitude = A	=	46 36 46	Semi-diam. = Sd	=	
	59 54.5				R, P, and Sd	=	
	18 01 19.5	$2m = L + Δ + A$	=	163 50 26	Observed 2 alt	=	93 15 13
	02 21.5	m	=	81 55 13	Index error	=	—
	03 14.	$m - A$	=	35 18 27			
720 00 00	04 13.5				2 alt. corrected	=	93 15 13
212 32 10	05 01.	log cos m	=	9.1478335			
	06 09.	log sin $(m-A)$	=	9.7619011	Altitude	=	46 37 36
932 32 10	18 07 02.				R, P, and Sd	=	50
		log cos m sin $(m-A)$	=	18.9097346			
93 15 13	18 02 25.5	log cos L sin Δ	=	9.8067296	True alt. = A	=	46 36 46
		log $\sin^2 \frac{1}{2} p$	=	19.1030050	log cos L	=	9.8332861
					log sin Δ	=	9.9734435
		log $\sin \frac{1}{2} p$	=	9.5515025			
				° ′ ″	log cos L sin Δ	=	9.8067296
		$\frac{1}{2} p$	=	20 51 29			
		p in arc	=	41 42 54			
				h. m. s.			
		p in time	=	2 46 51.6			
		✱ Æ	=	14 09 59.2			
		Equation of time	=				
		True time	=	16 56 50.8			
		Time by chron.	=	18 02 25.5			
		Chron. fast	=	1 05 34.7			

Determination of the latitude by observed double altitudes of Polaris off the meridian.

Station, Camp Lewis, Montana.—Date, July 25, 1875.—Ref. Circle, Gambay & Son, 212.—Chronometer, Bond & Son, 202.—Observer, Wood.—Computer, Wood.—Bar., 25in.95.—Ther., 58°.

Observed double altitudes.	Corresponding times.			
° ′ ″	h. m. s.			
	18 50 45.5	log cos p = 9.5393086	log sin p	9.97228
	51 37.	log Δ = 3.6895752	log Δ	3.68958
	52 44.5	log Δ cos p = 3.228-838	log Δ sin p	3.66186
	53 53.5	= 1694″		
	54 42.		log (Δ sin p)²	7.32372
	19 00 36.	° ′ ″	log a	4.32454
	01 30.5	1st term = 28 14	log tan A	0.02399
	02 30.5	Alt. = A = 46 34 55		
720 00 00	03 19.5	2d term = 54	log 2d term	1.73225
211 55 00	19 04 08.5		2d term	54″
931 55 00		Latitude = 47 04 03		
93 11 30	18 57 34.75			
46 35 45				
50				
46 34 55				

Refraction	50″
Chron. correction	1h 05m 36s.1
Dec	88° 38′ 27″
Δ	4893″

	h. m. s.
Æ Polaris	1 12 59.65
Sid. time at mean noon at this station	
Sid. interval from mean time of culmination	
Retardation of mean on sidereal time	
Mean time of culmination of star	
Error of chron. at time of observation	1 05 36.10
Time by chron. of culmination	2 18 35.75
Clock-time of observation	18 57 34.75
Hour-angle, p, in sid. time	7 21 01.
Sidereal equivalents in arc	110° 15′ 15″
p in arc	

Determination of latitude by circum-meridian altitudes.

Station, Camp Lewis, Montana.—Date, July 25, 1875.—Object observed, α Ophiuchi.—Sextant, Spencer Browning, 6536.—Index error, − 20″.—Chronometer, Bond & Son, 202.—Observer, Wood.—Computer, Wood.—Bar., 25in.95.—Ther., 58°.

Times of obs. by chron.	Mer. dist. = p.	$\frac{2 \sin^2 \frac{1}{2} p}{\sin 1''} = k$	$\frac{\cos l \cos D}{\cos a}$	Red. to mer. in arc = x.	Obs'd 2 circum-meridian altitudes.	Obs'd altitudes, corrected for index error.	True altitudes = a.	True mer. alt's deduced = $a + x$ = A.	Lat. deduced = 90° + D − A.
h. m. s.	′ ″	″		′ ″	° ′ ″	° ′ ″	° ′ ″	° ′ ″	° ′ ″
18 26 45.5	8 00.5	126.		2 27	111 07 30	55 33 35	55 33 01	55 35 28	47 03 39
27 16.	7 30.	110.		2 08	08 40	34 10	33 36	44	13
27 44.	7 02.	97.		1 53	08 00	33 50	33 16	09	58
28 10.	6 36.	85.5		1 39	08 50	34 15	33 41	20	47
28 36.5	6 09.5	74.3		1 26	09 40	34 40	34 06	32	35
29 14.5	5 31.5	60.		1 10	10 10	34 55	34 21	31	36
29 45.5	5 00.5	49.		57	11 00	35 20	34 46	43	24
30 26.	4 20.	37.		43	11 20	35 30	34 56	39	28
30 54.	3 52.	29.		34	11 20	35 30	34 56	30	37
31 49.5	2 56.5	17.		20	11 30	35 35	35 01	21	46
32 19.	2 27.	12.		14	11 30	35 35	35 01	15	52
32 47.	1 59.	8.	Constant multiplier, 1.176.	9	11 50	35 45	35 11	20	47
33 22.5	1 23.5	4.		5	12 20	36 00	35 26	31	36
34 12.5	33.5	0.6		1	12 00	35 50	35 16	17	50
34 53.	7.	0.		0	12 50	36 15	35 41	41	26
35 38.5	52.5	1.5		2	12 00	35 50	35 16	18	49
36 16.5	1 30.5	4.5		5	12 00	35 50	35 16	21	46
36 50.5	2 04.5	8.5		10	12 10	35 55	35 21	31	36
37 30.	2 44.	14.7		17	12 00	35 50	35 16	33	34
38 01.5	3 15.5	21.		24	11 30	35 35	35 01	25	42
38 35.	3 49.	28.6		33	11 00	35 20	34 46	19	48
39 05.	4 19.	36.6		42	10 50	35 15	34 41	23	44
40 18.	5 32.	60.		1 10	10 30	35 05	34 31	41	26
40 47.5	6 01.5	71.		1 23	10 00	34 50	34 16	39	28
41 39.	6 53.	93.		1 48	09 40	34 40	34 06	54	13
42 10.	7 24.	107.5		2 03	08 00	33 50	33 16	19	48
42 42.5	7 56.5	124.		2 24	08 00	33 50	33 16	40	27
18 43 17.	8 31.	141.8		2 45	111 07 30	55 33 35	55 33 01	55 35 46	47 03 21
Mean									47 03 37

	° ′ ″				h. m. s.		
App. lat. = l =	47 03 50.	cos 9.83326	Chron. correction	1 05 36	Semi-diam.		
Dec. =	12 39 07.4	cos 9.99932	Æ of ✱	17 29 10	Refraction 34″		
a =	55 35 20.	cos 0.24785		18 34 46	Parallax		
		0.07043					

6 w

Observation for time.

Station, Camp Lewis, Montana.—Date, September 10, 1875.—Object observed, Arcturus.—Sextant, Spencer Browning, 6536.—Chronometer, Bond & Son, 202.—Index error, 1′ 20″.—Observer, Wood.—Computer, Wood.—Bar., 25^{in}.75.—Ther., 50°.

Double altitudes observed.	Corresponding times.						
° ′ ″	h. m. s.		° ′ ″		° ′ ″
60 40 00	20 02 08.	Latitude = L	= 47 03 50	Refraction = R	= 1 26
	02 37.	N. polar dist. = Δ	= 70 10 00	Parallax = P	=
	03 06.5	True altitude = A	= 30 02 54	Semi-diam. = Sd	=
	03 36.			R, P, and Sd	=
	04 05.	2m = L + Δ + A	= 147 16 44	Observed 2 alt.	= 60 10 00
	04 35.5			Index error	= 1 20
59 40 00	20 05 04.5	m	= 73 38 22		
		m − A	= 43 35 28	2 alt. corrected	= 60 08 40
60 10 00	20 03 35.93	log cos m	= 9.4497575		
		log sin (m − A)	= 9.8385388	Altitude	= 30 04 20
				R, P, and Sd	= − 1 26
		log cos m sin (m − A)	= 19.2882963		
		log cos L sin Δ	= 9.8067069	True alt. = A	= 30 02 54
		log sin² ½ p	= 19.4815894	log cos L	9.8332634
				log sin Δ	9.9734435
		log sin ½ p	= 9.7407947		
			° ′ ″	log cos L sin Δ	9.8067069
		½ p	= 33 24 16		
		p in arc	= 66 48 32		
			h. m. s.		
		p in time	= 4 27 14.13		
		✶ Æ	= 14 09 58.65		
		Equation of time	=		
		True time	= 18 37 12.78		
		Time by chron.	= 20 03 35.93		
		Chron.	= 1 26 23.15		

Determination of the latitude by observed double altitudes of Polaris off the meridian.

Station, Camp Lewis, Montana.—Date, September 10, 1875.—Sextant, Spencer Browning, 6536.—Index error, − 1′ 20″.—Chronometer, Bond & Son, 202.—Observer, Wood.—Computer, Wood.—Bar., 25^{in}.75.—Ther., 50°.

Observed double altitudes.	Corresponding times.				
° ′ ″	h. m. s.	log cos p = 8.9318631		log sin p 9.99841	
93 50 30	20 14 34.5	log Δ = 3.6884198		log Δ 3.68842	
51 20	15 31.				
52 00	16 35.	log Δ cos p = 2.6202829		log Δ sin p 3.68683	
53 50	18 25.	= 417″.1			
54 10	19 53.5			log (Δs in p)² 7.37366	
55 10	20 32.		° ′ ″	log a 4.38454	
55 40	20 59.	1st term =	6 57.1	log tan A 0.02931	
56 00	21 37.	Alt. = A =	46 55 55.		
56 10	22 12.	2d term =	1 01.3	log 2d term 1.78751	
56 30	22 38.5			2d term 61″.3	
56 40	23 05.	Latitude =	47 03 53		
57 10	23 45.5				
93 57 30	20 24 17.5				
93 54 49	20 20 19.96				
1 20					
93 53 29					
46 56 45					
50					
46 55 55					

Refraction		50″
Chron. correction		1^h 26^m 23^s.15
Dec		88° 38′ 40″
Δ		4880″
		h. m. s.
Æ Polaris		1 13 33.66
Sid. time at mean noon at this station		
Sid. interval from mean time of culmination		
Retardation of mean on sidereal time		
Mean time of culmination of star		
Error of chron. at time of observation		1 26 23.15
Time by chron. of culmination		2 39 56.81
Clock-time of observation		20 20 19.96
Hour angle, p, in sid. time		6 19 36.85
Sidereal equivalents in arc		94° 54′ 13″
p in arc		

Determination of the time by observed equal altitudes of the sun's limb.

TO CORRECT THE CHRONOMETER AT NOON.

Station, Camp Baker, Montana.—Date, July 31, 1875.—Sextant, Spencer Browning, 6536.—Chronometer, Arnold & Dent, 1362.—Observer, Wood —Computer, Wood.

Observed double altitudes.	Corresponding times.		$t - t' =$ elapsed time.	Equation of equal altitudes $= x$.	Chron fast of mean time at appt. noon by each pair of equal altitudes.
	A. M. $= t$	P. M. $= t'$			
° ′ ″	h. m. s.	h. m. s.	h. m. s.	s.	h. m. s.
73 20 00	9 39 53.5	5 00 45.5			
	40 07.	00 30.5			
	40 23.5	00 15.			
	40 38.	00 00.5			
	40 52.5	4 59 45.5			
	41 07.	59 30.5			
	41 24.	59 16.5	7 18	+9.60	1 14 21.94
	41 37.5	59 01.			
	41 53.	58 45.5			
	42 08.5	58 31.			
	42 23.	58 16.			
	42 38.5	58 01.			
74 20 00	9 42 53.	4 57 46.			
	9 41 23.	4 59 15.73			

$T =$ 7ʰ 18ᵐ   log A (page 164) $= -9.4742$ log B $= 9.2355$ 16 59 15.73
$\delta =$ 37″.03   log $\delta = -1.5687$ log $\delta = -1.5687$ 9 41 23.
$L =$ 46° 40′ 40″   log tan $= 0.0254$ log tan D $= 9.5182$ 26 40 38.73
1st term $= +11ˢ.70$
2d term $= -2ˢ.10$ $= +1.0683$ $= -0.3224$ 13 20 19.36
    +   9.60
$x = +9ˢ.60 =$ equation of equal altitudes.   13 20 28.96
    12 06 07.02
    1 14 21.94

Determination of latitude by circum-meridian altitudes.

Station, Camp Baker, Montana.—Date, July 31, 1875.—Object observed, ☉.—Sextant, Spencer Browning, 6536.—Index error, −50″.—Chronometer, Arnold & Dent, 1362.—Observer, Wood.—Computer, Wood.—Bar., 25ⁱⁿ.20.—Ther., 85°.

Times of obs. by chron.	Mer. dist. $= p$.	$\frac{2\sin^2 \frac{1}{2} p}{\sin 1''} = k$.	$\cos l \cos D$ / $\cos a$.	Red. to mer. in arc $= x$.	Obs'd 2 circum-meridian altitudes.	Obs'd altitudes, corrected for index error.	True altitudes $= a$.	True mer. alt's deduced $= a + x = A$.	Lat. deduced $= 90° + D - A$.
h. m. s.	′ ″	″		′ ″	° ′ ″	° ′ ″	° ′ ″	° ′ ″	° ′ ″
1 10 37.5	9 51.5	190.8		4 21	123 33 10	61 46 10	61 30 01	61 34 22	46 40 43
11 11.5	9 17.5	169.5		3 52	122 30 50	61 15 00	30 27	34 19	40 46
11 43.	8 46.	151.0		3 25	123 34 50	61 47 00	30 51	34 16	40 49
12 12.	8 17.	134.7		3 04	122 32 00	61 15 35	31 02	34 06	40 59
12 35.5	7 53.5	122.2		2 50	123 35 00	61 47 30	31 21	34 11	40 54
13 01.5	7 27.5	109.3		2 29	122 32 50	61 16 00	31 27	33 56	40 69
13 42.5	6 46.5	90.0		2 03	123 37 20	61 48 15	32 06	34 09	40 56
14 19.5	6 09.5	74.5		1 42	122 35 00	61 17 05	32 32	34 14	40 51
14 47.5	5 41.5	63.6		1 27	123 38 40	61 48 55	32 46	34 13	40 52
15 22.5	5 06.5	51.2		1 10	122 35 40	61 17 25	32 52	34 02	40 63
16 03.	4 26.	38.6		53	123 40 20	61 49 45	33 36	34 29	40 36
16 31.	3 58.	31.0		42	122 36 30	61 17 50	33 17	33 59	40 66
17 06.5	3 22.5	22.4		31	123 41 00	61 50 05	33 56	34 27	40 38
17 47.	2 42.	14.3		20	122 37 10	61 18 10	33 37	33 57	40 68
18 15.	2 14.	9.8		13	123 41 20	61 50 15	34 06	34 19	40 46
18 45.5	1 43.5	5.8		8	122 37 50	61 18 30	33 57	34 05	40 60
19 21.5	1 07.5	2.4		3	123 42 10	61 50 40	34 31	34 34	40 31
19 55.	34.	0.6		1	122 38 10	61 18 40	34 07	34 08	40 57
20 32.	3.	0.0		0	123 42 00	61 50 35	34 26	34 26	40 39
20 58.5	29.5	0.5		1	122 38 00	61 18 35	34 02	34 03	40 62
21 33.5	1 04.5	2.3		3	123 42 00	61 50 35	34 26	34 29	40 36
22 16.	1 47.	6.3		8	122 38 00	61 18 35	34 02	34 10	40 55
22 44.5	2 15.5	10.0		14	123 41 20	61 50 15	34 06	34 20	40 45
23 23.5	2 54.5	16.6		23	122 37 20	61 18 15	33 42	34 05	40 60
23 55.	3 26.	23.0		32	123 41 10	61 50 10	34 01	34 33	40 32
24 32.	4 03.	32.2		44	122 37 40	61 17 55	33 22	34 06	40 59
25 00.	4 31.	40.1		55	123 40 40	61 49 55	33 46	34 41	40 24
25 30.5	5 01.5	49.5		1 08	122 36 00	61 17 35	33 02	34 10	40 55
25 56.	5 27.	58.3		1 19	123 39 00	61 49 05	32 56	34 15	40 50
26 21.5	5 52.5	67.8		1 33	122 39 50	61 17 00	32 27	34 00	40 65
26 52.	6 23.	80.0		1 49	123 37 30	61 48 20	32 11	34 00	40 65
27 24.5	6 55.5	94.1		2 09	122 34 30	61 16 50	32 17	34 26	40 39
27 57.5	7 28.5	109.7		2 30	123 37 30	61 48 20	32 11	34 41	40 24
28 29.5	8 00.5	126.0		2 52	122 32 20	61 15 45	31 12	34 04	40 61
29 11.5	8 42.5	149.0		3 24	123 35 10	61 47 10	31 01	34 25	40 40
29 42.5	9 13.5	167.0		3 48	122 39 40	61 14 55	30 22	34 10	40 55
30 12.	9 43.	185.4		4 14	123 33 20	61 46 15	30 06	34 20	40 45
1 30 41.5	10 12.5	204.5		4 40	122 29 20	61 14 15	61 29 42	61 34 22	46 40 43
Mean									46 40 49

90   ° ′ ″   h. m. s.   ″   ′ ″
18 15 05   App. lat. $= l =$ 46 40 40   cos 9.83639   Chron. correction 1 14 21.94   Semi-diam. − 15 47.9 + 15 47.9
108 15 05   Dec. $=$ 18 15 05   cos 9.97758   Equation of time 6 07.02   Refraction − 24.9 − 24.9
    $a =$ 41 33   cos 0.32204   1 20 28.96   Parallax + 4.2 + 4.2
    1.3677   0.13601   − 16 08.6 + 15 27.2

Determination of the latitude by observed double altitudes of Polaris off the meridian.

Station, Camp Baker, Montana.—Date, July 31, 1875.—Ref. Circle, Gambay & Son, 212.—Chronometer, Bond & Son, 202.—Observer, Wood. Computer, Wood.—Bar., 25in.24.—Ther., 60°.

Observed double altitudes.	Corresponding times.					
° ′ ″	h. m. s.					
	18 35 49.5	log cos p	= 9.6527431		log sin p	9.95098
	36 48.	log Δ	= 3.6894864		log Δ	3.68949
	37 22.					
	37 57.	log Δ cos p	= 3.3422295		log Δ sin p	3.64047
	38 22.5		= 2199″			
	38 53.				log $(\Delta \sin p)^2$	7.28094
	39 23.		° ′ ″		log a	4.38454
	40 32.	1st term	= 36 39		log tau Δ	0.01601
720 00 00	41 19.5	Alt. = A	= 46 03 21			
201 22 20	18 41 54.	2d term	= 48		log 2d term	1.68149
					2d term	48″
921 22 20	18 38 50.05	Latitude	= 46 40 48			
92 08 14						
46 04 07						
46						
46 03 21						

Refraction .... 46″
Chron. correction .... — 1ʰ 12ᵐ 35ˢ.05
Dec .... 1° 21′ 32″
Δ .... 4892″

                                                                      h. m. s.
Æ Polaris 1 13 05
Sid. time at mean noon at this station ....
Sid. interval from mean time of culmination ....
Retardation of mean on sidereal time ....
Mean time of culmination of star ....
Error of chron. at time of observation 1 12 35

Time by chron. of culmination 2 25 40
Clock-time of observation 18 38 50

Hour-angle, p, in sid. time 7 46 50
   Sidereal equivalents in arc .... 116° 42′ 30″

p in arc ....

Determination of latitude by circum-meridian altitudes.

Station, Camp Baker, Montana.—Date, August 1, 1875.—Object observed, ☉.—Sextant, Spencer Browning, 6536.—Index error, — 33″.—Chronometer, Arnold & Dent, 1362.—Observer, Wood.—Computer, Wood.—Bar., 25in.20.—Ther., 85°.

Times of obs. by chron.	Mer. dist. $=p$.	$\frac{2\sin^2\frac{1}{2}p}{\sin 1''}$ $=k$.	$\cos l \cos D \over \cos a$	Red. to mer. in arc $=x$.	Obs'd 2 circum-meridian altitudes.	Obs'd altitudes, corrected for index error.	True altitudes $=a$.	True mer. alt's deduced $=a+x=$ A.	Lat. deduced $=90°+$D—A.
h. m. s.	′ ″	″		′ ″	° ′ ″	° ′ ″	° ′ ″	° ′ ″	° ′ ″
1 14 17.	6 09	74.3		1 41	122 05 00	61 02 13	61 17 40	61 19 21	46 40 44
14 53.5	5 33	60.5		1 22	123 08 30	61 33 59	61 17 50	61 19 12	46 40 53
15 40.5	4 46	44.6		1 01	122 06 40	61 03 03	61 18 30	61 19 31	46 40 34
16 26.	4 00	31.4		43	123 09 40	61 34 34	61 18 25	61 19 08	46 40 57
16 48.	3 38	26.0		35	122 06 40	61 03 03	61 18 30	61 19 05	46 40 60
17 21.5	3 05	18.7		25	123 10 30	61 34 59	61 18 50	61 19 15	46 40 50
17 49.	2 37	13.4		18	122 07 20	61 03 23	61 18 50	61 19 08	46 40 57
18 33.5	1 53	7.0		9	123 10 40	61 35 04	61 18 55	61 19 04	46 40 61
19 11.5	1 15	3.0	Constant multiplier, 1.36.	4	122 07 40	61 03 33	61 19 00	61 19 04	46 40 61
19 40.	46	1.0		1	123 11 10	61 35 19	61 19 10	61 19 11	46 40 54
20 13.5	13	0.0		0	122 08 00	61 03 43	61 19 10	61 19 10	46 40 55
20 44.	18	0.0		0	123 11 10	61 35 19	61 19 10	61 19 10	46 40 55
21 09.5	43	1.0		1	122 07 50	61 03 36	61 19 03	61 19 04	46 40 61
21 40.5	1 14	3.0		4	123 11 00	61 35 14	61 19 05	61 19 09	46 40 56
22 04.	1 38	5.2		7	122 07 50	61 03 36	61 19 03	61 19 10	46 40 55
22 36.	2 10	9.2		12	123 10 40	61 35 04	61 18 55	61 19 07	46 40 60
23 09.	2 43	14.5		20	122 07 10	61 03 18	61 18 45	61 19 05	46 40 60
23 41.	3 15	20.7		28	123 10 10	61 34 48	61 18 39	61 19 07	46 40 58
24 25.	3 59	31.1		42	122 06 40	61 03 03	61 18 30	61 19 12	46 40 53
25 02.	4 36	41.5		56	123 09 40	61 34 24	61 18 15	61 19 11	46 40 54
25 38.	5 12	53.1		1 12	122 05 30	61 02 28	61 17 55	61 19 07	46 40 58
26 05.	5 39	62.7		1 25	123 08 30	61 33 59	61 17 50	61 19 15	46 40 50
26 29.5	6 03	71.9		1 38	122 04 40	61 02 03	61 17 30	61 19 08	46 40 57
1 26 48.5	6 22	79.6		1 48	123 07 40	61 33 34	61 17 25	61 19 13	46 40 52
				24) 15 12	122 38 20				
				38	33				
					2) 122 37 47				
					61 18 53.5				
					21				
					61 18 32.5				
					38				
					61 19 10.5				
					108 00 04.7				
					46 40 54.2				
Mean									46 40 54.4

```
90 00 00.0                                                              h.  m.  s.                    ′    ″          ′    ″
18 00 04.7      App. lat. = l = 46 40 45.   cos 9.83638   Chron. correction 1 14 22.38   Semi-diam.— 15 48.   +15 48.
─────────       Dec.      =     18 00 04.7  cos 9.97820   Equation of time      6 03.83   Refraction —   25.2  —  25.2
108 00 04.7     a         =     61 18 30.   cos 0.31867                       ─────────    Parallax   +    4.2  +   4.2
 61 19 21.                                  ─────────                      1 20 26.21                  ─────────  ─────────
─────────                                   0.13325                                                    —16 09.   +15 27.
 46 40 44.
```

Determination of latitude by circum-meridian altitudes.

Station, Camp Baker, Montana.—Date, August 3, 1875.—Object observed, ☉.—Sextant, Spencer Browning, 6536.—Index error, — 25″.—Chronometer, Arnold & Dent, 1362.—Observer, Wood.—Computer, Wood.—Bar., 25in.20.—Ther., 86°.

Times of obs. by chron.	Mer. dist. $= p$.	$\frac{2 \sin^2 \frac{1}{2} p}{\sin 1''} = k$.	$\cos l \cos D / \cos a$.	Red. to mer. in arc $= x$.	Obs'd 2 circum-meridian altitudes.	Obs'd altitudes, corrected for index error.	True altitudes $= a$.	True mer. alt's deduced $= a + x = A$.	Lat. deduced $= 90° + D - A$.
h. m. s.	′ ″	″		′ ″	° ′ ″	° ′ ″	° ′ ″	° ′ ″	° ′ ″
1 12 59.5	7 20	105.6		2 26	122 05 00	61 02 17	61 46 07	61 48 33	46 40 38
13 28.5	6 51	92.1		2 07	121 02 20	60 30 58	46 25	48 32	39
13 53.5	6 26	81.3		1 53	122 06 00	61 02 47	46 37	48 30	41
14 24.5	5 55	68.7		1 35	121 03 10	60 31 23	46 50	48 25	46
14 51.5	5 28	58.7		1 21	122 07 00	61 03 17	47 07	48 28	43
15 23.	4 56	47.8		1 06	121 04 10	60 31 53	47 20	48 26	45
16 01.	4 18	36.3		50	122 08 10	61 03 52	47 42	48 32	39
16 32.	3 47	28.1		39	121 05 00	60 32 18	47 45	48 24	47
17 00.	3 19	21.6		29	122 08 40	61 04 07	47 57	48 26	45
17 27.5	2 52	16.1		22	121 05 30	60 32 33	48 00	48 22	49
18 04.5	2 15	10.0		14	122 09 40	61 04 37	48 27	48 41	30
18 28.	1 51	6.7	Constant multiplier, 1.385.	9	121 05 30	60 32 33	48 00	48 09	62
19 00.5	1 19	3.4		4	122 09 50	61 04 42	48 32	48 36	35
19 30.5	49	1.3		1	121 06 20	60 32 58	48 25	48 26	45
20 00.5	19	0.0		0	122 09 40	61 04 37	48 27	48 27	44
20 30.5	11	0.0		0	121 06 10	60 32 53	48 20	48 20	51
21 52.5	1 33	4.7		6	122 09 20	61 04 27	48 17	48 23	48
22 37.	2 18	10.4		14	121 05 40	60 32 38	48 05	48 19	52
23 09.	2 50	15.8		22	122 09 00	61 04 17	48 07	48 29	42
23 34.	3 15	20.7		29	121 05 20	60 32 28	47 55	48 24	47
24 03.	3 44	27.4		38	122 08 20	61 03 57	47 47	48 25	46
24 36.	4 17	36.0		50	121 04 50	60 32 13	47 40	48 30	41
25 08.	4 49	45.5		1 03	122 07 40	61 03 37	47 27	48 30	41
25 50.	5 31	59.8		1 22	121 03 30	60 31 33	47 00	48 22	49
26 42.5	6 23	80.0		1 51	122 06 10	61 02 52	46 42	48 33	38
27 14.5	6 55	94.0		2 10	121 02 00	60 30 48	61 46 15	61 48 25	46 40 46
Mean									46 40 44

```
                    °   ′   ″
90 00 00   App. lat.= l  = 46 40 40   cos 9.83648    Chron. correction  1 14 23.7    Semi-diam. — 15 48.3   + 15 48.3
17 29 11   Dec.          = 17 29 11   cos 9.97945    Equation of time     5 55.5    Refraction  —    25.6   —    25.6
----------        a       = 61 48      cos 0.32555                      -----------  Parallax    +     4.3   +     4.3
107 29 11                                                                1 20  -9.2                          ---------
61 48 33                    1.385        0.14148                                                — 16 09.6   + 15 27.0
---------
46 40 38
```

Determination of latitude by circum-meridian altitudes.

Station, Camp Baker, Montana.—Date, August 4, 1875.—Object observed, α Ophiuchi.—Sextant, Spencer Browning, 6536.—Chronometer, Bon & Son, 202.—Observer, Wood.—Computer, Wood.—Bar., 25in. 22.—Ther., 57°.

Times of obs. by chron.	Mer. dist. $= p$	$\frac{2 \sin^2 \frac{1}{2} p}{\sin 1''} = k$	$\cos l \cos D / \cos a$	Red. to mer. in arc $= x$.	Obs'd 2 circum-meridian altitudes.
h. m. s.	′ ″	″		″	° ′ ″
18 31 34.	10 12.	204.2			111 50 40
32 20.	9 26.	174.7			51 30
33 07.5	8 38.5	146.6			53 00
33 51.	7 55.	123.1			53 50
34 32.5	7 13.5	102.5			54 50
35 09.	6 37.	86.0			55 20
36 11.	5 35.	61.2			56 00
37 14.5	4 31.5	40.2			56 50
38 06.	3 40.	26.4			57 30
38 43.5	3 02.5	18.2			58 00
39 22.	2 24.	11.3	Constant multiplier, 1.196.		58 10
40 13.	1 33.	4.7			58 20
41 00.5	45.5	1.1		85.1	58 50
41 53.5	07.5	0.0			58 20
42 54.	1 08.	2.5			58 30
43 51.5	2 05.5	8.6			58 20
44 38.5	2 52.5	16.2			58 10
45 25.	3 39.	26.2			57 50
46 10.	4 24.	38.0			56 40
46 55.5	5 09.5	52.3			56 20
47 32.5	5 46.5	65.5			56 00
48 16.	6 30.	83.0			55 10
48 53.	7 07.	99.7			54 20
49 31.	7 45.	117.9			54 00
50 34.5	8 48.5	152.3			52 30
18 51 32.	9 46.	187.3			111 51 50
					111 55 48
					60
					111 54 48
					55 57 24
					32
					55 56 52
					1 25.1
		71.14			55 58 17.1
					102 39 08.6
					46 40 51.5

```
                  °   ′   ″
App. lat. = l  = 46 40 40.    cos 9.83648     Chron. correction   1 12 35.65    Semi-diam.
Dec.           = 12 39 08.6   cos 9.98932     * Æ                17 29 10.38    Refraction — 32″
  a            = 55 57        cos 0.25188                                        Parallax
                  1.196         0.07768        Equation of time  18 41 46.03
```

TO YELLOWSTONE NATIONAL PARK.

Determination of the latitude by observed double altitudes of Polaris off the meridian.

Station, Camp Baker, Montana.—Date, August 4, 1875.—Ref. Circle, Gambay & Son, 212.—Chronometer, Bond & Son, 202.—Observer, Wood.—Computer, Wood.—Bar., 25in.22.—Ther., 57°.

Observed double altitudes.	Corresponding times.			
° ′ ″	h. m. s.			
	19 37 17.	log cos p = 9.2947207	log sin p	9.991395
	37 59.5	log Δ = 3.6893977	log Δ	3.689398
	38 48.	log Δ cos p = 2.9841184	log Δ sin p	3.680793
	39 26.	= 964″.1		
	39 58.5		log (Δ sin p)^2	7.36159
	40 32.	° ′ ″	log a	4.38454
	41 17.5	1st term = 16 04.1	log tan A	.02125
	41 53.	Alt. = A = 46 24 05.		
208 17 00	42 25.	2d term = 58.5	log 2d term	1.76738
720 00 00	19 42 56.		2d term	58″.5
10)928 17 00	19 40 15.25	Latitude = 46 41 07.6		
92 49 42				
46 24 51				
46				
46 24 05				

Refraction	46″
Chron. correction	1h 12m 35s.65
Dec.	88° 38′ 29″
Δ	4891″

	h. m. s.
Æ Polaris	1 13 08.00
Sid. time at mean noon at this station	
Sid. interval from mean time of culmination	
Retardation of mean on sidereal time	
Mean time of culmination of star	
Error of chron. at time of observation	1 12 35.65
Time by chron. of culmination	2 25 43.65
Clock-time of observation	19 40 15.25
Hour-angle, p, in sid. time	6 45 28.4
Sidereal equivalents in arc	101° 22′ 06″
p in arc	

Determination of latitude by circum-meridian altitudes.

Station, Camp Baker, Montana.—Date, August 4, 1875.—Object observed, η Serpentis.—Sextant, Spencer Browning, 6536.—Index error, — 30″.—Chronometer, Bond & Son, 202.—Observer, Wood.—Computer, Wood.—Bar., 25in.22.—Ther., 57°.

Times of obs. by chron.	Mer. dist. = p.	$\dfrac{2 \sin^2 \frac{1}{2} p}{\sin 1''}$ = k.	$\dfrac{\cos l \cos D}{\cos a}$	Red. to mer. in arc = x.	Obs'd 2 circum-meridian altitudes.
h. m. s.	′ ″	″		″	° ′ ″
19 23 18.5	4 10.5	34.3			80 49 00
24 07.	3 22.	22.3			49 00
24 49.	2 40.	14.0			49 00
25 37.5	1 41.5	5.7			49 10
26 42.5	46.5	1.2	Constant multiplier, .879.		49 10
27 19.5	09.5	.0			49 30
28 01.	32.	.6		13	49 30
28 42.	1 13.	2.9			49 20
29 19.	1 50.	6.6			49 10
30 04.5	2 35.5	13.2			49 00
30 46.	3 17.	21.2			49 00
31 24.	3 55.	30.1			48 10
19 32 11.	4 42.	43.4			80 47 40
		15.0			80 48 58
					30
					80 48 28
					40 24 14
					57
					40 23 17
					13
					40 23 30
					87 04 12
					46 40 42

	° ′ ″			h. m. s.	
App. lat. = l =	46 40 40.	cos 9.83648	Chron. correction	1 12 35.65	Semi-diam.
Dec. = S.	2 55 48.3	cos 9.99943	⋆ Æ	18 14 53.22	Refraction 57″
a =	40 23 20.	cos 0.11824		19 27 28.87	Parallax
	.879	9.94415			

Observation for time.

Station, Camp Baker, Montana.—Date, August 5, 1875.—Object observed, Altair.—Ref. circle, Gambay & Son, 212.—Chronometer, Bond & Sons, 202.—Observer, Wood.—Computer, Wood.—Bar., 25in.30.—Ther., 53°.

Double altitudes observed.	Corresponding times.								
° ′ ″	h. m. s.				° ′ ″				″
	18 24 55.5	Latitude = L	=	46 40 40		Refraction = R	=		56.8
	25 47.5	N. polar dist. = Δ	=	81 27 33		Parallax = P	=		
	26 16.	True altitude = A	=	40 19 44		Semi-diam. = Sd	=		
	27 06.5					R, P, and Sd	=		
	27 37.	$2m = L + \Delta + A$	=	168 27 57		Observed 2 alt.	=		
	28 07.5					Index error	=		
	28 40.	m	=	84 13 58.5		2 alt. corrected	=		
	29 15.5	$m - A$	=	43 54 14.5		Altitude	=		
86 53 30	29 46.	log cos m	=	9.0021000		R, P, and Sd	=		
720 00 00	18 30 24.5	log sin $(m-A)$	=	9.8410167		True alt. = A	=		
———		log cos m sin $(m-A)$	=	18.8431167		log cos L	=		9.8363878
806 53 30	18 27 47.6	log cos L sin Δ	=	9.8315447		log sin Δ	=		9.9951569
80 41 21		log sin² ½ p	=	19.0115720		log cos L sin Δ	=		9.8315447
40 20 40.5		log sin ½ p	=	9.5057860					
56.8				° ′ ″					
———		½ p	=	18 41 29					
40 19 44		p in arc	=	37 22 58					
				h. m. s.					
		p in time	=	2 29 31.87					
		✱ Æ	=	19 44 43.9					
		True time	=	17 15 12.					
		Time by chron.	=	18 27 47.6					
		Chron. fast	=	1 12 35.6					

Observation for time.

Station, Camp Baker, Montana.—Date, August 5, 1875.—Object observed, Arcturus.—Ref. circle, Gambay & Son, 212.—Chronometer, Bond & Son, 202.—Observer, Wood.—Computer, Wood.—Bar., 25in.30.—Ther., 53°.

Double altitudes observed.	Corresponding times.								
° ′ ″	h. m. s.			° ′ ″					″
	18 51 44.	Latitude = L	=	46 40 40		Refraction = R	=		58
	52 56.5	N. polar dist. = Δ	=	70 10 00		Parallax = P	=		
	53 30.	True altitude = A	=	39 25 30		Semi-diam. = Sd	=		
	54 07.					R, P, and Sd	=		
	54 34.	$2m = L + \Delta + A$	=	156 16 10		Observed 2 alt.	=		
	54 59.5					Index error	=		
	55 29.	m	=	78 08 05		2 alt. corrected	=		
	55 55.5	$m - A$	=	38 42 35		Altitude	=		
68 49 30	56 28.5	log cos m	=	9.3130467		R, P, and Sd	=		
720 00 00	18 56 55.5	log sin $(m-A)$	=	9.7961406		True alt. = A	=		
———		log cos m sin $(m-A)$	=	19.1091873		log cos L	=		9.8363878
10)788 49 30	18 54 39.95	log cos L sin Δ	=	9.8098313		log sin Δ	=		9.9734435
78 52 57		log sin² ½ p	=	19.2993560		log cos L sin Δ	=		9.8098313
39 26 28.0		log sin ½ p	=	9.6496780					
58				° ′ ″					
———		½ p	=	26 30 36					
39 25 30		p in arc	=	53 01 12					
				h. m. s.					
		p in time	=	3 32 04.8					
		✱ Æ	=	14 09 59.1					
		True time	=	17 42 03.9					
		Time by chron.	=	18 54 39.95					
		Chron. fast	=	1 12 36.0					

TO YELLOWSTONE NATIONAL PARK.

Determination of latitude by circum-meridian altitudes.

Station, Camp Baker, Montana.—Date, August 5, 1875.—Object observed, a Ophiuchi.—Ref. circle, Gambay & Son, 212.—Chronometer, Bond & Son, 202.—Observer, Wood.—Computer, Wood.—Bar., 25^{in}.30.—Ther., 53°.

Times of obs. by chron.			Mer. dist. $= p$.		$\dfrac{2 \sin^2 \frac{1}{2} p}{\sin 1''} = k$.	$\dfrac{\cos l \cos D}{\cos a}$	Red. to mer. in arc $= x$.	Observed 2 circum-meridian altitudes.		
h.	m.	s.	′	″	″		″	°	′	″
18	35	33.5	6	13	75.9					
	37	54.5	3	52	29.4					
	38	51.	2	55	16.7					
	39	51.	1	55	7.2					
	40	52.5		54	1.6	Cons't multiplier, 1.196.	40.8			
	41	59.5		13	....					
	43	10.5	1	24	3.9					
	44	18.	2	32	12.6					
	45	17.	3	31	24.3					
	46	41.	4	56	47.8					
	47	58.5	6	12	75.5			623	26	40
18	49	24.	7	38	114.4			720	00	00
					34.1			12)1343	26	40
								111	57	13.3
								55	58	36.6
										33
								55	58	03.6
										40.8
								55	58	44.4
								102	39	08.7
								46	40	24

	°	′	″			h.	m.	s.		
App. lat. $= l$	46	40	40	cos 9.83648	Chron. correction	1	12	35.8	Semi-diam.	
Dec.	12	39	08.7	cos 9.98932	Equation of time	17	29	10.4	Refraction	33″
a	55	58		cos 0.25206					Parallax	
		1.196		0.07786		18	41	46.2		

Determination of latitude by circum-meridian altitudes.

Station, Camp Baker, Montana.—Date, August 5, 1875.—Object observed, η Serpentis.—Ref. circle, Gambay & Son, 212.—Chronometer, Bond & Son, 202.—Observer, Wood.—Computer, Wood.—Bar., 27^{in}.30.—Ther., 53°.

Times of obs. by chron.			Mer. dist. $= p$.		$\dfrac{2 \sin^2 \frac{1}{2} p}{\sin 1''} = k$	$\dfrac{\cos l \cos D}{\cos a}$	Obs'd 2 circum-meridian altitudes.		
h.	m.	s.	′	″	″		°	′	″
19	23	15.	4	14.	35.2				
	24	53.5	2	35.5	13.2				
	25	55.	1	34.	4.8				
	26	55.5		33.5	0.6	Constant multiplier, .879.			
	27	56.5		27.5	0.4				
	28	54.	1	25.	3.9				
	30	24.5	2	55.5	16.8				
19	31	34.	4	05.	32.7		8) 646	29	00
					13.45		80	48	37.5
							40	24	18.7
									56.4
							40	23	22.3
									11.8
							40	23	34.1

	°	′	″			h.	m.	s.		
App. lat. $= l$	46	40	40	cos 9.83648	Chron. correction	1	12	35.8	Semi-diam.	
Dec.	2	55	48.3	cos 9.99943	$*$ Æ	18	14	53.2	Refraction	56″.4
a	40	23	20	cos 0.11824					Parallax	
	.879			9.94415		19	27	29.0		

Determination of the latitude by observed double altitudes of Polaris off the meridian.

Station, Camp Baker, Montana.—Date, August 5, 1875.—Ref. circle, Gambay & Son, 212.—Chronometer, Bond & Son, 202.—Observer, Wood.—Computer, Wood.—Bar., 25ⁱⁿ. 30.—Ther., 53°.

Observed double altitudes.	Corresponding times.			
° ′ ″	h. m. s.			
	19 34 18.5	$\log \cos p$ = 9.3227046		$\log \sin p$ 9.99018
	34 48.	$\log \Delta$ = 3.6893977		$\log \Delta$ 3.68940
	35 31.			
	36 30.	$\log \Delta \cos p$ = 3.0121023		$\log \Delta \sin p$ 3.67958
	37 06.5	= 1028″.3		
	37 37.5		° ′ ″	$\log (\Delta \sin p)^2$ 7.35916
	38 08.5	1st term =	17 08.3	$\log a$ 4.38454
	38 44.	Alt. = A =	46 22 43.2	$\log \tan A$ .02091
207 50 00	39 17.5	2d term	58.2	$\log$ 2d term 1.76461
720 00 00	19 39 57.5			2d term 58″.2
10) 927 50 00	19 37 11.9	Latitude =	46 40 49.7	
92 47 00				
46 23 30				
46.8				
46 22 43.2				

Refraction	46″.8
Chron. correction	1ʰ 12ᵐ 35ˢ.8
Dec	88° 38′ 29″
Δ	4891″
	h. m. s.
Æ Polaris	1 13 08.76
Sid. time at mean noon at this station	
Sid. interval from mean time of culmination	
Retardation of mean on sidereal time	
Mean time of culmination of star	
Error of chron. at time of observation	1 12 35.8
Time by chron. of culmination	2 25 44.56
Clock-time of observation	19 37 11.9
Hour-angle, p, in mean time	6 48 32.66
Sidereal equivalents in arc	102° 08′ 10″
p in arc	

Determination of the latitude by observed double altitudes of Polaris off the meridian.

Station, Camp Baker, Montana.—Date, August 5, 1875.—Sextant, Spencer Browning, 6536.—Index error, −60″.—Chronometer, Bond & Son, 202.—Observer, Wood.—Computer, Wood.—Bar., 25ⁱⁿ. 30.—Ther., 53°.

Observed double altitudes.	Corresponding times.			
° ′ ″	h. m. s.			
92 30 30	19 11 51.5	$\log \cos p$ = 9.4822605		$\log \sin p$ 9.97901
31 10	12 44.	$\log \Delta$ = 3.6893977		$\log \Delta$ 3.68940
31 20	13 24.5			
31 50	14 01.5	$\log \Delta \cos p$ = 3.1716582		$\log \Delta \sin p$ 3.66841
32 10	14 40.	= 1484″.8		
32 40	15 23.		° ′ ″	$\log (\Delta \sin p)^2$ 7.33682
33 20	16 10.5			$\log a$ 4.38454
34 00	16 49.5	1st term =	24 44.8	$\log \tan A$ 0.01896
34 15	17 21.5	Alt. = A =	46 15 00.7	
92 34 35	19 18 06.5	2d term =	55.0	$\log$ 2d term 1.74032
92 32 35	19 15 03.25			2d term 55″.0
1 00		Latitude =	46 40 40.5	
92 31 35				
46 15 47.5				
46.8				
46 15 00.7				

Refraction	46″.8
Chron. correction	1ʰ 12ᵐ 35ˢ.8
Dec	88° 38′ 29″
Δ	4891″
	h. m. s.
Æ Polaris	1 13 08.76
Sid. time at mean noon at this station	
Sid. interval from mean time of culmination	
Retardation of mean on sidereal time	
Mean time of culmination of star	
Error of chron. at time of observation	1 12 35.8
Time by chron. of culmination	2 25 44.56
Clock-time of observation	19 15 03.25
Hour-angle, p, in sid. time	7 10 41.3
Sidereal equivalents in arc	107° 40′ 20″
p in arc	

Determination of the latitude by observed double altitudes of Polaris off the meridian.

Station, Camp Baker, Montana.—Date, August 5, 1875.—Ref. Circle, Gambay & Son, 212.—Chronometer, Bond & Son, 202.—Observer, Wood.—Computer, Wood.—Bar., 25ⁱⁿ.30.—Ther., 53°.

Observed double altitudes.	Corresponding times.							
° ′ ″	h.	m.	s.					
	19	01	49.5	$\log \cos p$	= 9.5388061		$\log \sin p$	9.97235
		02	41.5	$\log \Delta$	= 3.6893977		$\log \Delta$	3.68940
		03	07.5	$\log \Delta \cos p$	= 3.2282038		$\log \Delta \sin p$	3.66175
		03	53.5		= 1691″.2		$\log (\Delta \sin p)^2$	7.32350
		04	24.5		° ′ ″		$\log a$	4.38454
		05	07.	1st term	= 28 11.2		$\log \tan A$	0.01817
		05	54.	Alt. = A	= 46 11 53.7			
		06	32.	2d term	= 53.2		$\log$ 2d term	1.72621
204 13 30		07	00.				2d term	53″.2
720 00 00	19	07	45.	Latitude	= 46 40 58.1			
10) 924 13 30	19	04	49.45					
92 25 21								
46 12 40.5								
46.8								
46 11 53.7								

Refraction .... 46″.8
Chron. correction 1ʰ 12ᵐ 35ˢ.8
Dec. .... 88° 38′ 29″
Δ .... 4891″

	h.	m.	s.
Æ Polaris	1	13	08.76
Sid. time at mean noon at this station			
Sid. interval from mean time of culmination			
Retardation of mean on sidereal time			
Mean time of culmination of star			
Error of chron. at time of observation	1	12	35.8
Time by chron. of culmination	2	25	44.56
Clock-time of observation	19	04	49.45
Hour-angle, p, in mean time	7	20	55.1
Sidereal equivalents in arc	110°	13′	47″

p in arc ....

Summary table of daily instrumental observations with deduced altitudes, latitude, and longitude of each camp, and of the Montana posts, distances traveled, &c.

Station.	Date.	Start.	Arrive.	Barometer.	Elevation.	Latitude.	Longitude.	Day's march.	Total distance.
	1875.	h.	h.	Inches.	Feet.	° ′ ″	° ′ ″	Miles.	Miles.
Carroll	July 13	9.00 a. m.		27.50	2,247	47 34 48	108 24 00		
Little Crooked Creek	July 13		1.30 p. m.	26.80	2,923	47 30 01	108 34 30	13	13
Crooked Creek	July 16	8.00 a. m.	10.00 a. m.	26.95	2,776	47 28 00	108 41 30	6	19
Box Elder Creek	July 18	7.00 a. m.	2.30 p. m.	26.28	3,437	47 20 43	109 02 00	19.5	38.5
Camp Lewis	July 25	6.00 a. m.	5.00 p. m.	25.83	3,890	47 03 47	109 26 30	36	74.5
Ross's Fork	July 26	7.30 a. m.	4.30 p. m.	25.54	4,186	46 47 03	109 44 00	27	101.5
Haymaker's Creek	July 27	7.00 a. m.	4.20 p. m.	25.07	4,673	46 30 00	110 06 40	29	130.5
North Fork Musselshell	July 28	7.30 a. m.	2.00 p. m.	24.70	5,063	46 33 13	110 28 30	19.25	149.75
Brewer's Springs	July 29	7.45 a. m.	4.00 p. m.	24.80	4,957	46 32 50	110 55 40	27	176.75
Camp Baker	July 30	8.30 a. m.	1.15 p. m.	25.20	4,538	46 40 44	111 11 00	16.75	193.5
Moss Agate Springs	Aug. 7	8.00 a. m.	5.00 p. m.	24.66	5,106	46 23 40	110 53 30	27	220.5
Twenty-five Yard Creek	Aug. 8	6.30 a. m.	5.30 p. m.	24.58	5,191	46 00 05	110 48 40	32	252.5
Fort Ellis	Aug. 9	6.15 a. m.	5.00 p. m.	25.00	4,747	45 40 15	110 59 04	28.75	281.25
Drane's Dam	Aug. 10	8.00 p. m.	8.45 p. m.					1.5	282.75
Boteler's Ranch	Aug. 11	6.30 a. m.	7.30 p. m.	24.88	4,873			33.25	316
Rocky Cañon	Aug. 12	6.30 a. m.	12.30 p. m.	24.90	4,958			15.5	331.5
Mammoth Springs	Aug. 13	7.45 a. m.	6.40 p. m.	23.73	6,114			18	349.5
Meadow Brook	Aug. 15	8.20 a. m.	3.00 p. m.	23.80	6,037			15	364.5
Cascade Creek	Aug. 16	8.40 a. m.	5.00 p. m.	22.28	7,767	44 43 40		19.5	384
Mud Volcano	Aug. 18	8.20 a. m.	11.45 a. m.	22.40	7,626	44 37 17		11	395
Yellowstone Lake and return	Aug. 19	9.30 a. m.	2.30 p. m.					16	411
Lower Geyser Basin	Aug. 20	8.30 a. m.	5.00 p. m.	22.73	7,238			26	437
Upper Geyser Basin	Aug. 21	1.10 p. m.	4.20 p. m.	22.64	7,347	44 27 40		9	446
Jay Creek	Aug. 24	8.40 a. m.	7.30 p. m.	22.40	7,626			40	486
Meadow Brook	Aug. 25	8.00 a. m.	3.50 p. m.					23	509
Mammoth Springs	Aug. 26	7.50 a. m.	12.30 p. m.					15	524
Rocky Cañon	Aug. 27	12.30 p. m.	5.30 p. m.					18	542
Boteler's Ranch	Aug. 28	8.30 a. m.	12.30 p. m.					15	557
Sprague's Ranch	Aug. 29	8.50 a. m.	1.50 p. m.					16.5	573.5
Fort Ellis	Aug. 30	9.15 a. m.	1.50 p. m.					18.5	592
Bridger Creek	Sept. 2	3.00 p. m.	7.50 p. m.					6	598
Bridger Creek	Sept. 3	10.30 a. m.	4.00 p. m.	24.28	5,513	45 45 27	110 53 45	4	602
Bridger Pass	Sept. 4	8.20 a. m.	6.00 p. m.	23.70	6,147	45 53 40	110 53 30	10.25	612.25
Cottonwood Creek	Sept. 5	1.10 p. m.	7.00 p. m.	24 37	5,416	46 05 30	110 45 15	16	628.25
Deep Creek	Sept. 6	6.45 a. m.	5.30 p. m.	24.25	5,545	46 20 12	110 45 30	16.5	644.75
South Fork of Musselshell	Sept. 7	7.30 a. m.	4.00 p. m.	24.61	5,160	46 26 08	110 24 50	21.75	666.25
Hopley's Hole	Sept. 8	7.00 a. m.	6.15 p. m.	24.86	4,894			27.25	693.5
Buffalo Creek	Sept. 9	6.30 a. m.	1.30 p. m.	25.37	4,360			24	717.5
Camp Lewis	Sept. 10	6.45 a. m.	1.45 p. m.	25.83	3,890			21.5	739
Arnell's Creek	Sept. 11	6.30 a. m.	3.30 p. m.	25.90	3,820	47 19 12	109 12 00	26	765
Dog Creek	Sept. 12	7.30 a. m.	3.45 p. m.	26.05	3,668	47 25 10	109 20 30	16.25	781.25
Judith River	Sept. 13	7.00 a. m.	7.30 p. m.	27.40	2,343	47 41 30	109 39 30	28	809.25
Near Dog Creek	Sept. 16	6.30 a. m.	3.30 p. m.	26.50	3,220	47 31 17	109 27 30	17.5	826.75
Armell's Creek	Sept. 17	6.30 a. m.	4.30 p. m.					23	849.75
Crooked Creek	Sept. 18	7.00 a. m.	4.45 p. m.					26	875.75
Carroll	Sept. 19	7.30 a. m.	2.15 p. m.					22.5	898.25
Fort Shaw						47 30 33	111 48 19.5		
Fort Benton						47 49 38	110 39 48		

Distances on the Missouri River from Bismarck to Benton, from a survey by Lieut. F. V. Greene, United States Engineers, under direction of Capt. W. J. Twining, Corps of Engineers.

From Bismarck.	To—	From Fort Benton.
Miles.		Miles.
805.4	Fort Benton	....
787.7	Marias River	17.7
764.9	Little Sandy River	40.5
756.4	Citadel Rock	49
745.9	Cathedral Rock	59.5
743.4	Hole in the Wall	62
731.4	Arrow River	74
725.3	Drowned Man's Rapids	80.1
723.1	Old Camp Cook	82.3
722.4	Judith River	83
718.8	Holmes Rapids	86.6
707.6	Dauphin Rapids	87.8
693.7	Lone Pine Rapids	111.7
689.6	Sturgeon Island	115.8
681.9	Cow Island	123.5
671.4	Grand Island	134
665.3	Two Calf Island	140.1
657.8	Emile or Harriett Island	147.6
647.9	Little Rock Creek	157.5
638.9	Carroll	166.5
621.7	Beauchamp's Creek	183.7
619.4	Boyd's Island	186
600.9	Musselshell River	204.5
486.2	Fort Peck	319.2
468.6	Milk River	336.8
453.4	Porcupine Creek	352
373.4	Frenchmen's Point	432
355.8	Big Muddy River	449.6
321.9	Little Muddy River	483.5
309.4	Fort Union	496
305	Yellowstone River	500.4
302.9	Fort Buford	502.5
267.8	Muddy River	537.6
205	White Earth River	600.4
186.4	Little Knife River	619
131.6	Little Missouri	673.8
108.4	Fort Berthold	697
84	Fort Stevenson	721.4
60.4	Big Knife River	745
52.5	Fort Clark	752.9
....	Bismarck	805.4

REPORT OF A RECONNAISSANCE OF JUDITH BASIN, AND OF A TRIP FROM CARROLL TO FORT ELLIS, VIA YELLOWSTONE RIVER.

By Lieut. R. E. Thompson.

Fort Stevenson, Dak., *March* 8, 1876.

Sir: I have the honor to forward herewith a report of the reconnaissance of the Judith Basin, made during the past summer, in accordance with your orders, and an account of my subsequent return from Carroll, Mont., to Fort Ellis, by way of the Yellowstone River.

The trip to the Judith River, which was laid out as part of the summer's work, on condition that it could be completed before the close of navigation on the Upper Missouri, was ordered from the camp on Armell's Creek, September 11. Its object was the examination of the country in the vicinity of the Judith, with regard to its topographical features, to accurately locate its position, but more particularly to afford an opportunity for a thorough search for fossil remains in the cut banks of its valley, which offer so extensive an exposure. The party consisted of a sergeant and one private of the Engineer Battalion, charged with running the trail by compass and odometer; a detachment of a sergeant and seven privates of the Second Cavalry as escort; and Reynolds as guide.

Mr. G. B. Grinnell and Mr. Ludlow accompanied the party; the former interested in the paleontology and zoology of the country. Sextant-observations were made by Mr. W. H. Wood whenever practicable.

Including myself, the party numbered fifteen men, all mounted, save the teamster, the sergeant in charge of the odometer-cart, and the man charged with the care of the chronometers.

On the morning of September 12, the party was put *en route* across a stretch of rolling prairie country. The general course was toward Square Butte, a landmark in the vicinity of Benton, considerably west of the point to be reached; but it was deemed advisable, from lack of knowledge of the country, and from the broken appearance to our right, to make the divide between Dog Creek and the Judith, and to follow this up till opportunity offered to descend to the valley of the latter stream near its mouth. The headwaters of Dog Creek were reached in the afternoon. Here I was joined by Reed, who had volunteered his services as guide. Camped at a pool near this creek.

In the morning (September 13), a course more to the north was taken, bearing nearly on Bear's Paw Mountains. The divide was kept from necessity, either valley being impassable for wagon. Shortly after leaving camp, the broken character of the Judith Bad Lands began to appear to our left and front.

For twenty miles back from the mouth of the stream, the country immediately tributary to it is washed and cut into the wildest and most rugged shapes. The soil is of that clayey character capable of supporting itself at steep inclines; and where ordinarily the drainage would be conducted in simple valleys or natural depressions, here gulches and ravines, with precipitous sides, are formed by the flow of the water. The worst of these were avoided, and to within ten miles of the mouth of the Judith our path was over a country such that a heavily-loaded wagon-train could have been conducted with but little difficulty.

The Judith and Dog Creeks from their sources converge gradually, and, at their junction with the Missouri, are but three miles apart. The valley of Dog Creek is broken in a manner similar to that of the Judith; and, back ten miles from their mouths, this erosion, from long-continued action of water, has gone to such extent that the summit of the divide between these two streams is a simple backbone of a few feet in width, and the passage of this ridge with a single wagon, lightly loaded and conducted with care, nearly entailed the loss of the team. This difficult piece of road lasted but a few hundred yards. For six miles farther on the valleys keep apart, and give a good stretch of prairie.

A descent into the valley of the Judith was made at a point four miles from its mouth. Camped on the river; abundance of wood; grazing poor.

The Judith is a swift-running stream, from 60 to 80 feet in width, and has a depth of water varying from 2 to 4 feet. Its sources in the Judith Mountains are clear, cold springs, but the character of the water changes completely in its course to the Missouri. Its temperature is very much increased, and a considerable amount of earthy matter is taken up and held in suspension. Though all its upper branches are plentifully stocked with trout, none of these fish were taken in the main stream. Its valley proper, from bluff to bluff, is about a mile wide, well timbered with a young growth of cottonwood. Scrub pines and cedars are sparsely scattered over the highlands, principally on the sides and at the heads of ravines. From the rate at which the wood is now being taken out for the supply of steamboats, the whole will be exhausted before many years.

September 14, moved camp half a mile down stream for better grazing; visited Fort Claggett, a small Indian trading-post on the Missouri, a short distance above the Judith. It consists of two log buildings facing each other; their ends joined by a stockade, with a small flanking arrangement at the alternate angles. A few Indians were seen about; their tepees standing near the fort.

From the ruins of old Camp Cooke, in the west angle between the Judith and Missouri, the plan of the post can be distinctly traced; some of the adobe walls still withstanding the effects of the weather.

The 15th and 16th were consumed in a vigorous search for fossils by nearly all the party. Observations were made by Mr. Wood.

On the night of the 16th, a courier arrived from Carroll, with orders from you for the return of the party. Preparations were made accordingly. As it is highly probable that a more lengthened search in this vicinity than our time had allowed would be richly rewarded, and, in order to afford every facility for the improvement of the time that could be gained, a mackinaw was procured, by which Mr. Grinnell, at whose disposal it was placed, with Messrs. Ludlow and Reynolds, was enabled to remain somewhat longer upon the ground, and then make Carroll by way of the Missouri as soon as the overland party.

The return trip began on the 17th. My old trail was necessarily taken for part of the way back; but, as soon as opportunity offered, a course to the east of it was taken; but little was gained by this, however, for from the nature of the ground I was compelled to pass near the old camp on Armell's Creek.

But little game was seen on the Judith. The Indians, as well as white men in that vicinity, kill for hides alone for purposes of trade. The consequence is very apparent. But three or four herds of buffalo and a few antelope were seen there; antelope becoming more plentiful as we left the river behind us.

Carroll was reached the afternoon of the 20th; the party by boat making the landing soon after.

This trip demonstrated the practicability of a wagon-road through the Judith Basin to the Missouri; though for general use a considerable amount of work would first needs be done.

The trail was carefully kept; the principal topographical features being sketched in. The data for the plotting of the course and the astronomical notes are already in your hands.

Every facility was afforded Mr. Grinnell in his collection of fossils. It is to be regretted that longer time could not have been taken in this work.

After the departure of the main party from Carroll for the East, it devolved upon me to conduct the transportation back to Ellis.

The party under my charge consisted of but two sergeants and ten privates of the Second

Cavalry, and it was my intention to follow the road previously passed over by the party; but on my arrival at the forks of the Musselshell River, I found a company of the Second Cavalry, commanded by Lieut. L. H. Jerome, under orders to scout the country east of the Crazy Mountains as far as the Yellowstone, and thence to return to Fort Ellis by way of that river.

Through the courtesy of Lieutenant Jerome, I was enabled to avail myself of the opportunity (which the small force at my disposal rendered it imprudent to attempt) to strike the Yellowstone at Big Timber Creek, a point within about seventy miles of that to which General Forsyth had ascended with his expedition in the spring.

Camp at the forks of the Musselshell was struck on the 28th of September, crossed to the south side of the Musselshell a mile below the forks, followed the general course of this stream for about four miles to the Little Elk—a well-wooded stream, crossed from this creek to the Big Elk (seven miles) in a course a little east of south, passed this stream, and three-quarters of a mile farther on a branch of the same. About eight miles more of travel brought us to the Porcupine (or American Fork). Here camped.

Throughout this day's march, an exceedingly large number of antelope were observed, and at our camp on the Porcupine the woods and underbrush were alive with deer, showing in a very marked manner the absence of the skin-hunter.

September 29.—Traveled seven miles to Summit Creek; four miles farther on crossed the Sweet Grass, a tributary to the Yellowstone. It is fed by springs and melted snow from Crazy Mountain, and flows a volume of water nearly equaling that of the Musselshell.

Beyond this, several small streams were passed: Beaver Creek, standing in pools at this season, two miles; a branch of same, half a mile; three miles farther on, Williamson's Creek, and a mile from this, Burnt Creek, all emptying into the Sweet Grass.

The first crossing of Big Timber Creek was at three miles; we recrossed half a mile beyond, and camped on left bank. This stream is about 20 feet wide, clear and cold. The valley is *very* heavily timbered.

On the department maps, several small streams are noted as running into Big Timber from the north. There are no streams of any moment after passing Burnt Creek going south on this trail.

October 1.—Traveled down left bank of Big Timber for about five miles; crossed within half a mile of its mouth. Here observed indications of Indians, probably Crows.

Two large tripods, 20 feet or more in height, had been erected, and from the legs of these were suspended hundreds of moccasins, some of them beautifully beaded. It was remarkable that none of these moccasins were more than 5 inches in length; the most of them averaging about 3 inches; probably some offering, or medicine. Traveled up Yellowstone on its left bank. Little Timber about four miles and a half from Big Timber, about a third of the size of the latter; well wooded. The country between these two streams is very poor, almost no grazing; sage-brush being the main production. Half a mile farther on crossed a branch of Little Timber; the two unite about three hundred yards from the Yellowstone. Three miles beyond, Cherry Creek. In succession, we passed Duck Creek three miles on, Hot Spring Creek three miles beyond, and Cold Spring Creek a mile beyond that. Went into camp on the Yellowstone near the latter.

October 2.—General course still along Yellowstone. Crossed Yellowstone ten miles from camp at a point nearly opposite old Crow agency. The ford was very circuitous, ranging back and forth along the bars to avoid deep water. At this season, the greatest depth on this ford brings the water nearly to the wagon-body.

The old Crow agency, recently abandoned, is at the foot of the Yellowstone Mountains, opposite to, and about four miles from, the mouth of Shield's River. It consists of a collection of rude buildings, principally adobe. Recrossed the Yellowstone about five miles above the agency. There are two fords equally good, one above and one below "Benson's Ferry." Formerly, the passage of the stream at high water was made by a ferry-boat conducted by means of a cable stretched across the river. At the time of my crossing, the ferry was not in existence. Its place is marked by two stones on the left bank. Camped two miles below, just opposite one of the highest points of the Yellowstone Mountains, called Medicine Peak.

October 3.—After leaving camp, crossed Fleshman's Creek about eight miles from Shield's River.

Half a mile beyond is a small stream, which I followed up for about twelve miles, then pulled over a high divide; at this point the only difficult road was encountered. Across the divide, the head of the Middle Fork of the Gallatin River was struck, and a general course with that of the stream was followed to Fort Ellis.

In the progress up the Yellowstone River, a very noticeable feature presented itself; the change of the character of the country adjacent to it. Throughout its whole length on the lower stream, the elevations on either side never attain to more than the dignity of "buttes." But from the moment of passing Crazy Mountain, the scenery of the river becomes more in keeping with the grandeur to which it attains above.

Very respectfully, your obedient servant,

R. E. THOMPSON,
Second Lieutenant Sixth Infantry.

Capt. WILLIAM LUDLOW,
Corps of Engineers, Saint Paul, Minn.

RECONNAISSANCE FROM CARROLL, MONTANA, TO YELLOWSTONE NATIONAL PARK.

ZOOLOGICAL REPORT.

BY

GEO. BIRD GRINNELL.

LETTER OF TRANSMITTAL.

YALE COLLEGE, NEW HAVEN, CONN.,
June 1, 1876.

SIR: I beg leave to hand you herewith, as a partial report on the zoology of the region traversed by your expedition last summer, a list of the mammals and birds observed on the trip. In making out this list, I have taken care to give only such species as I actually saw and identified either in life or by their remains. I have added a list of such species as have been noticed in the immediate vicinity of the Yellowstone Park, combining the observations made by Mr. Merriam, of Hayden's survey, 1872, with my own during the past summer.

It may not be out of place here, to call your attention to the terrible destruction of large game, for the hides alone, which is constantly going on in those portions of Montana and Wyoming through which we passed. Buffalo, elk, mule-deer, and antelope are being slaughtered by thousands each year, without regard to age or sex, and at all seasons. Of the vast majority of the animals killed, the hide only is taken. Females of all these species are as eagerly pursued in the spring, when just about to bring forth their young, as at any other time.

It is estimated that during the winter of 1874-'75 not less than 3,000 elk were killed for their hides alone in the valley of the Yellowstone, between the mouth of Trail Creek and the Hot Springs. If this be true, what must have been the number for both the Territories? Buffalo and mule-deer suffer even more severely than the elk, and antelope nearly as much. The Territories referred to have game laws, but, of course, they are imperfect, and cannot, in the present condition of the country, be enforced. Much, however, might be done to prevent the reckless destruction of the animals to which I have referred, by the officers stationed on the frontier, and a little exertion in this direction would be well repaid by the increase of large game in the vicinity of the posts where it was not unnecessarily and wantonly destroyed. At one or two points, notably Camp Baker, efforts have been made to drive off the skin hunters, and with such success that the officers have very fine hunting within easy reach. The general feeling of the better class of frontiersmen, guides, hunters, and settlers, is strongly against those who are engaged in this work of butchery, and all, I think, would be glad to have this wholesale and short-sighted slaughter put a stop to. But it is needless to enlarge upon this abuse. The facts concerning it are well known to most Army officers and to all inhabitants of the Territory. It is certain that, unless in some way the destruction of these animals can be checked, the large game still so abundant in some localities will ere long be exterminated.

I am, sir, very respectfully, your obedient servant,

GEO. BIRD GRINNELL.

Col. WM. LUDLOW,
    Chief Engineer Department Dakota, St. Paul, Minnesota.

ZOOLOGICAL REPORT.

By Geo. Bird Grinnell.

LIST OF MAMMALS AND BIRDS.
CHAPTER I.
MAMMALS.

FELIDÆ.

1. FELIS CONCOLOR, *Linn.*

Mountain Lion; Cougar.

Although not a common species, a few of these animals are killed in the mountains every winter.

The skins of the Cougar were formerly imported in large quantities from the east and from California for purposes of trade with the Indians. A few years since, a good skin was sometimes sold for seven or eight buffalo-robes; but at present they have little or no commercial value. A single individual of this species was seen by our party on the Yellowstone River, near the mouth of Alum Creek.

2. LYNX RUFUS, *Raf.*

Bay Lynx; Wildcat.

Very abundant in the mountains.

3. LYNX CANADENSIS, *Raf.*

Canada Lynx; Catamount.

Not a common species, though taken occasionally. I saw a few skins at Fort Peck, and was told that it was sometimes killed in the Yellowstone Park.

CANIDÆ.

4. CANIS OCCIDENTALIS, *Rich.*

Gray Wolf; Timber Wolf.

Although the Gray Wolf is always killed whenever the opportunity offers, it still exists in considerable numbers wherever the Buffalo are abundant. On the return march, just before entering the Judith Gap, I saw one pack of twelve, another of nine, and, besides these, many individuals singly or by twos and threes. Buffalo were very numerous here, and, although not much hunted, enough were killed to furnish abundant food for the wolves. This species was also abundant near the Judith River, and during the hours of darkness their howlings were heard almost constantly.

Wolfing, as it is called, is an established industry in Montana; and, being pursued only in winter, it gives employment and support to a large number of teamsters, steamboat-hands, and others who are necessarily idle at this season. The method is sufficiently simple. The wolfer, starting out, kills a deer, a buffalo, or some other large animal, and, thoroughly poisoning it with strychnine, leaves it for a day or two. When he returns to it, he finds from one to a dozen wolves coyotes, and foxes lying dead about the carcass. As wolf-skins, large and small, *i. e.*, gray wolves and coyotes, bring $2.50 apiece at the trader's store, it is not unusual for two men to make $1,000 or $1,500 at this work in a winter.

Almost all the dogs seen among the Assinaboines, Crows, and Gros Ventres of the Prairie, appeared to have more or less wolf-blood in their veins, and many of them would have been taken for true wolves had they been seen away from the Indian camps.

5. CANIS LATRANS, *Say.*

Prairie Wolf; Coyote.

This species is abundant between Carroll and Fort Ellis; being, I think, much more common on the prairie than in the mountains. I have always found it most numerous in a plain country, where there are deep washed ravines, to which the animals may retire during the day, and in holes in the sides of which the young are brought forth. When searching for fossils in such places during the past summer, I have often come upon an old female lying at the mouth of a hole in the bank, and surrounded by her litter, of from four to eight half-grown pups. At my appearance, the family would spring to their feet, stare at me for a few seconds, and then two or three would dart into the hole, as many wildly scramble up the bank, and the rest would start off up the ravine at a good round pace, looking back over their shoulders every few steps, as if there were a constant struggle between their fears and their curiosity.

A puppy, perhaps three months old, was captured while we were in camp on Crooked Creek He had taken refuge in a hole in the bluffs, and was dug out and brought to camp. Although so young, he was utterly wild and vicious; snapping at any one that ventured to touch him, and refusing to eat. His unceasing efforts to escape were at length successful, and one morning we found that during the night he had gnawed off his fastenings and departed.

6. VULPES ALOPEX MACRURUS, *Baird.*

Prairie Fox.

This is an abundant species throughout the country traversed by our party. It is often found dead near the carcasses poisoned for wolves.

7. VULPES VELOX, *Aud & Bach.*

Swift; Kit Fox.

This pretty little fox is common on the prairies of Dakota and Montana, and, as it is a species that has but few enemies, it is often quite tame. I have sometimes come upon one of these animals as it lay sleeping in the sun at the mouth of its burrow, and have been amused to see it, after a brief examination of me, stretch, yawn, and then with its tail held straight up in the air, and an appearance of the utmost unconcern, trot slowly into the hole. This has generally two openings; and sometimes, while you are examining one entrance, the Swift may be seen inspecting you from the other.

MUSTELIDÆ.

8. MUSTELA AMERICANA, *Turton.*

MARTEN.

The Marten is said to be quite abundant in the mountains of the Yellowstone Park, and it doubtless is found some distance down the Missouri River. I saw skins at Fort Peck which I was told had been taken in the immediate neighborhood.

9. PUTORIUS VISON, *Rich.*

MINK.

This species was quite abundant all through the mountains. Some very fine dark specimens were seen along Bridger Creek near Fort Ellis.

10. GULO LUSCUS, *Sabine.*

WOLVERENE; SKUNK-BEAR.

No living individuals of this species were seen by any of the party; but we noticed their tracks quite often while in the park, and saw many skins in Bozeman. Hunters there informed me that they were seldom killed, except in the severest weather of the winter. In this region, they were spoken of as the "Skunk-bear"; farther south they are called "Carcajou". The young, when first born, are said to be snow-white in color. Although this species is seldom found far from the mountains, an indivdual was killed during the winter of 1872–'73 near Fort Stevenson on the Missouri River. It had probably wandered out on to the prairie from the high Bad Lands of the Little Missouri.

11. LUTRA CANADENSIS, *Sab.*

OTTER.

Although nowhere a very abundant species, the Otter occurs perhaps as frequently on the Missouri River as on the purer mountain-streams. The furs taken on this river, however, are by no means so valuable as those which come from the mountains; being much lighter in color and less glossy. This difference is regarded by trappers and dealers in furs to be due to the muddy character of the Missouri water. Whether this be the case, or whether it is merely an exemplification of the law which obtains with regard to the birds and mammals of the plains as contrasted with those of the mountains, I am unable at present to determine. It seems quite possible, however, that the former explanation is the true one, since animals like the Otter and Beaver, to which latter the above remarks also apply, from the conditions of their lives are but slightly exposed to the modifying influences which act on animals living on the uplands and more or less diurnal in their habits.

The fur of the Otter is highly prized by the Indians; being used by them to tie up the hair, to ornament their "coup-sticks", to cover bow-cases and quivers, and for a variety of other purposes.

12. MEPHITIS MEPHITICA, *Baird.*

SKUNK.

This species is exceedingly abundant throughout Eastern Montana. While ascending the Missouri River, we often saw them on the low benches of alluvium left bare by the rapid falling of the waters. Having slipped or climbed down the almost vertical banks to get to the water, they seemed unable to retrace their steps, and could only escape from their prison by swimming.

At Camp Lewis, these animals were so numerous as to have become a terrible nuisance. Mr. Reed, the post-trader, told me one morning that during the previous night he had been obliged to rise four times to kill Skunks.

13. TAXIDEA AMERICANA, *Baird.*

BADGER.

The Badger was quite common all through the prairie country over which we passed, but was most often seen in the vicinity of the prairie-dog towns. It is a slow animal, and may easily be overtaken by a man on foot. If unable to reach its hole in time to escape, it will turn and rush toward its pursuer in the most courageous manner; snapping and snarling in such a way as to inspire one with a wholesome respect for it.

URSIDÆ.

14. PROCYON LOTOR, *Storr.*

RACCOON.

This species occurs occasionally along the Missouri River.

15. URSUS HORRIBILIS, *Ord.*

GRIZZLY BEAR.

The Grizzly is rather common in some localities along the Missouri; and from the upper deck of the steamer I saw three one evening digging roots in a wide level bottom. In the Bridger Mountains and in the Yellowstone Park, they were numerous, so much so that we would often see several sets of fresh tracks in a morning's ride. From their abundance in the vicinity of Fort Ellis and Bozeman, it was evident that they were not much disturbed by hunters.

In Bozeman, I was shown two cubs about six months old; and two more sullen and vicious little brutes I never saw. A Black Bear cub of about the same age was as friendly and playful as a puppy; but no one dared to venture within reach of the Grizzlies.

But little seems to be known about the breeding-habits of this bear. It is pretty well established, however, that the young are brought forth about the 15th of January, and that they are then very small, scarcely larger than new-born puppies.

16. URSUS AMERICANUS, *Pallas.*

BLACK BEAR.

Not nearly so common as the preceding species. Only one living specimen was seen. At a ranch near the bridge over the Yellowstone River, however, I was shown a single skin of the so called Cinnamon Bear, which, I was told, had been taken in the Park.

SCIURIDÆ.

17. SCIURUS HUDSONIUS, *Pallas.*

RED SQUIRREL; PINE SQUIRREL.

Red Squirrels were abundant wherever pine timber was found. In the mountains, they seem to feed chiefly on the seeds of the pine; and I frequently came upon little heaps of cones gathered together by the squirrels just as they collect nuts in the East. Most specimens taken in the Yellowstone Park seem to be referable to var. *Richardsonii*, but several killed in the Fire Hole Valley are not to be distinguished from ordinary Connecticut specimens.

18. TAMIAS QUADRIVITTATUS, *Rich.*

MISSOURI GROUND SQUIRREL.

This pretty little squirrel seems equally at home among the most desolate Bad Lands, where no vegetation is to be found save a few straggling sage-bushes, and amid the dense pine forests and luxuriant undergrowth of the mountains. They are very gentle and unsuspicious, and would play about in the most unconcerned manner while I was standing within a few feet of them.

Although by no means tree-climbers, in the strict acceptation of the term, I often saw them, while at play or when frightened, ascend the pines to a height of 20 or 30 feet. It would seem that they are not exclusively vegetarian in their diet; for I interrupted one of them while making a meal of the dried carcass of a *Hesperomys*. It sat up, holding the food in its fore feet in the ordinary manner, and gnawing the meat from the back and shoulders. No doubt, in some localities it feeds, partially at least, on grasshoppers, as many of the small rodents of the West are known to do.

19. SPERMOPHILUS TRIDECIM-LINEATUS, *Mitchell*.

STRIPED PRAIRIE SQUIRREL.

This species was common everywhere on the prairies. When anything unusual attracts its attention, it raises itself up on its haunches to examine the object of its curiosity. As this approaches, the squirrel gradually lowers itself until at last it is quite flattened out upon the ground. In this position, if the eye is removed from it for a moment, it is very difficult to find it again, as its colors harmonize admirably with the yellowish gray of the soil.

20. SPERMOPHILUS RICHARDSONII, *Cuv*.

RICHARDSON'S GROUND SQURREL.

This species was not seen until after we had passed Camp Lewis in Montana. Along the North Fork of the Musselshell River it was abundant in the valley, and it was observed in considerable numbers about Camp Baker and Fort Ellis.

In their habits, they resemble the Prairie-dog (*Cynomys*) more nearly than any other species with which I am acquainted. They live in communities, act as do the Prairie-dogs when approached, and are equally hard to secure when shot near the entrance of their burrows. A young one, killed with a charge of fine shot at short range, moved himself over two feet along the smooth surface of a flat rock, on which he had been lying when shot, by convulsive pushes of his hind feet. After I had taken him in my hand, these kickings continued for half a minute or more, although the animal could not have been conscious after the shot struck him.

I several times saw the young of this species playing with one another very prettily. One standing over the other would hold him down and pretend to bite his head and neck, just as we often see young puppies play together.

At Camp Baker, there were many of these animals in and about our camp, and they soon became very tame. Often they would come to the open tent-door, and, sitting on their haunches, would watch the occupants with an appearance of the greatest curiosity. We often tried to catch them alive, but were never successful. They would always manage to slip into some hole that we did not know of, just as our hands were on them. Between Fort Ellis and Bozeman there is quite a large settlement of these animals, and they were more tame here than at any other locality where we met with them.

21. CYNOMYS LUDOVICIANUS, *Baird*.

PRAIRIE-DOG.

Quite abundant on the plains near the foot of the mountains.

22. ARCTOMYS FLAVIVENTER, *Bach*.

WESTERN WOOD-CHUCK.

Common in the mountains, but rather a shy species, more often heard than seen.

23. CASTOR CANADENSIS, *Kuhl*.

BEAVER.

While ascending the Missouri, we saw the houses and "slides" of the Beaver very frequently, and often, just at evening, the animals themselves were observed, sitting on the banks gazing at the steamer, or feeding on the tender shoots of the cottonwood and willow. They were by no means shy, and would sometimes permit the vessel to pass within a few yards of them without taking to the water.

The streams in the mountains through which we passed were sometimes dammed by the Beavers for miles, and the backwater spreading out over the level valleys makes wide ponds. These in the course of time are partially filled up with the mud carried down by the stream, and when this takes place are deserted by the Beavers, which move away and build another dam somewhere else. As the pond fills, a rank growth of rushes and underbrush springs up, and before long, what was a pretty little lake has become an impassable morass.

The value of the fur of the Missouri River Beaver is diminished by the same causes spoken of in reference to that of the Otter.

SACCOMYIDÆ.

24. THOMOMYS TALPOIDES, (Rich.) Baird.

GOPHER.

An individual of this species was taken among the high mountains near the head of Gardiner's River. It was running over the snow-drifts when captured.

MURIDÆ.

25. ZAPUS HUDSONIUS, Coues.

JUMPING MOUSE.

This species was observed several times in the Bridger Mountains, and again on Cascade Creek near the Yellowstone River.

26. MUS DECUMANUS, Pallas.

BROWN RAT.

The common Wharf-rat is sufficiently abundant in all the settlements on the Missouri River to be a great nuisance and to do considerable damage. In the trader's store at Fort Peck, they were very numerous, so much so that the trader told me that he had recently poisoned one hundred and fifty in one week.

27. MUS MUSCULUS, Linn.

HOUSE MOUSE.

Abundant in towns and large settlements, but in isolated ranches replaced by the following species.

28. HESPEROMYS LEUCOPUS SONORIENSIS, LeConte.

WESTERN WHITE-FOOTED MOUSE.

This species was very abundant along the North Fork of the Musselshell River and along the Yellowstone. In many places, they had deserted the woods and fields and taken to the ranches, where they are quite as annoying as the common House Mouse.

29. ARVICOLA RIPARIA, Ord.

MEADOW MOUSE.

Very common along the Yellowstone River.

30. FIBER ZIBETHICUS, (L.) Cuv.

MUSKRAT.

Abundant on streams flowing into the Missouri.

HYSTRICIDÆ.

31. ERITHIZON EPIXANTHUS, *Brandt.*

YELLOW-HAIRED PORCUPINE.

Quite common along the Missouri and in the "bottoms" of streams flowing into that river. We saw signs of its presence also in the National Park along the Yellowstone River.

LEPORIDÆ.

32. LEPUS CAMPESTRIS, *Bachman.*

PRAIRIE HARE.

This species is very abundant in some localities, while in others, quite as favorable for it, it is not found at all. In fact, the abundance or scarcity of the Prairie Hare in any district depends almost altogether on the number of wolves to be found in the same tract of country. Where all the coyotes and gray wolves have been killed or driven off, the hares exist in great numbers; but where the former are abundant, the latter are seldom seen. We saw none near the Missouri River, where the buffaloes, and consequently the wolves, were numerous; but at Camp Baker, where there were scarcely any wolves, the hares were very common.

33. LEPUS ARTEMISIA, *Bachman.*

SAGE RABBIT.

Very abundant west of the Missouri in suitable localities, but its numbers controlled by the same causes spoken of in regard to the preceding species.

CERVIDÆ.

34. ALCE AMERICANA, *Jardine.*

MOOSE.

This species is quite abundant in suitable localities in the Yellowstone Park, although, like all the large game, it has been driven away from the neighborhood of the trail by the constant passage of travelers. We saw signs of its presence in the Bridger Mountains, and were told that there was a famous country for Moose about fifteen miles from the mouth of Trail Creek.

The only living specimen that we saw was a young calf that had been captured by the son of a settler when it was but a few days old. When seen by us, it was probably about three months old, and was a most grotesque object. It was very tame, and would come at the call of its owner.

35. CERVUS CANADENSIS, *Erxleben.*

ELK.

Elk were rather abundant all through the country which we traversed. They were seen in considerable numbers along the Missouri River, among the Bridger Mountains, and in the Yellowstone Park. Those killed early in September, at the commencement of the rutting-season, were fat and well flavored, furnishing us with delicious meat.

The Elk rut in September, and the young are brought forth late in May or early in June.

The "whistling" of the Elk is heard only for a few days during the early part of September. It is made up of several parts, and is so peculiar a cry that it can hardly be described, much less imitated. The first part consists of a prolonged, shrill whistle, which seems to come to the hearer from a long distance, even though the animal uttering it be quite near at hand. This is followed by a succession of short grunting brays or barks, three or four in number, and the call is completed by a low, smooth bellow. Sometimes the whistle is sounded without the succeeding parts. Withal, the cry is an odd one, and one that once heard will always afterward be recognized.

36. CERVUS VIRGINIANUS, *Boddaert.*

RED DEER; WHITE-TAILED DEER.

This species was by no means abundant in the country through which we passed. We saw a few along the Missouri, and I noticed one in the Judith Mountains; but on the whole they were seldom seen.

37. CERVUS MACROTIS, *Say.*

MULE DEER; BLACK-TAILED DEER.

The Black-tailed Deer, as it is usually called in the Missouri River country, is an abundant species in Eastern Montana. It is quite unsuspicious, and, except where it has been much hunted, will often permit the hunter to fire two or three shots at it before it takes to flight. This species, and the same may be said of all large game in that section of the country, is at present most recklessly slaughtered for the hides alone. It will soon, unless some means are taken for its protection, be unknown in the regions where it is now so plentiful.

ANTELOPIDÆ.

38. ANTILOCAPRA AMERICANA, *Ord.*

PRONG-HORNED ANTELOPE.

Everywhere abundant on the plains, the antelope forms one of the most pleasing and attractive features of those barren wastes. Although where they have been much hunted they are difficult to approach, they are very unsuspicious and curious where they have been accustomed to seeing and mixing with large animals. About Camp Baker and between that post and Fort Ellis, there are large droves of cattle which roam at will over the prairie. The antelope become used to the presence of these large animals, and are often seen mingling with the herds when feeding or resting.

One day while out from Camp Baker in search of Tertiary fossils, my companion and myself stopped on the borders of a little stream to rest and cook some food. The saddle-horses and pack mule were picketed near at hand; a fire had been kindled, and we were discussing some broiled venison, when two antelope suddenly appeared over the brow of a bluff about seventy-five yards distant. On seeing us, they scarcely hesitated, but trotted gracefully on toward us and would, I have no doubt, have come quite up to us, if it had not been that my companion shot them both when they were still about forty yards distant. When in the buffalo country, antelope, if the wind was right, would often approach very near me, several times coming to within a few yards of where I was standing.

It is well known that the female antelope sometimes has horns and is sometimes without them. Observations extended over several years, together with the testimony of several plainsmen, among them Charles Reynolds, a hunter of seventeen years' experience and a man of close observation, lead me to conclude that the horned does are always barren. I have myself examined a great number of doe antelopes with and without horns, and have never seen one of the former class that gave evidence of having produced or being about to have young. Nor have I ever seen a hornless doe that was barren. The horns on the does vary from one to three inches in length, have no prong, and are soft and easily bent. Their length no doubt depends in a measure upon the age of the animal. Those that I have seen lack the hard bony core which is found in the horns of the perfect males.

The barren does are always fat, and on this account are, when it is possible, selected by the hunter in preference to the other members of the herd.

OVIDÆ.

39. OVIS MONTANA, *Cuv.*

BIGHORN; MOUNTAIN SHEEP.

The Bighorn occurs in considerable numbers in the Judith Mountains and in the Yellowstone Park, away from the trail; but they are so wary that they are not often seen. As is well known, they affect the most rugged and barren country, and they are perhaps more plentiful in the Bad Lands of the Judith and Missouri Rivers than anywhere else.

On the Cone Butte and Sweet Grass Mountains, which are covered for half their height with a talus of platter-like blocks of trachyte, the sheep in their passage up and down the sides of the hills have worn regular paths among and over the loose blocks, and it is only by following these paths that the ascent can be made on the east and south.

BOVIDÆ.

40. BOS AMERICANUS, *Gmelin*.

BUFFALO; BISON.

No Buffalo were seen while we were ascending the Missouri River until just before we reached Carroll. From that place westward, they were occasionally observed until we reached the Judith Gap, although, owing to the presence in the region through which we were passing of the Sioux and Crows, they were not abundant. On our return march, we saw great numbers of them before reaching the Gap, but none afterward until we were quite near the Missouri.

The statement that the herds of bulls that are everywhere met with during the autumn consist of individuals driven away from the main herd by their stronger rivals may, I think, be doubted It is said that these assemblages are not seen in spring before the rutting-season. It seems more probable that during the late summer and autumn, many of the old and strong bulls exhausted by the fatigues of the rutting-season, thin in flesh, and generally run down, are unable to keep up with the active and constantly-moving herd of cows and young animals, and devote all their energies to recruiting for the winter. Early in the spring, they rejoin the herd, and remain with it until the end of July.

During the past autumn the Buffalo have proceeded down the Missouri River much farther than is usual. They have been quite numerous a few miles north of Fort Berthold, Dakota, and a few stragglers have been seen near Painted Woods, about twenty-five miles above Bismarck.

The so-called "Mountain Buffalo" was abundant in the Yellowstone Park.

CHAPTER II.

BIRDS.

TURDIDÆ.

1. TURDUS MIGRATORIUS, *Linn.*

ROBIN.

This species was abundant along the Missouri River, and was also seen in considerable numbers in the mountains about Camp Baker and in the Yellowstone Park.

2. TURDUS SWAINSONI, *Cab.*

OLIVE-BACKED THRUSH.

Quite common along the Missouri above Bismarck.

3. OREOSCOPTES MONTANUS, (*Towns.*) *Bd.*

MOUNTAIN MOCKINGBIRD.

I first saw this species on Little Crooked Creek, thirteen miles west of Carroll. It was abundant, and doubtless had bred there, as I took some very young birds. It was generally started from the ground, whence it would fly to the top of some little sage-bush, where it would sit jerking its tail and constantly uttering low cries of anxiety. They were quite shy, and I was often obliged to follow them for some distance before I could secure them.

This species was abundant in the valley of the Yellowstone River.

4. MIMUS CAROLINENSIS, (*Linn.*) *Gray.*

CATBIRD.

Quite common along the Missouri River, and very abundant in the Yellowstone Park and in the mountains generally.

5. HARPORHYNCHUS RUFUS, (*Linn.*) *Cab.*

BROWN THRUSH; THRASHER.

This species was seen occasionally in the Missouri River bottom.

CINCLIDÆ.

6. CINCLUS MEXICANUS, *Sw.*

WATER-OUZEL; DIPPER.

On Cascade Creek, near the Upper Falls of the Yellowstone, we first met with this interesting species. Although tolerably familiar with the accounts of its habits given by various authors, I must confess to having experienced a ludicrous feeling of astonishment the first time I saw the bird walk unconcernedly down a sloping rock until its head disappeared under the water. It repeated this performance several times, occasionally rising to the surface as if forced up by the water, and then immediately diving again. When carried down a few yards by the force of the current, it would fly a short distance up the stream and dive from the wing.

With the help of a good glass I saw from the top of the cañon two of these little birds flying about over the river where it boiled and surged along below the Lower Falls.

SAXICOLIDÆ.

7. SIALIA ARCTICA, Sw.

Arctic Bluebird; Western Bluebird.

One of the most abundant birds in the wooded region through which we passed. It was especially numerous in the Yellowstone Park late in August and early in September, when it formed a large division of the army of small birds that were being constantly started from the ground.

PARIDÆ.

8. PARUS ATRICAPILLUS SEPTENTRIONALIS, (Harris) Allen.

Long-tailed Chickadee.

Common along the Missouri River and in the mountains.

9. PARUS MONTANUS, Gamb.

Mountain Chickadee.

A few birds of this species were seen searching for food among the pines that grow among the Bad Lands near the mouth of the Judith River. In habits, they seemed to resemble closely the preceding species; but the note was slightly different, being more slowly uttered, almost drawled in fact.

SITTIDÆ.

10. SITTA CAROLINENSIS ACULEATA, (Cass.) Allen.

Slender-billed Nuthatch.

Common in the Yellowstone Park and in the mountains toward the Missouri River.

TROGLODYTIDÆ.

11. SALPINCTES OBSOLETUS, (Say) Cab.

Rock Wren.

Very abundant in the Bad Lands along the Missouri and among the sandstone bluffs near the Judith Mountains. These birds were also common in the Little Belt Mountains near White-tailed Deer Creek, darting about among old stumps and wood-piles, just as they do among the bluffs of the Bad Lands. A nest found near Haymaker's Creek was nothing more than a short burrow under a flat rock. The little chamber at the end contained three nearly full-grown young.

12. TROGLODYTES AËDON PARKMANNI, (Aud.) Coues.

Western House Wren.

Abundant on the Missouri near Bismarck.

13. CISTOTHORUS PALUSTRIS, (*Wils.*) *Baird.*

Long-billed Marsh Wren.

This species was seen but once, on a reedy slough near the bridge over the Yellowstone River.

ALAUDIDÆ.

14. EREMOPHILA ALPESTRIS LEUCOLÆMA, (*Forst.*) *Coues.*

Horned Lark; Shore Lark.

Abundant everywhere on the plains.

MOTACILLIDÆ.

15. ANTHUS LUDOVICIANUS, (*Gm.*) *Licht.*

Titlark.

A single individual of this species was seen among the snows on the highest point of the Bridger Mountains.

16. NEOCORYS SPRAGUEI, (*Aud.*) *Scl.*

Missouri Skylark.

This little-known bird was not uncommon between Camp Lewis and Camp Baker. It was most often seen in the road searching for food, and, when alarmed, running along in the ruts as the Shore Larks are often seen to do. It was usually seen in company with these latter, and seems somewhat to resemble them in its habits.

SYLVICOLIDÆ.

17. DENDRŒCA ÆSTIVA, (*Gm.*) *Baird.*

Yellow Warbler; Summer Yellowbird.

Abundant and breeding along the Missouri River.

18. DENDRŒCA AUDUBONII, (*Towns.*) *Baird.*

Audubon's Warbler.

A family of this species, the young of which had but just left the nest, was seen among the pines near the Yellowstone Bridge.

19. (?) SEIURUS AUROCAPILLUS, (*Linn.*) *Sw.*

Golden-crowned Thrush.

The characteristic song of this species was often heard along the Missouri; but I was unable to secure any specimens, or even to see the birds.

20. GEOTHLYPIS TRICHAS, (*Linn.*) *Cab.*

Maryland Yellowthroat.

Seen quite often along the Missouri.

21. GEOTHLYPIS PHILADELPHIA MACGILLIVRAYI, (*Wils.*) *Allen.*

WESTERN MOURNING WARBLER.

A female of this species was found dead on the shore of the Yellowstone Lake.

22. ICTERIA VIRENS, (*Linn.*) *Baird.*

YELLOW-BREASTED CHAT.

Abundant along the Missouri River. Its familiar notes were heard whenever we passed a wooded bottom, and its curious antics often seen.

23. SETOPHAGA RUTICILLA, (*Linn.*) *Sw.*

REDSTART.

Seen on several occasions in the Missouri River bottom.

TANAGRIDÆ.

24. PYRANGA LUDOVICIANA, (*Wils.*) *Bon.*

LOUISIANA TANAGER.

Observed quite frequently in the Yellowstone Park.

HIRUNDINIDÆ.

25. HIRUNDO HORREORUM, *Barton.*

BARN SWALLOW.

Abundant throughout the region which we traversed.

26. HIRUNDO THALASSINA, *Sw.*

VIOLET-GREEN SWALLOW.

Very numerous about Fort Ellis, and more or less abundant throughout the Yellowstone Park.

27. PETROCHELIDON LUNIFRONS, (*Say*) *Scl.*

CLIFF SWALLOW.

Extremely abundant along the Missouri River, breeding on many of the high bluffs between which it flows. They were also common in the mountains, and especially so about Camp Baker.

Early one morning late in July, while traveling along the road near the Judith Mountains, I was surprised to see great numbers of these birds feeding on the ground. A little investigation showed me that they were picking up insects that had been chilled by the severe frost of the previous night, and were as yet unable to fly.

28. COTYLE RIPARIA, (*Linn.*) *Boie.*

SAND MARTIN; BANK SWALLOW.

Observed in large numbers on the Missouri River; often breeding in the same bluffs to which the preceding species had attached their nests.

29. PROGNE SUBIS, *Baird.*

PURPLE MARTIN.

Abundant in the mountains, where it breeds.

AMPELIDÆ.

30. AMPELIS GARRULUS, *Linn.*

BOHEMIAN WAXWING.

At Camp Baker, I saw the remains of an individual of this species which, I was informed by Major Freeman, had been taken there in winter. It is said to be common there at that season.

31. AMPELIS CEDRORUM, (*Vieill.*) *Gray.*

CEDAR-BIRD.

Quite common along the Missouri.

LANIIDÆ.

32. COLLURIO LUDOVICIANUS EXCUBITOROIDES, (*Sw.*) *Coues.*

WHITE-RUMPED SHRIKE.

Common along wooded ravines on the plains west of the Missouri.

FRINGILLIDÆ.

33. CARPODACUS CASSINI, *Baird.*

CASSIN'S PURPLE FINCH.

A single individual of this species was taken at the Mud Volcano in the Yellowstone Park.

34. LOXIA CURVIROSTRA AMERICANA, (*Wils.*) *Coues.*

RED CROSS-BILL.

This species was found in great numbers near the Falls of the Yellowstone in August. It had undoubtedly bred in the immediate vicinity, as I saw old birds feeding young just from the nest. Their food seemed to consist entirely of the seeds of the pine. The males uttered almost constantly a short monotonous whistle.

35. CHRYSOMITRIS PINUS, (*Wils.*) *Bp.*

PINE FINCH.

Though this species was noticed several times while in the park, it did not seem to be common there. The birds were seen among the pines or else feeding on thistle-blows, after the manner of *C. tristis.*

36. CHRYSOMITRIS TRISTIS, (*Linn.*) *Bp.*

YELLOW-BIRD; THISTLE-BIRD.

Abundant along the Missouri and on the plains near the mountains.

37. PLECTROPHANES ORNATUS, *Towns.*

CHESTNUT-COLLARED LONGSPUR.

Abundant, and one of the most characteristic birds of the high plains. The most eastern point at which I saw it was Jamestown, Dak. From that place west, it was more or less common until we left the plain country. Late in July, I took, near Box Elder Creek, young birds that had but just left the nest.

38. PLECTROPHANES MACCOWNII, *Lawr.*

MACCOWN'S LONGSPUR.

Abundant, breeding on the plains in company with the preceding. I secured many fully-fledged birds of the year late in July.

39. PASSERCULUS SAVANNA, (*Wils.*) *Bp.*

SAVANNAH SPARROW.

Quite common about Camp Baker.

40. POOCÆTES GRAMINEUS CONFINIS, (*Gm.*) *Baird.*

GRASS FINCH; BAY-WINGED BUNTING.

Abundant everywhere on the plains.

41. COTURNICULUS PASSERINUS PERPALLIDUS, (*Wils.*) *Ridgway.*

YELLOW-WINGED SPARROW.

Common on the plains near the Missouri.

42. MELOSPIZA MELODIA FALLAX, (*Wils.*) *Ridgway.*

WESTERN SONG SPARROW.

Common in the mountains, especially in low brush along the banks of streams, but so shy as to be quite difficult of approach.

43. JUNCO OREGONUS, (*Towns.*) *Scl.*

OREGON SNOWBIRD.

Very abundant in the mountains of the Yellowstone Park.

44. SPIZELLA MONTICOLA, (*Gm.*) *Baird.*

TREE SPARROW.

Three or four individuals of this species were seen in the Bridger Mountains early in September.

45. SPIZELLA SOCIALIS ARIZONÆ, (*Wils.*) *Coues.*

WESTERN CHIPPY.

Abundant in the mountains.

46. SPIZELLA PALLIDA, (*Sw.*) *Bp.*

CLAY-COLORED SPARROW.

Abundant on the plains in bushy ravines and along the river-bottoms.

47. ZONOTRICHIA LEUCOPHRYS, (*Forst.*) *Sw.*

WHITE-CROWNED SPARROW.

This species was abundant in the Yellowstone Park. It was seen during August and September in small flocks of ten or twelve individuals, old and young, feeding on the ground in company with *S. arctica* and a host of small sparrows.

48. CHONDESTES GRAMMACA, (*Say*) *Bp.*

LARK FINCH.

Very abundant on the plains near the Missouri River and westward.

49. CALAMOSPIZA BICOLOR, (*Towns.*) *Bp.*

WHITE-WINGED BLACKBIRD.

Very abundant on the plains, especially in somewhat broken country along ravines and dry water-courses, and also in the neighborhood of isolated buttes. I found it breeding near Little Crooked Creek.

50. EUSPIZA AMERICANA, (*Gm.*) *Bp.*

BLACK-THROATED BUNTING.

A breeding female taken in the Missouri River bottom near Bismarck early in July was the only individual of this species seen.

51. CYANOSPIZA AMŒNA, (*Say*) *Baird.*

LAZULI FINCH.

This beautiful species was abundant along the Missouri River bottom.

52. PIPILO MACULATUS ARCTICA, (*Sw.*) *Coues.*

ARCTIC TOWHEE.

Abundant, breeding in the Missouri River bottom, and often seen about Camp Baker.

ICTERIDÆ.

53. DOLICHONYX ORIZIVORUS, (*Linn.*) *Sw.*

BOB-O-LINK; RICE-BIRD.

This species was breeding in large numbers in the wide river-bottom near Bismarck when we passed through early in July. I saw none except here during the trip.

54. MOLOTHRUS PECORIS, (*Gm.*) *Sw.*

COW-BUNTING.

Abundant everywhere.

55. AGELÆUS PHŒNICEUS, (*Linn.*) *Vieill.*

RED-WINGED BLACKBIRD.

Noticed on several occasions along the Missouri River.

56. STURNELLA MAGNA NEGLECTA, (*Linn.*) *Allen.*

WESTERN MEADOW LARK.

Abundant all through the open country. We heard their sweet songs all through the summer and as late as September 18.

57. SCOLECOPHAGUS CYANOCEPHALUS, (*Wagl.*) *Cab.*

BLUE-HEADED GRAKLE.

I found this species very abundant near Carroll, and, in fact, everywhere on the plains. At Little Crooked Creek, their nests were found placed on little "greasewood" bushes only two or three feet in height. The young were most of them so well grown at this time (July 15) that they would leave the nest at my approach and fly a few yards to another bush, where they would sit uttering the sharp cry that we hear from all young blackbirds at that age. When I approached the nests or young, flocks of a dozen or more old birds would fly over me uttering constantly cries of anxiety.

About Camp Baker, they were very numerous; the flocks being so large as fairly to blacken the ground where they alighted. The birds were familiar enough and readily ventured up to our tent doors.

CORVIDÆ.

58. CORVUS CORAX, *Linn.*

RAVEN.

Rather common on the plains west of Carroll.

59. CORVUS AMERICANUS, *Aud.*

CROW.

Extremely abundant on the streams flowing out of the Sweet Grass Hills. They were breeding here in the tall undergrowth that fringed Box Elder and Armell's Creek, and on the return march were seen in large flocks feeding on the dead buffalo that strewed the prairie. It is hardly necessary to remark that they were very tame, in striking contrast to their eastern relatives.

60. PICICORVUS COLUMBIANUS, (*Wils.*) *Bp.*

CLARK'S CROW.

I first noticed this species near Camp Baker, but it did not become very abundant until we reached the Yellowstone River on our road to the park. Its striking plumage and loud harsh voice makes this bird one of the most noticeable features of the animal life of this region.

61. PICA MELANOLEUCA HUDSONICA, (*Sab.*) *Coues.*

MAGPIE.

Abundant everywhere in the mountains, and universally execrated by hunters and trappers on account of the injury it does in winter to the fresh skins that are stretched out to dry, and the annoyance that it causes to their sore-backed animals.

62. CYANURUS STELLERI MACROLOPHUS, (*Baird*) *Allen.*

LONG-CRESTED JAY.

Abundant from the Bridger Mountains through the Yellowstone Park. In habits, this species resembles most closely *C. cristatus;* but its notes are quite different, being harsh and grating, more like those of *P. columbianus.*

63. PERISOREUS CANADENSIS CAPITALIS, *Baird.*

GRAY JAY.

I found this species extremely abundant all through the mountains of the Yellowstone Park. They are noisy restless birds, continually passing to and fro among the branches of the pines with easy, graceful movements. They are at all times bold and even impudent, remaining in the trees, beneath which we encamped, and frequently descending to the ground within a few feet of some one of the party to pick up a piece of meat or a crumb of bread. When a morsel of food has been secured, it is taken to a low limb and there leisurely broken up and devoured.

This species is said to cause considerable annoyance to trappers by removing the bait from their mink and marten traps.

TYRANNIDÆ.

64. TYRANNUS CAROLINENSIS, (*Gm.*) *Temm.*

KINGBIRD.

Abundant along the Missouri and on the plains to the west.

65. TYRANNUS VERTICALIS, *Say.*

ARKANSAS FLYCATCHER.

Abundant along the Missouri and on the plains.

66. SAYORNIS SAYUS, (*Bp.*) *Baird.*

SAY'S FLYCATCHER.

I saw but two or three individuals of this species, all of them near Crooked Creek.

67. CONTOPUS VIRENS RICHARDSONII, (*Sw.*) *Allen.*

WESTERN WOOD PEWEE.

I frequently noticed this species while in the Geyser Basins, but did not observe it at any other point on the route. In the Lower Geyser Basin, I saw one of these birds taken by a Sharp-shinned Hawk, which was immediately attacked with the utmost fury by another Pewee. The latter kept up the chase for a considerable distance; finally following his enemy into the woods.

CAPRIMULGIDÆ.

68. CHORDEILES VIRGINIANUS HENRYI, (*Gm.*) *Coues.*

WESTERN NIGHTHAWK.

This species was common on the plains. Near Little Crooked Creek, late in July, I took a female sitting on two eggs, which were far advanced toward hatching.

ALCEDINIDÆ.

69. ALCEDO ALCYON, (*Linn.*) *Boie.*

KINGFISHER.

Abundant on all streams which we passed, though apparently less common on the Missouri below Carroll than elsewhere. This is probably due to the fact that the river below this point is very muddy, and the Kingfishers are hence unable to find and pursue their prey as successfully as in the clear streams of the mountains.

CUCULIDÆ.

70. COCCYZUS ERYTHROPHTHALMUS, (*Wils.*) *Bp.*

BLACK-BILLED CUCKOO.

Common along the Missouri, at least as far as Wolf Point, forty miles below Fort Peck.

PICIDÆ.

71. PICUS VILLOSUS HARRISII, (*Linn.*) *Allen.*

HARRIS' WOODPECKER.

Seen once in the Little Belt Mountains near Camp Baker.

72. PICUS PUBESCENS, *Linn.*

DOWNY WOODPECKER.

Occasionally noticed in the Yellowstone Park near the bridge.

73. SPHYRAPICUS THYROIDEUS, (*Cass.*) *Baird.*

BLACK-BREASTED WOODPECKER.

Observed but once, near Tower Creek in the Yellowstone Park.

74. MELANERPES ERYTHROCEPHALUS, (*Linn.*) *Sw.*

RED-HEADED WOODPECKER.

Very common wherever there was timber.

75. MELANERPES TORQUATUS, (*Wils.*) *Bp.*

LEWIS' WOODPECKER.

We first saw this species in the mountains near Camp Baker, where it was quite abundant. It was afterward seen in considerable numbers near the mouth of Trail Creek, and along other little timbered streams running into the Yellowstone River. These birds were several times seen searching for food upon the ground after the manner of *Colaptes*.

76. COLAPTES AURATUS, (*Linn.*) *Sw.*

GOLDEN-WINGED WOODPECKER; FLICKER.

Abundant along the Missouri River, at least as far up as Fort Buford.

77. COLAPTES MEXICANUS, *Sw.*

RED-SHAFTED WOODPECKER.

Abundant about Camp Baker and in the Yellowstone Park.

STRIGIDÆ.

78. BUBO VIRGINIANUS, (*Gm.*) *Bp.*

GREAT HORNED OWL.

Seen once near Carroll.

79. OTUS PALUSTRIS, (*Bechst.*) *Gould.*

SHORT-EARED OWL.

Common on the plains.

80. SPHEOTYTO CUNICULARIA HYPOGÆA, (*Bp.*) *Coues.*

BURROWING OWL.

Seen occasionally on the plains.

FALCONIDÆ.

81. CIRCUS CYANEUS HUDSONIUS, (*Linn.*) *Schl.*

MARSH HAWK.

Very common throughout the country which we passed over.

82. NISUS FUSCUS, (*Gm.*) *Kaup.*

SHARP-SHINNED HAWK.

This species was seen but twice; one specimen having been taken on the shores of the Yellowstone Lake, and another observed in the Lower Geyser Basin.

83. NISUS COOPERI, (*Bp.*) *Ridgway.*

COOPER'S HAWK.

A single individual of this species was seen while we were ascending the Missouri.

84. FALCO LANIARIUS POLYAGRUS, (*Cass.*) *Ridgway.*

AMERICAN LANNER FALCON.

This species, although not common in the country through which we passed, was occasionally seen, and no doubt bred on the mountains. I felt quite sure that a pair had a nest on Cone Butte, but was unable to find it. While at Camp Baker, a bird of this species used to fly over our camp every morning to a corral just beyond, where he would secure a blackbird or two for breakfast, and then return to the mountains.

85. FALCO COMMUNIS ANATUM, (*Gm.*) *Ridgway.*

DUCK HAWK.

While ascending the Missouri, we several times saw the nests of this species placed on little ledges of the high washed clay bluffs by which the river is bordered. These nests all contained unfledged young. One or both of the parents was always to be seen sitting near the nest. This species was abundant in the valley of the Yellowstone above Emigrant Peak, and had no doubt bred there, as I took a very young bird.

86. FALCO COLUMBARIUS (?) RICHARDSONI, (*Linn.*) *Ridgway.*

RICHARDSON'S FALCON.

A Pigeon Hawk, probably to be referred to this variety, was seen September 5, hovering low over the summit of the Bridger Mountains.

87. FALCO SPARVERIUS, *Linn.*

SPARROW HAWK.

Abundant on the plains and along the Yellowstone River.

88. BUTEO BOREALIS, (*Gm.*) *Vieill.*

RED-TAILED HAWK.

Seen on several occasions on the Missouri River.

89. BUTEO BOREALIS CALURUS, (*Gm.*) *Cass.*

WESTERN RED-TAILED HAWK.

This was the most common hawk seen in the mountains. We must have seen fifteen or twenty the day that we passed through Bridger's Pass; and they were equally abundant in some parts of the Yellowstone Park.

90. BUTEO SWAINSONI, *Bp.*

SWAINSON'S HAWK.

Rather numerous in the valley of the Yellowstone.

91. ARCHIBUTEO LAGOPUS SANCTI-JOHANNIS, (*Gm.*) *Ridgway*.

ROUGH-LEGGED HAWK.

Abundant about Gardiner's Springs and in the valley of the Yellowstone.

92. ARCHIBUTEO FERRUGINEUS, (*Licht.*) *Gray*.

FERRUGINOUS HAWK.

This striking species was common on the plains from the Missouri River westward until we reached the mountains. It was often seen sitting on the little mounds raised by the prairie-dogs, gazing intently at the entrance of the burrow, apparently waiting to seize the first one that should appear.

93. PANDION HALIAËTUS, (*Linn.*) *Cuv*.

FISH-HAWK.

The Fish-hawk, although occasionally seen on the Missouri, is not, in my experience at least, common on that river below the point where it becomes muddy. Above Carroll, however, the river is quite clear, and there it seems much more numerous. It was nowhere so abundant as on the Yellowstone River; and while traveling along that stream I saw from six to twelve of these birds every day. At the falls of the Yellowstone, this species was constantly in sight, sometimes sailing like a black speck close to the water far below us, or balancing itself on some dead pine that grew half-way up the sides of the cañon.

94. AQUILA CHRYSAËTOS, *Linn*.

GOLDEN EAGLE.

Occurs more or less frequently all through the country which we traversed, but is most often seen in the mountains and on high wooded buttes. I saw it at the Forks of the Musselshell, near Bridger Pass, and once over the Missouri River.

95. HALIAËTUS LEUCOCEPHALUS, (*Linn.*) *Sw*.

WHITE-HEADED EAGLE.

Seen several times on the Missouri.

CATHARTIDÆ.

96. CATHARTES AURA, (*Linn.*) *Ill*.

TURKEY BUZZARD.

Abundant on the plains.

COLUMBIDÆ.

97. ECTOPISTES MIGRATORIA, (*Linn.*) *Sw*.

PASSENGER PIGEON.

Seen in small companies in July along the Missouri River bottom, where it was doubtless breeding.

98. ZENÆDURA CAROLINENSIS, (*Linn.*) *Bp*.

COMMON DOVE; TURTLE DOVE.

Common everywhere.

TETRAONIDÆ.

99. TETRAO OBSCURUS, *Say*.

DUSKY GROUSE; BLUE GROUSE.

We found this species very abundant from the time that we reached the mountains until we left them again. The first seen were a mother with a brood of small young, taken in the Judith Mountains. From this point to and through the Yellowstone Park they were frequently met with.

There seems to be a wide variation in the time at which these birds deposit their eggs. In the Musselshell Cañon and along Deep Creek I saw many broods of half-grown chicks, and in some cases the young were nearly as large as the parent bird. This was late in July. On the 4th of August, I saw a brood on an extensive prairie in the Little Belt Mountains near Camp Baker, which must have been less than a week old; at all events, they were so young that I had no difficulty in catching several of them alive. Two weeks later I saw a brood on Trail Creek near the Yellowstone River, that were certainly not more than ten days or two weeks old.

The females with their young seem to pass the night in the creek-bottoms, and it is in such places that they must be looked for early in the morning and late in the afternoon. About 9 or 10 o'clock a. m., they proceed on foot to the uplands, where they remain until about two hours before sunset, when they come down to the stream to drink, and remain all night. In returning from the hills, they always fly. The young, when alarmed or uneasy, have a fashion of erecting the feathers of the sides of the neck just below the head, which, when seen at a little distance, gives them a very odd appearance. The female, when the young birds are nearly approached or captured, makes no attempt to draw away the enemy by any of the artifices employed by *Bonasa umbellus*, but contents herself with wandering anxiously about at a short distance, holding the tail quite erect, and clucking after the manner of the domestic hen under similar circumstances. The young when well grown are delicious eating, and many were killed by us for food when large game could not be obtained. When a brood has been scattered, the individuals which compose it lie well and furnish fair shooting. Though swift fliers, they are easily killed in the open, and I secured most of those that I killed with mustard-seed shot. The birds would sometimes let me approach within three or four feet of them before rising, and they were pretty objects as they crouched waiting for me to take one more step toward them. The body flattened out on the ground, the head and neck straight and pressed against the earth, the tail slightly elevated, and all the while the bright brown eye watching for the slightest sign that the bird's presence was discovered, together made up a picture which, though familiar enough, ever possesses a new interest for me.

But one brood was seen in heavy pine timber. In this case, the family, which consisted of the mother and six or eight well-grown young, took refuge in the lower limbs of a large pine, from which they refused to move until several shots had been fired at them.

Having in mind Dr. Cooper's statement that, in Oregon and Northern California, this species is not seen in winter, I made diligent inquiry among the settlers in the mountains of Montana for information on this point. All of those with whom I spoke informed me that the Blue Grouse was apparently quite as abundant in winter as in summer.

It is to be noticed that I found this species almost invariably in the open creek-bottoms, and sometimes in quite extensive prairies, although always among the mountains. This state of things, which is exactly the reverse of the experience of most other observers, was no doubt due, in part at least, to the fact that the birds had their tender young with them, and that these would be more safe in the valleys than on the mountain-sides.

During the trip, not a single adult male was secured. On the high mountains, however, at and near timber-line, I several times started single birds and small packs of this species. The only one secured in such situations was a barren female; but I think it probable that most of those seen here were old males.

The specimens preserved on the trip seem to be intermediate between varieties *obscurus* and *richardsoni*.

100. CENTROCERCUS UROPHASIANUS, (*Bp.*) *Sw.*

SAGE GROUSE.

We first saw this species near Wolf Point on the Missouri, where several were started from the river-bottom by the passage of the steamboat. On Box Elder Creek, where we remained in camp for several days late in July, they were extremely numerous, and broods of young were seen of all ages, from the little chicks that could fly but a few feet to the large strong-winged birds that almost equaled their parents in weight. All were painfully ignorant of the effect of fire-arms, and I have seen a brood of ten or a dozen well-grown birds walk quietly along before two men who were trying to shoot their heads off with rifles, until half their number had been killed. At each report, they would stretch up their necks and gaze around as if a little curious to find out whence the noise proceeded and what it meant, and would then move leisurely on toward the hills, feeding as they went. If, however, a ball touched, but did not fatally wound or cripple a bird, and it rose or fluttered about on the ground, the whole flock took the alarm and were off without delay.

About Box Elder, they seemed to pass the night on the uplands, coming down to the water morning and evening, and retiring to the higher ground before the sun became hot in the morning, and just about sunset in the evening. The young, even when nearly full grown, utter a plaintive peeping cry, which has the peculiar effect of appearing to come from a long distance off, even though the bird may be quite close at hand.

When seen during the summer, the birds were, of course, in families; but on our return march in September, they had commenced collecting together, and packs of from thirty to fifty individuals were several times seen.

101. PEDIŒCETES PHASIANELLUS COLUMBIANUS, (*Ord.*) *Coues.*

SHARP-TAILED GROUSE.

I saw this species only on the plains, a state of things which somewhat surprised me; for, although, of course, essentially a prairie bird, I found it during the summer of 1874 in great numbers among the Black Hills of Dakota. They were more numerous on Box Elder Creek than at any other point; and indeed they seem to prefer streams which have a wide bottom overgrown with rose-bushes and other shrubs, on the fruit of which they feed. The young birds were from one-half to two-thirds grown late in July.

During our passage down the Missouri River, we often saw this species on the dry sand-bars that dotted the river, rolling and dusting themselves in the sand. I did not see these birds roosting on trees until about September 10, at which time the weather at night was quite cold.

102. BONASA UMBELLUS UMBELLOIDES, (*Linn.*) *Baird.*

ROCKY MOUNTAIN RUFFED GROUSE.

Although this species was said to be extremely abundant in the Yellowstone Park, we saw very few of them, not twenty in all. In habits, they seem to resemble almost exactly the eastern variety. A female, with six or eight young only about a week old, was seen August 19. The young, instead of hiding, flew into the lowest branches of a dead pine, a distance of three or four feet, which they just managed to accomplish, while the female fluttered about at my feet as if in the death agony. I had not the heart to molest the charming little family, and after watching them for a short time I moved off, leaving them to their own devices.

CHARADRIIDÆ.

103. ÆGIALITIS VOCIFERUS, (*Linn.*) *Bp.*

KILLDEER PLOVER.

Abundant, breeding on the plains near water.

104. ÆGIALITIS MONTANUS, (*Towns.*) *Baird.*

MOUNTAIN PLOVER.

I did not find this species at all abundant in that portion of Montana which we traversed. Two females, each followed by a newly-hatched young one, were taken near Haymaker's Creek August 1, and were the only individuals observed during the trip. The mothers displayed much anxiety for their young, and endeavored to lead me away from them by the artifices usual with this family of birds. The young were pretty but rather awkward little objects, and tottered along with uncertain steps, as if their legs were too long and they found difficulty in balancing themselves upon them.

RECURVIROSTRIDÆ.

105. RECURVIROSTRA AMERICANA, *Gm.*

AVOCET.

This species abounds on the small alkaline pools that are so common in Dakota, and is quite common in that portion of Montana through which we passed. It was quite numerous on the Yellowstone River above the falls, where the stream is wide, and the wet, grassy banks slope gradually down to the water's edge; and many were seen on the shores of the lake. I also saw a large flock on a small pool near Fort Ellis. They were rather shy, rising in a thick flock at long gunshot, and making the air ring with their shrill cries. A wounded bird unable to fly attempted to escape by diving, making use of the wings for progression under water.

PHALAROPODIDÆ.

106. LOBIPES HYPERBOREUS, (*Linn.*) *Cuv.*

NORTHERN PHALAROPE.

A flock of thirty or forty of these graceful birds was seen on a small pool near Fort Ellis.

SCOLOPACIDÆ.

107. GALLINAGO WILSONII, (*Temm.*) *Bp.*

WILSON'S SNIPE.

One individual seen near Fort Ellis.

108. TRINGA MINUTILLA, *Vieill.*

LEAST SANDPIPER.

This species was only observed near Fort Ellis, where, however, it was abundant early in September.

109. TRINGA BAIRDII, *Coues.*

BAIRD'S SANDPIPER.

This species was noticed at Fort Ellis, at Gardiner's Springs, and in the Lower Geyser Basin. In the last-mentioned locality, it was seen in flocks of from fifty to sixty individuals.

110. TOTANUS SEMIPALMATUS, (*Gm.*) *Temm.*

WILLET.

Abundant on alkaline pools in Dakota and on the Yellowstone Lake.

111. TOTANUS MELANOLEUCUS, (*Gm.*) *Vieill.*

Great Yellowshanks; Telltale.

Abundant on the Yellowstone Lake, and, during September, on the Missouri and streams flowing into it.

112. TOTANUS FLAVIPES, (*Gm.*) *Vieill.*

Lesser Yellowlegs.

A few birds of this species were seen near Fort Ellis and on the shores of the Yellowstone Lake.

113. TOTANUS SOLITARIUS, (*Wils.*) *Aud.*

Solitary Sandpiper.

This species was observed but twice during the summer; once near Fort Ellis and once in the Upper Geyser Basin.

114. TRINGOIDES MACULARIUS, (*Linn.*) *Gray.*

Spotted Sandpiper.

Abundant along the Missouri River, and along mountain-streams as well. On the Missouri, when startled by the approach of the steamboat, they would fly a short distance, and then alight on the slender and pliable twigs projecting from the fresh beaver-houses, on which they would balance themselves with the oddest bobbings and noddings imaginable.

115. ACTITURUS BARTRAMIUS, (*Wils.*) *Bp.*

Bartramian Sandpiper; Upland Plover.

Abundant on the plains in Montana. Late in July,1 secured young birds nearly as strong on the wing as their parents, and at the same time noticed broods of newly-hatched young.

116. NUMENIUS LONGIROSTRIS, *Wils.*

Long-billed Curlew.

Abundant on the plains. Near Box Elder, and all along the base of the Judith Mountains, large scattering companies of these birds were seen feeding on the prairies. They were quite shy, and could not often be approached within gun-range except by strategy. As we drew near, they would rise, one after another, each uttering his loud, rolling note, until finally all were on the wing. They would then, in a dense flock, for a short time perform a variety of beautiful evolutions high in the air, finally re-alighting at a considerable distance.

ARDEIDÆ.

117. ARDEA HERODIAS, *Linn.*

Great Blue Heron.

This species was abundant along the Missouri River in July and September. Prominent objects as they stood on the bare sand-bars, they often drew half a dozen rifle-shots from the steamer as it passed.

GRUIDÆ.

118. GRUS CANADENSIS, (*Linn.*) *Temm.*

Sandhill Crane.

Very abundant all through the Yellowstone Park, but not seen on the plains.

RALLIDÆ.

119. FULICA AMERICANA, *Gm.*

COOT; MUD-HEN.

Abundant in Dakota.

ANATIDÆ.

120. (?) CYGNUS BUCCINATOR, *Rich.*

TRUMPETER SWAN.

A single swan seen in flight at the Yellowstone Lake was probably of this species. It was taken on this water by Mr. Merriam in 1872.

121. ANSER HYPERBOREUS, *Pall.*

SNOW GOOSE.

A flock of these birds were seen on the Yellowstone River near the lake; and the species was again observed in considerable numbers on the alkaline pools near the Missouri River in October.

122. BRANTA CANADENSIS, (*Linn.*) *Gray.*

CANADA GOOSE; COMMON WILD GOOSE.

The common wild goose was seen in the greatest abundance on the Missouri River, and was numerous on the Yellowstone Lake as well. Early in July, while on the way from Bismarck to Carroll, we saw many broods of young, and, when coming down the river late in September, hardly an hour passed without our seeing one or more large flocks of these birds. The young goslings are pretty little things, and the devotion to them of the mother is interesting. Four was the smallest number seen in a brood, and nine the largest. On one occasion I saw what seemed to be a union of two families. The two females swam in advance side by side, while the ganders brought up the rear, and the nine young ones followed directly behind the females.

When approached while in the water, the birds would gradually sink until nothing but the bill and upper part of the head appeared above the surface; the young would then disappear one after another, and last of all the old female would dive. The male always flew off to a safe distance before the diving commenced; but in no instance did I see the mother leave her brood.

123. ANAS BOSCHAS, *Linn.*

MALLARD.

Abundant, breeding along the Missouri and on smaller streams in the mountains.

124. DAFILA ACUTA, (*Linn.*) *Bp.*

PIN-TAIL DUCK.

Observed in considerable numbers on the Yellowstone Lake.

125. CHAULELASMUS STREPERUS, (*Linn.*) *Gray.*

GADWALL; GRAY DUCK.

Abundant on alkaline pools in Dakota; a female with a brood of newly-hatched young was seen on Box Elder.

126. MARECA AMERICANA, (*Gm.*) *Steph.*

AMERICAN WIDGEON.

Abundant on many of the streams in Dakota and Montana.

127. QUERQUEDULA CAROLINENSIS, (*Gm.*) *Steph.*

GREEN-WINGED TEAL.

Abundant, breeding on streams in Eastern Montana. On Deep Creek, early in August, I saw many broods of young apparently only a few days old.

128. QUERQUEDULA DISCORS, (*Linn.*) *Steph.*

BLUE-WINGED TEAL.

Seen in considerable numbers on the Missouri River in September.

129. SPATULA CLYPEATA, (*Linn.*) *Boie.*

SHOVELER.

Quite abundant on alkaline pools in Dakota.

130. FULIGULA AFFINIS, *Eyton.*

LESSER BLACKHEAD.

Abundant on alkaline pools in Dakota.

131. BUCEPHALA ALBEOLA, (*Linn.*) *Bd.*

DIPPER; BUFFLE-HEAD.

This species was rather common on the little mountain lakes and streams of Montana. On one of the forks of Deep Creek, a female with half a dozen young not yet able to fly, was seen, and several of the young secured. Afterward families of this species were quite frequently observed

132. (?) ŒDEMIA FUSCA, (*Linn.*) *Flem.*

WHITE-WINGED SURF DUCK.

Seen on the Yellowstone Lake in August. I mention this species with a query, because, although I recognized it satisfactorily to myself, I took no specimens. The locality is quite out of the range usually ascribed to this bird.

133. MERGUS MERGANSER, *Linn.*

GOOSANDER.

Observed in considerable numbers on the Yellowstone Lake. In August, the young were not yet able to fly.

134. MERGUS CUCULLATUS, *Linn.*

HOODED MERGANSER.

Rather common along the Missouri River.

PELECANIDÆ.

135. PELECANUS TRACHYRHYNCHUS, *Lath.*

WHITE PELICAN.

Very abundant on the Yellowstone Lake, but shy and difficult of approach.

LARIDÆ.

136. LARUS DELAWARENSIS, *Ord.*

RING-BILLED GULL.

Common on Yellowstone Lake and on the Missouri River.

COLYMBIDÆ.

137. COLYMBUS TORQUATUS, *Brunn.*

LOON; GREAT NORTHERN DIVER.

Observed frequently on alkaline pools in Dakota and on the Missouri River.

PODICIPIDÆ.

138. PODICEPS CORNUTUS, *Lath.*

HORNED GREBE.

Abundant during migrations on the Missouri, and all streams and pools in the mountains.

139. PODILYMBUS PODICEPS, (*Linn.*) *Lawr.*

PIED-BILLED GREBE.

Abundant on alkaline pools in Dakota.

PARTIAL LIST OF THE MAMMALS AND BIRDS OF THE YELLOWSTONE PARK.

This list, which is of course very incomplete, consists merely of the observations of Mr. C. Merriam in 1872 and those made by myself in 1875. Such species as were noticed by only c observer are followed by the initial letter of his name.

MAMMALS.

1. *Nycticejus crepuscularis*, Allen, M.
2. *Vespertilio lucifugus*, LeConte, M.
3. *Vespertilio yumanensis*, Allen, M.
4. *Felis concolor*, Linn, G.
5. *Lynx rufus*, Raf., G.
6. *Lynx canadensis*, Raf., G.
7. *Canis occidentalis*, Rich., G.
8. *Canis latrans*, Say, G.
9. *Mustela americana*, Turton, G.
10. *Putorius pusillus*, Aud. & Bach., M.
11. *Gulo luscus*, Sabine.
12. *Mephitis mephitica*, Baird, M.
13. *Mephitis bicolor*, Gray, M.
14. *Ursus horribilis*, Ord.
15. *Ursus americanus*, Pallas.
16. *Sciurus hudsonius*, Pallas.
17. *Tamias quadrivittatus*, Say.

18. *Spermophilus townsendi*, Bach., M.
19. *Arctomys flaviventer*, Bach.
20. *Castor canadensis*, Kuhl.
21. *Thomomys talpoides*, Rich.
22. *Zapus hudsonius*, Coues.
23. *Hesperomys leucopus sonoriensis*, LeConte.
24. *Arvicola riparia*, Ord.
25. *Erithizon epixanthus*, Brandt.
26. *Lepus bairdii*, Hayden, M.
27. *Lagomys princeps*, Rich., M.
28. *Alce americanus*, Jardine.
29. *Cervus canadensis*, Exleben. G.
30. *Cervus macrotis*, Say, G.
31. *Antilocapra americana*, Ord. M.
32. *Ovis montana*, Cuv., G.
33. *Bos americanus*, Gmelin, G.

BIRDS.

1. *Turdus migratorius*, Linn.
2. *Oreoscoptes montanus*, (Towns.) Baird.
3. *Mimus carolinensis*, (Linn.) Gray.
4. *Cinclus mexicanus*, Sw.
5. *Sialia arctica*, Sw.
6. *Regulus calendula*, (Linn.) Licht., M.
7. *Parus atricapillus septentrionalis*, (Harris) Allen, G.
8. *Parus montanus*, Gambel, M.
9. *Sitta carolinensis aculeata*, (Cass.) Allen.
10. *Troglodytes aëdon parkmanni*, (Aud.) Coues, M.
11. *Cistothorus palustris*, (Wils.) Baird, G.
12. *Anthus ludovicianus*, (Gm.) Licht., M.
13. *Dendrœca audubonii*, (Towns.) Baird.
14. *Geothlypis philadelphia macgillivrayi*, (Wils.) Allen, G.
15. *Myiodioctes pusillus*, (Wils.) Bp., M.
16. *Pyranga ludoviciana*, (Wils.) Bp.
17. *Hirundo horreorum*, Barton.
18. *Hirundo thalassina*, Sw.
19. *Petrochelidon lunifrons*, (Say) Scl.
20. *Carpodacus cassini*, Baird.
21. *Loxia curvirostra americana*, (Wils.) Coues, G.
22. *Chrysomitris pinus*, (Wils.) Bp.
23. *Poœcœtes gramineus confinis*, (Gm.) Bd.
24. *Melospiza melodia fallax*, (Wils.) Ridgway.
25. *Junco oregonus*, (Towns.) Baird.
26. *Spizella socialis arizonœ*, (Wils.) Coues.
27. *Zonotrichia leucophrys*, Sw.
28. *Zonotrichia leucophrys intermedia*, Ridgway, M.
29. *Chondestes grammaca*, (Say) Bp., M.
30. *Goniaphœa melanocephala*, (Sw.) Gray, M.
31. *Cyanospiza amœna*, (Say) Baird, M.
32. *Pipilo chlorurus*, (Towns.) Baird, M.
33. *Molothrus pecoris*, (Gm.) Sw., G.
34. *Icterus bullockii*, (Sw.) Bp., M.
35. *Picicorvus columbianus*, (Wils.) Bp., G.
36. *Pica melanoleuca hudsonica*, (Sab.) Coues.

37. *Cyanurus stelleri macrolophus*, (Baird) Allen.
38. *Perisoreus canadensis capitalis*, Baird.
39. *Tyrannus verticalis*, Say, M.
40. *Contopus borealis*, Baird, M.
41. *Contopus virens richardsonii*, (Sw.) Allen.
42. *Empidonax pusillus*, Cab., M.
43. *Ceryle alcyon*, (Linn.) Boie, G.
44. *Picus villosus harrisii*, (Linn.) Allen, M.
45. *Picus pubescens*, Linn., G.
46. *Picoides arcticus*, (Sw.) Gray, M.
47. *Picoides americanus dorsalis*, (Brehm) Baird, M.
48. *Sphyrapicus thyroideus*, (Cass.) Baird.
49. *Melanerpes erythrocephalus*, (Linn.) Sw., G.
50. *Melanerpes torquatus*, (Wils.) Bp.
51. *Colaptes mexicanus*, Sw.
52. *Otus vulgaris wilsonianus*, (Less.) Allen, M.
53. *Surnia ulula hudsonia*, (Gm.) Coues, M.
54. *Circus cyaneus hudsonius*, (Linn.) Schl.
55. *Nisus fuscus*, (Gm.) Kaup.
56. *Falco communis anatum*, (Gm.) Ridgway, G.
57. *Falco sparverius*, Linn.
58. *Buteo borealis calurus*, (Gm.) Ridgway.
59. *Buteo swainsoni*, Bp.
60. *Archibuteo lagopus sancti-johannis*, (Gm.) Ridgway, G.
61. *Pandion haliaëtus*, (Linn.) Cuv.
62. *Tetrao obscurus*, Say.
63. *Bonasa umbellus umbelloides*, (Linn.) Baird.
64. *Ægialitis vociferus*, (Linn.) Bp.
65. *Recurvirostra americana*, Gm., G.
66. *Tringa bairdii*, Coues.
67. *Totanus semipalmatus*, (Gm.) Temm., G.
68. *Totanus melanoleucus*, (Gm.) Vieill.
69. *Totanus flavipes*, (Gm.) Vieill., G.
70. *Totanus solitarius*, (Wils.) Aud., G.
71. *Grus canadensis*, (Linn.) Temm., G.
72. *Cygnus buccinator*, Rich.
73. *Anser hyperboreus*, Pallas, G.
74. *Branta canadensis*, (Linn.) Gray, G.
75. *Dafila acuta*, Jenyns, G.
76. *Bucephala albeola*, (Linn.) Baird, G.
77. (?) *Œdemia fusca*, (Linn.) Flem., G.
78. *Mergus merganser* Linn, G.
79. *Pelecanus trachyrhynchus*, Lath., G.
80. *Larus delawarensis*, Ord, G.
81. *Podiceps cornutus*, Lath., G.

RECONNAISSANCE FROM CARROLL, MONTANA, TO YELLOWSTONE NATIONAL PARK.

GEOLOGICAL REPORT.

BY

EDWARD S. DANA AND GEO. BIRD GRINNELL.

LETTER OF TRANSMITTAL.

YALE COLLEGE, NEW HAVEN, CONN.,
June 1, 1876.

SIR: We have the honor to hand you herewith a report on the geology of a "Reconnaissance from Carroll, Montana, to the Yellowstone Park, and return," made under your command during the months of July, August, and September, 1875.

In submitting the narrative of our examination of the country passed over, we wish to express to you our grateful appreciation of your uniform kindness, and constant willingness to facilitate our investigations by every means in your power. To Lieut. C. F. Roe, who commanded our escort from Carroll to Camp Baker, we are under obligations for many kindnesses. At Camp Baker, Fort Ellis, and Camp Lewis, we were the recipients of most generous hospitalities from the officers of those posts; and our brief delays at those points are remembered by us as being among the pleasantest days of the trip.

The vertebrate fossils collected during the summer were submitted to Prof. O. C. Marsh, and by him identified. The invertebrates were examined by Mr. R. P. Whitfield, of Albany, and his identifications, with occasional comments on the specimens, will be found in the body of the report. A paper by Mr. Whitfield, describing such new forms as were discovered during the summer, accompanies our report. To both of these gentlemen our thanks are due for the many favors that we have received from them.

We remain, sir, very respectfully, your obedient servants,

EDWARD S. DANA.
GEO. BIRD GRINNELL.

Col. WM. LUDLOW,
Chief Engineer of the Department of Dakota,
Saint Paul, Minn.

GEOLOGICAL REPORT.

By Edward S. Dana and Geo. Bird Grinnell.

PRELIMINARY REMARKS ON THE ALLUVIAL DEPOSITS OF THE UPPER MISSOURI RIVER.

The town of Carroll is situated in the alluvial bottom of the Missouri, which is at this point quite extensive, and well timbered with a fine growth of cottonwood. The course of the river-valley is here easterly, and it continues for a considerable distance with but little change in general direction, though the valley varies very considerably in width between the high walls of Cretaceous clays which rise on either side of it. The river sometimes winds along through a bottom two or three miles wide, and again is confined to a narrow passage between the steep washed bluffs several hundred feet in height.

The alluvial phenomena are those which are always observed under similar circumstances, though they take place here more rapidly and on a larger scale than is often the case, in consequence of the vast amount of solid matter which the river is constantly carrying down. On this account, the "muddy Missouri" offers peculiar advantages for the study of alluvial changes; and, could a series of observations be carried on at a few points during two or three seasons, a large amount of data might be collected which would lead to interesting and valuable conclusions. At Carroll, we have an example of a condition of things which may be observed at almost any point in this part of the river, and a few words of explanation may consequently not be out of place. At a, on the outer bank of the river, the current is strong, and has forced itself close up under the high bluffs, whose top forms the border of the broad prairie above. The older deposits, at points such as this, are directly acted upon by the running water, and are thus gradually undermined and worn away, the material being carried on by the current. Upon the opposite side of the stream, at c, the current is weaker, the water shallow and eddying, and the shore runs out to meet the water in a long low sand-bar. At b, there is a high bank of alluvial clays, 10 feet or more above the stream, deposited long before in time of flood, but now being rapidly torn away. Still again at a' the water washes at the foot of the older bluffs, while opposite is the never-failing sand-point.

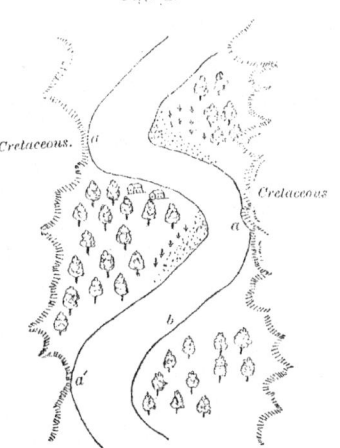

Fig. 1.

Thus the river winds on its course, touching the hills, which form the true limit of its valley, only here and there. For the greater part of its course, it is confined between the alluvial banks. It is safe to say that, except in the spring, the river deposits comparatively little solid matter, and this, chiefly on the sand-spits and bars, where the force of the moving water is small. The work of the river is at this season one of destruction more than deposition, tearing down what it has itself previously built up, and also to a less extent carrying away the older deposits. It acts alone, unaided by any minor tributary streams; for they are dry except in the early season. Even during the summer, however, the channel is constantly changing. The mud-and-sand bars which are everywhere formed do not long retain their positions, but are moved on down the river and heaped up again in other places. Thus the process is one of gradual transferral down the stream; the solid matter going to make one alluvial bank after another until it is finally deposited in the Gulf of Mexico.

It is interesting to note, in this connection, the explanation recently given by Prof. James Thomson (Proc. Royal Society, 1876) of the origin of the windings of rivers in alluvial plains. He shows that, upon hydraulic principles, the velocity of the stream must be greater on the inner bank than on the outer, and yet, as shown here, the wearing away takes place upon the outer bank, and the deposits are made on the inner bank. This is in part due to the centrifugal force, which tends to make the surface-water move away from the inner bank, while its place is taken by a partial upward current of the bottom water retarded much by friction. This current moves obliquely toward the inner bank, and serves to protect it from the rapid scour of the stream-line. On the outer bank, however, there is a tendency of the rapidly-moving surface-water, unimpeded by friction, downward against the solid bank; this it tends to wear away, the worn substance is carried down to the bottom, where the oblique current spoken of carries it toward the inner bank. Sooner or later it will reach this point, and more or less of it will find a resting-place.

These principles find an application in the flow of the Missouri through its alluvial plain. It is on the outer bank of the successive curves of the river that the wear is greatest, and that the river has forced its way up to the older bluffs, while on the inner bank the deposits are being made, more or less, all the time, sand or mud, or both, according to the relative velocities of the different parts of the stream.

As has been remarked, the work of the river in summer is destructive, and no additions are made at this time to the height of the alluvial banks. In spring, the case is very different, and it is at that time that the chief deposits of alluvium are made. The river is then full, the snows all over the wide area drained by the Missouri are melting, rains are frequent, and a vast amount of material is brought in from the surrounding country. The amount of solid matter held in suspension at this season is enormous. In floods, the waters rise many feet, overspreading the lower alluvial ground, and in subsiding and evaporating they deposit their load of sand and clay, sometimes covering a well-grown and fertile plain with a bed of alluvium a foot and more in thickness. This sometimes takes place for a number of successive years at the same points, as is shown by the fact that the roots of trees which must have been close to the surface of the ground when they commenced to grow were often seen buried beneath from four to six feet of alluvium. We could of course only observe this on the very edge of the bank, where the water had removed a part of the old alluvium, exposing to view the roots, and that part of the trunk which had been buried.

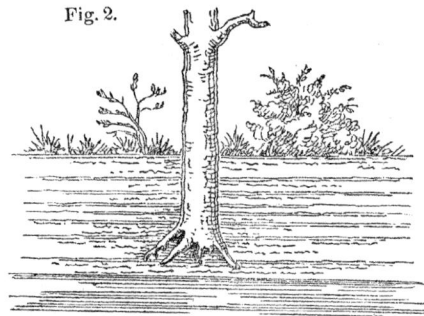
Fig. 2.

Some of these trees were quite small, not more than 3 or 4 inches in diameter, and most of them were still living; thus indicating how rapidly such deposits as those referred to are made. The trees were mostly cottonwoods and elms, species of rapid growth. That these deposits are made very rapidly is also shown by the thick layers to be noticed in any section of a bank so deposited, sometimes a foot or more, perfectly homogeneous. It is interesting to note the great variation in the height of the perpendicular alluvial banks. From point to point, in some cases, it is only three or four feet; in others twenty-five feet or more. This depends obviously on the strength of the current, and the extent to which the water is backed up. It bears upon the general subject of river-terraces. Not infrequently we observed a second terrace above, or rather a long line of high cut bluffs separated from the stream by another alluvial plain (see figure 3). This is all of recent origin, and merely means that the river stopped washing away the bluffs here, and commenced to fill up at its foot.

The energy of the stream is at all times directly proportional to the amount of the descending water; and hence is immensely greater in spring than in summer. This energy is probably all expended in overcoming friction, and in carrying the load of solid matter. The difference in the amount of detritus held in suspension by the stream in early July and in late September was very marked—at the latter time the stream seemed to have to a great extent cleared itself. This is doubtless due to the diminished volume of the water, in consequence of which the carrying power of the stream was so much diminished. A river of this character seems to act as a destructive agent rather through the weight and moving force of its own water than by means of the abrading power of the solid matter it carries with it.

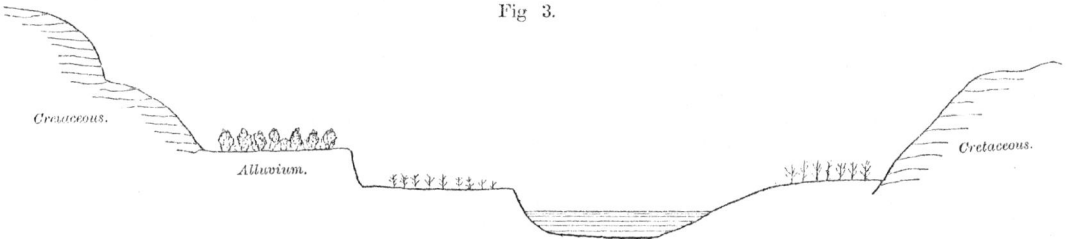

Fig. 3.

A true upper terrace was not observed at any point above the mouth of the Yellowstone. At points below, it was not uncommon to see one hugging the lignite bluffs, and separated from the river by a wide alluvial plain. Whether it be a true terrace or only a recent deposit is doubtful. Such a place was noticed a short distance below Fort Buford, where the water must once have spread over an immense area, pointing to the time when the Missouri was a much larger stream than it is at present.

Above Carroll, the river-bottom becomes much less wide, and, although sometimes flowing through valleys more or less broad, the stream generally passes along between and close beneath frowning banks of washed clays and sands. The undermining of the banks takes place here in the same manner as where they are alluvial; but, owing to the greater hardness and thickness of the older rocks upon which the water acts, the process is much more slow. It goes on constantly, however, so that at last a great mass of the rock above, perhaps a hundred feet in thickness, deprived of its support, slips down into the water. This has occurred at many points, and gives to the rocks, as viewed from the river, a great variety of dip, which has been considered by some observers as indicating an extensive disturbance of these beds, due to the elevation of the mountain-ranges of this section of the country. We cannot doubt, however, that all these apparent disturbances are purely local, and have been caused by the action of running water.

FROM CARROLL TO BOX ELDER CREEK.

Fort Pierre Group of the Cretaceous.

The clay bluffs at Carroll rise abruptly above the alluvial bottom on both sides of the river. They belong to what Dr. Hayden has called the Fort Pierre Group, Cretaceous No. 4. These bluffs consist of a dark-blue to purplish-black laminated clay, occasionally stained with iron, and sometimes containing very thin layers of white sand. They are remarkably constant in character from top to bottom. Dr. Hayden has stated in general that the clays of No. 4 are *not* laminated; but this is not true of those which came under our observation.

The characteristic features of this clay are (1) the large calcareous concretions, which will be spoken of more particularly in connection with Crooked Creek; (2) the plates and crystals of transparent gypsum, or selenite; and (3) the alkaline deposits.

The selenite plates are quite conspicuous, as they lie on the surface of the ground, and glisten brilliantly as the sun strikes them. In general, they are irregular crystalline fragments; but occasionally perfect crystals are found of the form common in the clay of Poland, Ohio. The surface of all these fragments is roughened and etched by the solvent action of the water which has flowed over them. These etchings are most distinct on the clinopinacoid, and are similar to those described by Baumhauer as having been produced artificially by the action of caustic potash. The selenite plates are found most abundantly near the level of the river, having been washed together here, but they occur also more or less frequently on the plains, twenty-five miles from the river, at a level nearly 1,000 feet above.

The alkaline deposits seem to be particularly abundant in some layers, exuding from the bluffs along the river in long white lines. Considerable deposits of it are seen at various points on the banks of the river, and all the little dry creek-bottoms leading into the Missouri are white, as if frosted with it. The following is an analysis of a particularly-pure specimen of the alkali collected near Carroll. For this analysis we are indebted to Mr. Fred. P. Dewey, of the Sheffield Scientific School of New Haven, and we would here express our acknowledgments to him:

	I.	II.	Mean.
MgO	11.69	11.91	11.80
Na_2O	15.81	16.20	16.00
CaO	0.53	0.68	0.60
Li_2O	0.88	0.88	0.88
SO_3	44.09	44.12	44.10
Cl	trace	trace	trace
H_2O	23.09	23.00	23.05
Insoluble	3.29	3.27	3.28
	99.38	100.06	99.71

As will be seen from this analysis, the alkali consists essentially of the sulphates of sodium and magnesium; in fact, the amount of sulphuric acid given is almost exactly what is required to unite with the several bases. The presence of the lithia is also to be noticed.

This alkali is a constant attendant of this member of the Cretaceous, wherever observed in the West, and is one of the causes of its barren character. The water of the Missouri is so entirely derived from pure mountain-sources—even the large rivers, as the Musselshell, which flow through the alkaline prairie, being nearly dry at their outlets—that it is little affected by the salt which is brought into it, though the white deposits on the alluvial banks show that the quantity is not small.

These Cretaceous clays have a laminated shaly structure wherever exposed: they weather down so readily, however, that often only the rounded beds of clay are seen. These are so soft and yielding, that the foot sinks deeply into them, and they have much the feeling of a bed of ashes. In the neighborhood of Carroll, there is more or less of a scanty vegetation; but farther down the river, perhaps one hundred and fifty miles, there seems to be no vegetation whatever, and the appearance of these black clay-beds is desolate in the extreme.

The height of the Cretaceous bluffs above the river is quite variable as viewed from the water; but, when we examine the total elevation attained in passing back from the river, we find that it is remarkably constant. The Helena road at Carroll rises in two or three very steep pitches the greater part of its final ascent, and, within two or three miles of where the road leaves the valley the high plateau is reached, which is kept, with little change of level, beyond Crooked Creek. The height here, as given by an aneroid, is 665 feet. On the other side of the river, the height of the corresponding plateau is 680 feet; though in this case the final elevation was found a little farther from the river, the rise of the plain being more gradual after the first steep ascent had been made.

The appearance of the surrounding country, as viewed from the top of the bluffs back of Carroll, is very forbidding. The whole landscape is of a somber, gray tint; the color of the soil and the sage-brush sparingly relieved by the dark green of the stunted pines that grow here and there on the summits of the bluffs and along the little ravines. There is little vegetation, except the *Artemisia*, and, altogether, the region seems incapable of affording sustenance to man or beast. Notwithstanding its uninviting appearance, the neighboring country abounds in game. This region has been, and still is, though to a less extent than formerly, the favorite feeding-ground of a portion of the great northern herd of buffaloes: antelope are numerous on the plains, and mule-deer and elk are found in the pine-timbered ravines. Farther back from the river, in the hill-country, the big-horn, or mountain-sheep, and the grizzly bear occur, though nowhere numerous.

On both sides of the Missouri, the high bluffs are cut into numberless ravines, which divide and subdivide again to a wonderful extent, thus carrying the surface-drainage back into the river. These ravines are often quite well wooded, and some of them contain a little strongly alkaline water.

As has been remarked, the height of the plateau varies but little as we proceed away from the river, though we soon pass over the divide which separates the immediate drainage of the Missouri from that of Crooked Creek, a tributary of the Musselshell River.

Little Crooked Creek, thirteen miles from Carroll, retains water in holes until midsummer, when it generally dries up entirely. Five miles beyond, a branch of Crooked Creek also affords a little poor water in the early summer; but, late in the season, the only water on the route is found in pools in the bed of Crooked Creek, and this is decidedly unpalatable. All these creeks, with their many dry branches, certainly contain swiftly-running water in the early season, when the spring rains unite with the melting snows to swell the streams. This is plainly shown by the high, cut banks and the large accumulations of drift pebbles in the turns in the creek-beds.

The surface of the prairie from Carroll to Crooked Creek (twenty-one [miles) and beyond, though this point is only about fifteen miles from the river in a direct line, is scattered with drift deposits. These are of two kinds: (1) large, mostly angular, blocks of syenite and other hornblendic rocks, with occasionally some semi-crystalline limestone; and (2) small, smoothly-rounded pebbles, consisting to 90 per cent. of a brown quartzite or jasper. Some fragments of fossil wood may here and there be found, and a large variety of pebbles of various kinds of rocks in small quantities. This drift is entirely *superficial*, no proper deposits having been observed at any point. The lithological character of the drift will be described more in detail hereafter, when it will be connected with observations made north of the Missouri River (p. 135).

At Carroll, in the lower levels of the Cretaceous No. 4, the only fossils observed were *Baculites ovatus*, Say, and a large *Inoceramus*. At Little Crooked Creek, where we made our first camp (July 13), we had more opportunity for search, and here, and farther on, at Crooked Creek, we found:

1. *Lucina ventricosa*, M. & H.
2. *Lucina occidentalis*, Morton.
3. *Mactra*, sp.?.
4. *Inoceramus tenuilineatus*, H. & M.
5. *Anchura*, sp. (specific features not shown).
6. *Ammonites Halli*, M. & H.
7. *Scaphites nodosus*, Owen.
8. *Baculites ovatus*, Say.

Inoceramus tenuilineatus, H. & M., *Ammonites Halli*, M. & H., and *Baculites ovatus*, Say, were extremely abundant at these localities, and the specimens secured comprise individuals of all ages.

These fossils, as far as our observations go, are found only in the concretions previously mentioned in connection with these beds. These concretions occur in great numbers from the level of the river to the highest point above it where these clays were seen. Those which contain fossils seem to be much more abundant in the upper layers than in those nearer the water's level. Fossils were occasionally found in concretions from the lower ravines; but such concretions were not seen in place. They were generally found imbedded in the loose, washed clays of the ravine, and had the appearance of having been carried down from some point above. The concretions are quite compact when found in place in the cut bank, though they yield readily to a blow of the hammer. Whenever exposed for any length of time, however, to atmospheric influences, they separate into hundreds of angular fragments; and here and there over the prairie may be seen the little piles of these blocks, a conspicuous feature among the low cactus-plants.

The concretions are generally a foot or two in diameter, though sometimes much larger, and are extensively cracked; the seams having been filled with crystallized calcite and sometimes with gypsum. One fine specimen of an *Ammonite* was found, the interior of which was lined with exceedingly delicate crystals of the selenite. The concretions, as a rule, are not distributed at random through the clays, but lie in layers, sometimes closely contiguous, so as to form an almost uninterrupted stratum. The large majority are destitute of fossil remains; but occasionally they are met with, containing large numbers of the shells, a considerable number forming the nucleus of a single concretion. It is to be noticed that these fossils, as a rule, are not clustered together in the center of the concretion, but lie in a single layer; and it is not uncommon to see this layer continued in line from one concretion to the others lying immediately adjoining it. This fact indicates the relation in point of time between the deposit of the shells and the formation of the concretions.

The most common fossil in this association, and one which is met with almost everywhere on the prairie, is the *Baculites ovatus*, Say. These remains are often called "fossil fish", "fossil ferns", &c., by the white inhabitants of that section of the Territory; and, as they are so well known and so often spoken of, it may not be amiss to make a remark in regard to them for the benefit of the unscientific. They are not fish-skeletons, but are simply the shell of an animal somewhat allied to the present *Nautilus*, but having the shell straight and tapering instead of curved in a spiral. The delicate lines on the shell show the divisional walls, or septa, of the successive chambers in the shell.

During a delay of a day at Crooked Creek, we were enabled to follow along the dry bed of the stream for several miles. This bed is filled with alluvial deposits of the black clay deposited by the stream, and through which it has again washed out its path, leaving steep walls three feet or more in height. The banks on either side show evidence of having been washed over, looking white, and a little sandy, and with the drift-pebbles collected in large numbers. Here and there the Cretaceous clays are exposed in high bluffs on either side of the creek-valley. These bluffs have sometimes a height of 50 to 75 feet above the stream-bed. The clays are not to be distinguished from those forming the immediate banks of the Missouri. They are blue-black or slate-colored, shaly, the layers being very distinct and everywhere characterized by the concretions. The layers of the clay are pretty uniformly horizontal, though an occasional slight dip is to be observed. At one point, we noticed a very low synclinal fold followed by a fault; the strata being displaced some 15 or 20 feet. This and other similar disturbances observed in this neighborhood we decided were undoubtedly local, being due to slips in the loosely-laminated clays, through the influence of running waters. Many similar disturbances were observed along the river which were obviously due to a similar cause (see p. 125).

From Crooked Creek, the road runs on nearly southwest, rising slightly till a point some few miles from Box Elder Creek is reached, when there is a more sudden rise of 50 feet up to a plateau, which on top, is very level, and the northern edge of which can be distinctly seen extending some distance in both directions.

The following cut (fig. 4) gives an ideal section * from Cone Butte to the Missouri along the line of the road, as obtained from measurements made by an aneroid. It is to be observed that the line runs obliquely, making the distance somewhat farther than in a direct line, as will be seen by reference to the map.

The highest point at which the undisturbed Fort Pierre Group was observed was 1,060 feet above the river; and deposits of this age were seen at various points along the Helena road until Camp Lewis was reached. The last point at which they were noticed was near the crossing of Warm Spring Creek, south of the Moccasin Mountains.

---

* The vertical distances are increased nine times to admit of being brought within the limits of the page. The horizontal scale is (as on the map) 6 miles to the inch; the vertical scale is ⅛ mile (3,520 feet) to the inch.

The rise of the land continues until we reach Box Elder Valley, where the high plateau is seen extending east and west, and here a descent of 80 feet is made to the level of the stream.

Box Elder Creek takes its rise in the Judith Mountains, and, after a northerly course of about seven miles, turns easterly and then southeasterly, finally reaching the Musselshell River. At the stage-station, where we camped for several days, its course is nearly east and west. It is a running stream and furnishes fair water. Our delay at this point gave us an opportunity to explore to some extent the Judith Mountains.

In the neighborhood of Box Elder, we pass from the Fort Pierre clays, Cretaceous No. 4 of Hayden, to the sandstones of the Fox Hills Group, or Cretaceous No. 5, overlying them. At a locality lying nearly south of Box Elder station and distant from it about a mile, we observed a ledge of sandstone containing some tolerably-preserved shells. The rock is a yellow ferruginous sandstone in rather thin beds, but quite firm. Occasional calcareous layers contain fossils similar to those in the sandstone, but much better preserved. The thickness of this yellow fossil-bearing sandstone is small; and beneath it is a friable white sandstone, easily rubbed into powder with the fingers. The dip of the exposed strata is slight, toward the northeast. The fossils found at this locality are as follows:

1. *Sanguinolaria oblata*, Whitf. (n. sp.).
2. *Liopistha (Cymella) undulata*, M. & H.
3. *Tellina isomma*, Meek.
4. *Tellina scitula*, M. & H.
5. *Mactra warreniana*, M. & H.
6. *Mactra maia*, Whitf. (n. sp.).
7. *Tapes montanensis*, Whitf. (n. sp.).
8. *Ostrea congesta*, Con.???.
9. *Lunatia concinna*, H. & M.
10. *Inoceramus*, sp.
11. *Fusus Galpinianus*, M. & H.

Sandstones of a similar character to that mentioned may be seen at a variety of points where the excavation of the deep coulées has laid bare the rock beneath. One striking locality was visited some four miles east of the station, where, on the east bank of a deeply-cut coulée, the sandstone is exposed at a height of 200 feet above the creek-bottom.

The section was as follows:

Two feet of a white sandstone, in thin layers;

Thirty feet of a white, soft, thickly-laminated sandstone, underlaid by an uncertain thickness of rusty-yellow sand-rock.

No fossils were found here, though they were searched for with care.

JUDITH MOUNTAINS.

Our examination of the Judith Mountains was hasty and incomplete, owing to lack of time at this point; and our movements were still further embarrassed by the necessity of taking some precautions against the hostile Sioux, known to be in the vicinity at the time.

The following cut (fig. 5) will give some idea of the extent and bearings of the Judith Mountains,

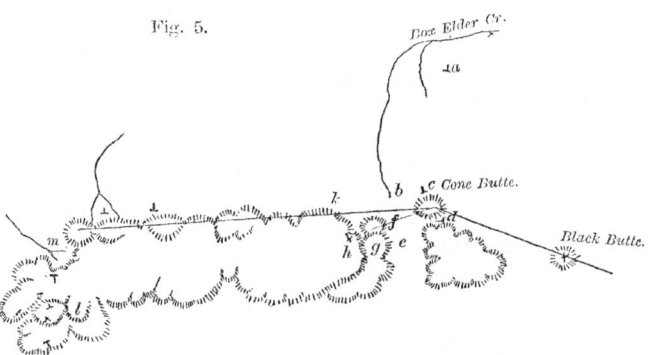

Fig. 5.

although it makes no pretensions to topographical accuracy. The few bearings which were taken from Cone Butte are indicated. It is to be noticed that these mountains do not lie north and south on the east bank of the Judith River, where they are generally represented on the maps of this region. On the contrary, their trend is essentially east and west, so that the axis of the range lies almost at right angles with the course of the river. The general appearance of the range as viewed from a point to the northeast is shown in figure 6.

Fig. 6.

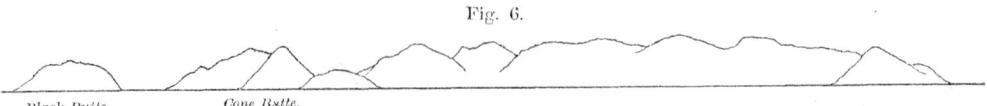

Black Butte. Cone Butte.

In the neighborhood of Box Elder, we pass, as has been stated, from the Fort Pierre clays to the sandstones of the Fox Hills Group overlying them. The rocks of this group extend widely east and west from this point, and from the hills which slope up to the foot of the Judith Mountains.

Near Box Elder station, the sandstone shows itself nearly on the level of the stream at a point hardly a mile distant from it to the south. This is the locality where the fossils above mentioned were found. From this point, in approaching the hills, we took a course nearly south up a coulée, then dry, but which had been deeply excavated by running water, and which in the spring is no doubt a considerable tributary of Box Elder Creek. The eastern bank of this coulée is quite high above the bed, perhaps 200 feet, and all the way has a very uniform slope up to the mountains. On the west side the terrace is quite low, but has also the same gradual slope upward; the surface being for the most part remarkably level. The slope is about 50 feet to the mile. The sandstone of No. 5 is seen at a number of points, both in the bed of the coulée and above in the high eastern bank just referred to. The slope upward on the east continues until within a mile or so of Cone Butte, where the sandstone strata are more upturned and the surface of the hill is more broken. Close to Cone Butte, at its foot (at c, fig. 5), we observed the sandstone, elevated 750 to 800 feet above Box Elder. It was here whitish, compact, weathering out into peculiar forms, with irregular layers of ferruginous sand; dip, 10°; strike north 80° west.

The thickness here, as elsewhere, is difficult to estimate, because of the insufficient exposure. It must be two or three hundred feet, or perhaps more. It may be mentioned here that the hills and terraces are so much covered with grass and soil that exposures of rock are rare. Below this point (at b, see map) is an exposure of blue laminated clays, with abundant concretions, probably the Fort Pierre Group again, though here 600 feet above the highest exposure observed below, and 400 feet above the sandstone identified as No. 5 (a, on map). The elevation is due to the upturning of the mountains, involving both members of the Cretaceous alike.

From here we made the ascent of Cone Butte. The immediate foot-hills, and indeed those at some distance from the peak, are made up of the talus from the mountain as far as the surface-exposure goes. Loose blocks of the trachyte, which forms the mass of the mountain, have been spread over the surrounding country to a remarkable extent, and the smaller fragments were found abundantly within a mile or two of Crooked Creek; that is, having crossed Box Elder Valley. Cone Butte is, as has been intimated, a trachytic hill, and according to the readings of our aneroid it is 2,200 feet above Box Elder, and 3,400 above the Missouri River. This is about the average height of what are called the Judith Mountains, though there are several points which are probably a little higher.

The summit of Cone Butte commands an extensive view over the prairies to the north. The Little Rocky Mountains and the Bear's Paw Mountains, though far in the distance, are the most conspicuous points to be noticed. Its commanding position is well appreciated by the Indians who use it as a lookout, for which it is most conveniently situated. A shelter which we found on the summit, formed of large flat blocks of trachyte resting upon the spreading branches of a stunted pine-tree, had doubtless been used as a resting-place by many an Indian scout.

Cone Butte is itself a conspicuous object from all the surrounding country, even as far north as the Little Rocky Mountains; its perfectly conical shape being very striking from any point on the Carroll road. Viewed from the west, the sides of the cone are broken, and not so symmetrical as shown in figure 6. The slopes are covered with loose blocks of trachyte, and at some points are precipitous. The angle of the cone is about 40° or 41°; indeed, it is so steep, and the loose blocks of trachyte furnish so insecure a foot-hold, that, were it not for the trails made by the mountain-sheep ascending and descending, it would be no easy task to climb it from the west side.

The mineralogical character of this trachyte deserves to be described a little in detail, as it may be taken as a type of the variety which occurs most widely in these mountains. It is in general of uniform texture, hard and firm, though occasionally showing minute cavities containing quartz crystals as a secondary product. It breaks on weathering into the large thin slabs which cover the sides of Cone Butte. The main constituent of the rock is a triclinic feldspar, as revealed by a thin section under the microscope, though occasional crystals of orthoclase of greater size may be observed. Hornblende follows next in order, the crystals being very distinct; and, further than this, magnetite plays an important rôle—this is distributed more generally than is common in similar rocks, and is seen by the microscope as extremely minute grains, whose metallic character is revealed only in reflected light. These particles of magnetite have suffered alteration to a considerable extent, and the feldspar is often stained red and yellow in a ring about them by the oxidized iron. It is to this alteration that the peculiar red color of the talus on the sides of the hills, as seen from a distance, is undoubtedly due. A critical examination shows that a little quartz is also present; but, as it was often otherwise noted in minute cavities, it may be questioned whether it is not merely a secondary product.

The descent from Cone Butte was made by way of the deep ravine which separates it from the trachytic hills to the south. The white trachyte is carried down nearly to the gap, where (see fig. 7) we passed a transverse dike, east and west in direction, of a hard green trachyte, with a cubical fracture breaking into large angular blocks, in striking contrast with the loose slabs of the other trachyte which cover the slopes of Cone Butte. This is probably a later dike, subsequent to the formation of the other hills. This trachyte, as well as that of Cone Butte, was found in fragments abundantly over the prairie, even to a distance of fifteen miles from the mountains. It is characterized by large crystals of a glassy orthoclase, which give it a porphyritic structure. Under the microscope, these crystals are found to be more or less clouded, in consequence of incipient alteration: this is also shown by the indistinct colors obtained in polarized light. Accompanying the large crystals of orthoclase are smaller thin-bladed crystals in large numbers. The other essential constituent is the hornblende, which is seen in simple distinct prisms: it has a deep-green color, and is strongly dichroic. No quartz was observed. The most interesting feature of the rock

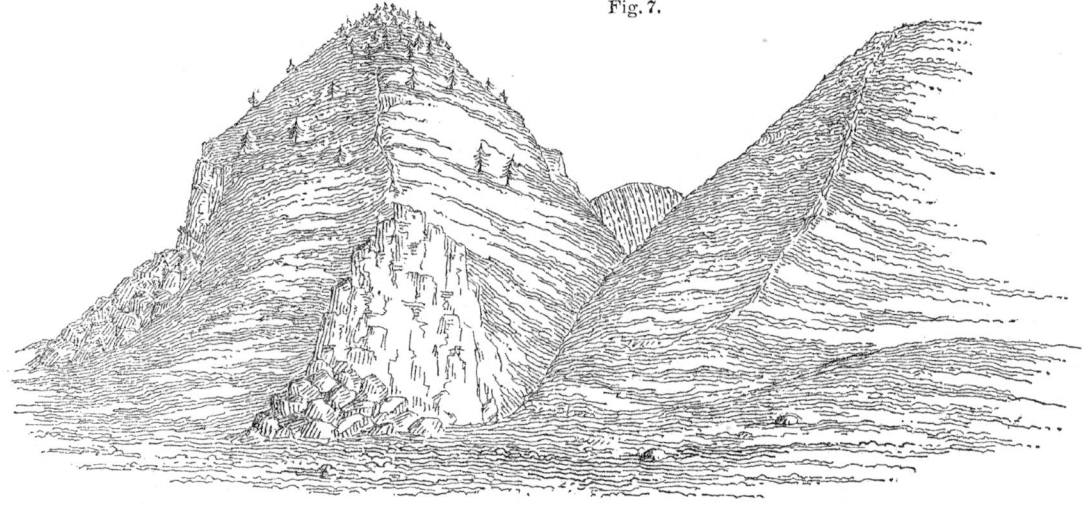

Fig. 7.

is the green base, which, under a low magnifying power, seems to be without structure, but, when magnified highly, is resolved into countless minute, acicular crystals, jumbled together in a confused mass. They show very little color in polarized light. They may be zeolitic; but a chemical analysis, which the circumstances do not now admit of, would be required to settle the point.

In the ravine spoken of, 355 feet below the summit of Cone Butte, we were surprised to find a series of slates and sandstones. The cut (Fig. 7) will give some idea of the relations of the rocks, it being a sketch taken from a point below to the west. The total width of the gap is about 70 yards; the trachyte rising abruptly on both sides. The trachyte of the hill to the south is quite similar to that of Cone Butte. The section in the gap is as follows:

Coarse ferruginous sandstone, vertical	3 feet.
Fine blue shale, vertical	20 feet.
Slate, sometimes shaly, sometimes a good slate, and very sandy, in layers; color whitish and yellowish; dip 70° south	180 to 200 feet.

The strike of these slates is east and west.

The age of these rocks is uncertain, as the only fossils found in them were some cycloidal fish-scales, with occasional impressions of fish-vertebræ and spines, which were quite numerous in some layers in the slate. It is hardly to be doubted, however, that they are Cretaceous; and the position of some rocks, also containing fish-scales and probably identical with these, observed at another point, as noted below, suggests that they are probably Upper Cretaceous, perhaps No. 5.

The present position of these slates is very remarkable: they lie far above (about 600 feet) the rocks visible in the hills below, and doubtless owe their elevation to the eruption of the trachyte, having been squeezed up between the two great masses of igneous rock. They show little trace of the influence of heat upon them.

The hills to the south and east, forming the eastern extremity of the Judith Mountains, are, as far as observed, trachyte. Black Butte, or Buffalo Heart Mountain, was not visited; but its position and similar appearance show that it is also eruptive, probably exclusively so. The sandstones dip away from it even more distinctly than from Cone Butte. It may be remarked here that the trachytic hills are very distinctly marked in appearance, and may be recognized with certainty even at a considerable distance. Their sides are covered with the loose blocks of the rock, and have a distinct reddish color, due to the oxidation of the iron which exists in considerable quantities in the trachyte (see description), which is quite conspicuous and characteristic.

West of Cone Butte (see e, fig. 5), there is a break in the hills, and a low pass called "Ross's Cut-off" gives passage to frequent Indian parties. It is free from timber, and of gradual slope, so that upon one occasion wagons were brought through without serious trouble. It is from this low pass that Box Elder takes its rise.

In this gap, the observations made were unimportant; the rocks being mostly covered up with soil and grass. It was interesting, however, to note that the even, gradual slope of the terrace before mentioned extends quite into the pass, with the same character well preserved. At e, (Fig. 5,) just on the edge of the hills which rise on the west side of the gap, a series of black shales were observed, vertical, and with a strike nearly north and south. These hills at g and to the south are all trachyte. We crossed them at one point, dragging our horses over the loose talus, much to their and our own discomfort, and found the height a little less than that of Cone Butte. On their western side, the trachyte shows itself in a series of columns, which are very regular and well formed; much more so than is common in this rock. This trachyte differs somewhat from the others described in the larger proportion of hornblende present. As before, the orthoclase appears in distinct crystals of large size, and the triclinic feldspar in thin-bladed fragments. The whole has a pasty base. A little valley, in which rises a small stream of cool water, lies just to the west, and on the other side is a high limestone hill (at h), the only exposure of the older sedimentary rocks which we met with in this part of the hills.

This limestone rises in a series of sharp ridges, very distinct, and seen from a distance as a number of white lines running up the sides of the hills. It dips 50° northeast; the strike being northwest. The upper layers are white, semi-crystalline, and very profuse in flinty fragments. These are exposed by the weathering, and, on the surface, the rock has quite a coralline aspect. Lower layers are firmer, blue, and also cherty, though not to the same extent as those above. A very careful search showed that fossils were very rare, though a few were found, enough to determine the age of the rock to be Carboniferous. The following is a list of the fossils obtained at this point:

1. Crinoidal remains too indistinct to be identified.
2. *Terebratula* or *Cryptonella*.
3. *Spirifera (Martinia) lineata*, Martin.
4. *Spirifera centronata*, Winch.
5. *Orthoceras ? ? ?*, possibly filling of outer chamber.

Spirifera centronata, Winch., was the most abundant and characteristic form noticed here.

The thickness of these limestone beds must be very considerable; at least 300 or 400 feet were seen on this side of the hill, but as we were unable to follow them farther, we cannot venture to estimate their whole extent. This limestone is intersected at one point by a ridge of hard trachyte. On the other side of the little creek valley, the limestone also appears, containing here only a few imperfect crinoidal stems. Here it is apparently overlaid by a sandstone which has all the appearance of dipping under the hill, or, in other words, is overlaid by the trachyte. The outlying hill, *f*, is made up of sandstone, or a sandy slate; its summit is 1,200 feet above Box Elder, and hence a thousand feet lower than the adjoining trachytic hill. The observed thickness of this slate is 200 feet; dip 10° a little east of north, and strike nearly east and west. It can hardly be conformable to the limestone described; but the eruption of the trachyte, which doubtless accompanied the elevation of the mountains, has very much complicated the relations of the beds..

This slate contained large numbers of poorly-preserved fish-scales, which would seem to show its probable identity with the elevated slates in the ravine behind Cone Butte. Further than this, its position seems to suggest that it may be nearly parallel with the sandstones near Cone Butte, which are, as has been stated, Upper Cretaceous. No trace was seen at this point of any rocks between the Cretaceous and the Carboniferous limestone.

FROM BOX ELDER TO CAMP LEWIS.

The road from Box Elder to Camp Lewis follows along the foot of the mountains, but at such a distance from them that very few observations could be made. The character of the country is much better than that nearer the Missouri, but cannot be very highly praised. The Judith Mountains give rise to several running streams, which occupy wide valleys, and the region seems well adapted for stock-raising. Near Armell's Creek, a mile to the north of the road-crossing, gray clays are conspicuous, forming high bluffs with perpendicular faces, quite different from anything seen near Crooked Creek. This exposure was visited later, on the way to the mouth of the Judith River, but yielded no fossils, and its age is therefore uncertain. It is probably, however, near the top of the Cretaceous.

Our road approached quite near the mountains at Bald Butte (see *m* on map), and here, and at several points beyond, we observed a considerable thickness of a soft white sandstone, fine-grained and even-textured, but without fossils. It is in very thick beds, and weathers out in vertical walls, taking fantastic shapes, which are like those of the "Quader Sandstein" of the Saxon Switzerland. This is undoubtedly Upper Cretaceous. From this point, the road bears away from the hills again, crossing the divide between the Musselshell and Judith Rivers, and passing between the Judith and Moccasin Mountains. As has been before remarked, the dark clays of the Fort Pierre Group are seen again south of the Moccasin Mountains and just before reaching Warm Spring Creek. At this point, there was a considerable exposure of these beds, and, although no fossils were collected here, the characteristic features of the deposit were unmistakable. Farther on, a cut bank on the creek gave the following section:

Yellow clays, somewhat sandy .... 20 feet.
Hard gray shaly clays seen .... 20 feet.

These beds had a very slight dip a little east of north.

The Moccasin Mountains we were unable to visit; but their appearance, as viewed from various points on the road, and again from the northeast, indicated that, like the Judith Mountains, they are largely trachytic.

Camp Lewis is situated on Trout Creek, or Big Spring Branch, as it is sometimes called, which is the largest branch of the Judith River. This is a wide stream of clear, very cold, water, which takes its rise in a spring about five miles from where the camp is situated. The immediate valley of the stream is covered with excellent grass, and when the country becomes safe from the incursions of hostile Indians—far from being the case at present—it must prove of high value for settlement.

About Camp Lewis there are considerable deposits of red clay. This is the case on both sides of the stream, but most conspicuously on the east bank, where the bluffs for a considerable distance are of a deep-red color. It is rare to find any exposures of the beds which give rise to these red slopes. In general, they are so washed down that only the red surface-deposits are seen. In some ravines, however, on the east bank of Trout Creek, we found the hardened red clays in place. No fossils could be discovered, though they were searched for with care. These beds seemed to be somewhat irregular and of rather local character. In the place where opportunities for observation were most favorable, we found 10 feet of red laminated clay, underlaid by a gray shale and overlaid by a sandy slate of a brown color. A little farther north, other layers of sandstone were observed, and beneath these some very thick bedded sandstone deposits; the red clays running out entirely. There was nothing to settle positively the age of these deposits. Except in color, they do not resemble the "red beds" of the West, generally referred to the Triassic; and as similar deposits were seen on the slopes of the Snow Mountains, twenty-five miles distant, overlying sandstones containing Cretaceous fossils (the same was true elsewhere), as noted later, it is more than probable that they are all Cretaceous in this vicinity. From this point, on our return journey, we made a detour and crossed the west end of the Judith Mountains; and, as we have just stated our observations in the neighborhood of Cone Butte, it may be interesting to add the others in this place.

Passing on from the red beds just mentioned, we crossed a low divide, and came down into the wide valley of a branch of Trout Creek, passing over some more red clays at a little higher level than those seen before. From here, our course was about north; our objective point being some white limestone bluffs conspicuous on the summit of the range. The foot-hills first passed over consisted, as indicated by one or two rock-exposures, of a brown, firm sandstone, in which no fossils were found. It had a dip of 20° away from the hills. These hills, in both directions, are covered with timber and grass, and the rock is rarely seen on the surface.

The limestone bluffs (*l*, fig. 5) were reached without much clue to the structure of the intervening country having been gained. This limestone stands up in a series of high buttresses, which, with their vertical fronts, are quite conspicuous objects. They show no evidence of stratification or structure. The rock contains occasionally masses of flint, though they are not so conspicuously cherty as those seen near Cone Butte. Some few fossils show that the rock is of Carboniferous age.

The following is a list of those obtained:

    1. *Zaphrentis centralis*, Ev. & Shum.
    2. *Syringapora mult-attenuata*, McChes.
    3. *Stictopora*, sp.
    4. *Spirifera centronata*, Winch.

On the hill to the west of this, a broad band of stratified limestone is exposed, in which some similar fossils were found. This same band apparently appears again on the north side of the hill, but here with a changed dip, northwest instead of southwest, pointing to a fold over at this point.

We crossed the higher ridge here, from which we could see off to the east, noting, as before, that the hills to the north are mostly trachyte, while those behind them to the south are as uniformly limestone. Near the source of Deer Creek, we descended into a broad, green meadow, quite surrounded by the hills. At one point, a patch of bright-red soil suggested a return to the red clays before seen. Crossing over by Bald Butte, a hill of trachyte, we reached the road again. The excursion was not altogether a satisfactory one, though showing the presence of the limestone at this point, but, as an investigation into the further structure of the hills, it was not successful. The difficulty lies in the fact that the hills are principally of igneous origin, and the thrusting in of the trachyte between the sedimentary rocks has destroyed the regular succession in the strata which would otherwise exist. Further than this, while the trachytic hills are mostly bare and rocky, the other hills are, with the exception of the occasional sharp ridges of limestone, covered with grass and timber, so that little can be seen by one who must hurry on and make few stops. Probably two-thirds of the area of the hills is covered with trachyte, of which that found at Cone Butte may be taken as the type.

CAMP LEWIS TO THE JUDITH GAP.

From Camp Lewis, the road passes on thirty miles to the Judith Gap, crossing a portion of the country which has some promise of becoming valuable in time. Quite a number of running streams pass through it, of which Cottonwood Creek, Little Trout Creek, and Buffalo Creek are the most important. The latter becomes dry late in the season. Little Trout Creek is famous for the number and beauty of the trout which it contains. In the immediate vicinity of the streams, the grass is excellent; but, on the higher prairie, it is rather thin. The streams flow fresh and cold from the neighboring Snow Mountains, and could doubtless be used extensively in irrigation. This Judith Basin is a region that has been highly spoken of, and it will no doubt in time furnish farms for hundreds of settlers.

Very little opportunity for geological work is afforded over this portion of the route; for the prairie is much of it almost level, sloping away to the northwest to the Judith River, and giving no exposures of the underlying rocks. Considerable surface-drift is found here, which is entirely local, consisting, for the most part, of pebbles and masses of a blue limestone, some of them containing Carboniferous fossils. The source of this limestone is to be found in the Snow Mountains, whcih rise ten or twelve miles to the east, and from which it has been very abundantly carried off.

A short distance before reaching Ross's Fork, a bluff was examined, of a black shale, containing many reddish iron concretions, but no fossils; and a little farther on, to the left of the road, were seen some washed exposures of light-gray shales, also without fossils. Not far beyond, the soil becomes red again; and, for a distance of several miles up to the Judith Gap, the presence of beds of red clay is indicated. Associated with them was a limestone, impure and knotty, with many veins of calcite. These red-clay beds appear also at the foot of the Snow Mountains, and, as has been said, also at the foot-slopes of the western end of the Judith Mountains. Their thickness seems to be small. They appear to belong to the Cretaceous, which doubtless extends under the grassy prairie from Camp Lewis to the Judith Gap.

SNOW MOUNTAINS.

From Buffalo Creek, ten miles before reaching the Judith Gap (that is, north of it), we made a short detour, to examine the west end of the Snow Mountains. This range extends in an approximately east and west direction for a distance of some twenty miles. It is low, like all the other minor ranges. The average height can hardly be more than 2,000 feet above the surrounding prairie. Buffalo Creek takes its rise in the north side of the west end of the range. Following up the stream for a mile and a half from where the road crosses it, we found some outcrops of sandstone, with indistinct vegetable remains, undoubtedly Upper Cretaceous. A little farther—this on the north side—on the hill-tops, there was a gray sandstone, and below it, on the hill-side, a sandstone of a deep yellow color. Both of these broke into irregular, wavy fragments. Dip 10° westerly; strike north 20° east. These, which are in thickness perhaps 60 feet, are probably Upper Cretaceous.

On the opposite (south) side of the stream appears a thinly-laminated sandstone, with a southwesterly dip of 10°, but a strike north 30° west. Beneath this followed the slopes of red soil, pointing to the presence of thin beds of clay beneath, like those at Camp Lewis. Following and underlying this was a firm, thick sandstone, breaking into massive slabs, which covered the top and sides of the hill, giving it much the appearance of having been paved; the strike was as before. Beyond, also south of the creek, a hard, gritty sandstone was noticed, with layers containing a large number of poorly-preserved shells. These were not specifically recognizable, but have been identified as Cretaceous by Mr. Whitfield. Beneath this was what seemed to be a second deposit of the red-clay beds. These last are visible, though not so distinctly, on the opposite side of the creek, where they are followed by about 5 feet of a firm limestone, and that by a considerable thickness of green and black shales, which last may be traced for a short distance on both sides of the stream. It is to be noticed that the strike and hence the dip of similar layers on both sides of the stream is quite different; and, though further study is needed to make out all the facts, we think it can hardly be doubted that at this western end of the mountains there is a distinct fold; the axis probably running a little north of west.

Continuing up to the source of the stream, we found the limestone here with a very slight dip to the northwest; strike northeast. The final point which we reached was a little cañon, with high and bold limestone walls, from which we obtained a few not very perfect Carboniferous fossils, viz:

1. *Zaphrentis centralis* (?), Ev. & Shum.
2. *Streptorhynchus Keokuk*, H.
3. *Spirifera centronata*, Winch.
4. *Stictopora*, sp.

To reach these Carboniferous rocks, we had doubtless passed over in succession the Cretaceous rocks, having perhaps a thickness of 900 feet, and also the Jurassic, if it exists here. We found no fossils belonging to this age, and doubt the existence of any considerable thickness of Jurassic beds. The limestone with the green and black shales noted above may possibly belong here.

Leaving the ridge, we turned at right angles to it; that is, nearly north. Here we passed over, first, the limestone dipping northwest, then successive beds of sandstone with beds of red clay interstratified. Near the foot of the hill, a reversal of the dip occurs in the sandstones, pointing to a minor fold parallel to the general course of the range. No older rocks than the Carboniferous limestone were observed; and from the numerous limestone pebbles containing Carboniferous fossils, picked up at different points along the sides of the mountains, it is safe to conclude that the range, as a whole, is made up of Carboniferous limestone; the younger rocks lying on its outer slopes. No evidence of any older rocks than the Carboniferous was noted; certainly not of any crystalline rocks. The trachyte, so common in the neighboring Judith Mountains, seems to be almost or entirely absent.

LITTLE BELT MOUNTAINS.

The Judith Gap is the divide between the Judith and the Musselshell Rivers. At this point the Little Belt Mountains and the Snow Mountains approach one another quite closely. The former are quite an extended and somewhat irregular range, reaching for a long distance north and west. Of its general geology, we can say little, as we can speak only of a few widely-separated points where we were able to visit it. One of these points was the extremity of the range at the Judith Gap. Near the Gap, we have already spoken of finding, on the north side, beds of red clay, which are associated with a little limestone, and nearer the hills with an underlying sandstone. Crossing the hills, which form the extreme eastern end of the range, perhaps a mile west of the Gap, we found a bed of yellow sandstone, which contained *Ostrea congesta*, Con.; then, some distance up the slope, a limestone containing corals, and dipping in a northerly direction; then some thin layers of limestone containing *Productus*.

The fossils found here were as follows; the identification by Mr. Whitfield:

1. *Ostrea congesta*, Con.
2. Cyathophylloid coral.
3. *Campophyllum torquium*, Owen??.
4. *Spirifera centronata*, Winch.
5. *Spirifera*, sp. May possibly be *Spiriferina Kentuckensis*.
6. *Productus*, sp. Resembles *P. Wortheni*, H.; but perhaps more nearly related to *P. multistriata*, Meek.
7. *Schizodus*, sp. Nearly or quite *S. Rossicus*, (DeVern.,) M. & W.

Here were seen 20 feet of green and black shales, dipping 50° northeast. From here, as we go up and across the hills, the strike gradually changes, and with it the dip, so that on the south side of the hill we have strata dipping southeast instead of northeast. The succession observed here is from below up:

Limestone, dip 65° south, strike north 70° east .... 2 feet.
Red clays, with purple slates underlying it .... 10 feet.

These beds bend around some 50°, so that in a vertical section they describe a quarter circle.

The upper and central part of the hill consists of limestone, overlaid by a considerable thickness of slates and sandstones, dipping mostly east-southeast. The hill alluded to forms the extremity of this portion of the Little Belt Mountains. Farther along to the west, in the main range, is a limestone which has every appearance of dipping under all the rocks thus far mentioned; it probably corresponds to the firm limestone which forms the lower portion of the Carboniferous as developed in this region. The structure of this hill, thus imperfectly made out (a hasty run across it while the party was going round being all that circumstances admitted of), may be better understood upon the statement that it is an anticlinal fold; the axis pointing about north 30° west, and somewhat elevated in this direction. The south side of the fold is apparently the steeper.

JUDITH GAP TO THE MUSSELSHELL CAÑON.

From the Judith Gap to the Musselshell Cañon, a distance of rather more than forty miles, the underlying rock belongs for the most part to the Upper Cretaceous; the only fossils found having been referred by Mr. Whitfield, as stated below, to No. 5. This district is remarkable, perhaps more so than any other seen by us, for the deep and wide valleys which have been cut through the nearly horizontal rocks, and which lead away from the neighboring range, the Little Belt Mountains. There are now no streams running from the mountains, with the exception of Haymaker's Creek near the Forks of the Musselshell, and yet the otherwise remarkably level prairie is broken by a number of striking ravines or valleys. These are all alike in that they show no evidence of any important action by recent running water, but, on the contrary, point to agencies which must have done their work in glacial times. The beds of these valleys, and also, though to a less extent, the prairie above them, are strewn with pebbles and masses of limestone, whose source is in the mountains, only a few miles distant.

Three very conspicuous valleys, one of them a mile wide, with steep banks more than one hundred feet in height, are crossed before going twelve miles from the gap. Hopley's Hole is by far the most remarkable of these. A section is given in the following cut (fig. 8).

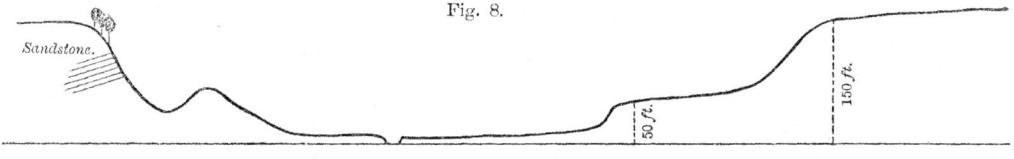

A Section across Hopley's Hole.

The width of the coulée at the top is about 1,000 yards. From the level of the prairie on either side, there is a steep plunge down; the total depth to the dry bed of the little stream being, according to aneroid measurements, 150 feet. On the west side, a second terrace of 50 feet in height is very distinct, while on the eastern slope a similar terrace, at about the same height, seems to be indicated; at present, however, there remains only a series of little conical hills all lying in a continuous line and presenting quite a peculiar appearance. This ravine is now dry, with the exception of a few springs of moderately good water on the west side. The water from these springs moistens the ground for a little distance about the point where they appear, but soon sinks out of sight. In the early part of the year, after the melting of the snow, more or less water evidently runs in the bed of the stream, which is dry in summer; but its erosive power is small, and there is nothing in the present relations which will explain the existence of such an extended valley. Hopley's Hole is important to those who pass over this road, not only as furnishing one of the few sources of water in this part of the route, but also because along the eastern edge of the valley there is here and there a little timber; a few straggling pine-trees which have ventured out into the prairie from the adjoining hills, and which show, by their appearance, that they have here a hard struggle for existence. The western slopes of this ravine, over which the limestone pebbles before mentioned are thickly scattered, are more gradual than the eastern; and, while the former are covered with thin grass, the latter shows a line of exposure of the sandstone which underlies the level prairie here. The upper part of this is yellow and quite ferruginous; that below whitish and a little shaly. It varies somewhat at different points; in one place turning into a soft, dark-colored slate in very thin layers. The whole exposure may be 15 or 20 feet in thickness; the sandstone having a very slight southeasterly dip. No fossils could be found, and the rock seemed to be without any special characteristic features, with the exception of pipe-stem pieces of carbonate of lime, which were quite common. They occupied a vertical position, sometimes curving more or less, and were 6 to 15 inches in length; possibly they were holes in the sand made by borers and subsequently filled up.

West of Hopley's Hole, the plain is nearly level for a long distance, broken only by one or two gullies. The general slope of the whole is very gradual to the south toward the Musselshell River and far beyond. In this direction, there is nothing to break the view, and the eye wanders unrelieved over a vast range of dry, parched prairie, from which, at midday, the heated vapors arise, producing the illusive phenomena of the mirage.

Haymaker's Creek, twenty-five miles from the gap, offers another example of the extensive erosion which has taken place in this region. The stream at present carries very little water, and that quite strongly alkaline, especially late in the summer, at which time it barely moves at all. On the west side, the terrace is high and distinctly marked. It may be traced from the mountains to the Musselshell River with the same gradual slope noticed elsewhere; here also quite independent of the dip of the strata, which make a small angle with its upper surface. On the east side, the slope is very gradual; the final height not being attained for several miles.

A short distance below the road-crossing, the sandstone is exposed. For the most part, it is a fine-grained rock of even texture, and of a light-bluish color, becoming yellow on exposure to the weather. Much of this lies in exceedingly thin, paper-like layers. There are also a few layers of a blue, impure limestone, and toward the top a bed of coarse sandstone, almost a conglomerate, containing some indistinct plant-remains, shells, and a few sharks' teeth and vertebræ, which show the beds to be Cretaceous No. 5. The remains are too poorly preserved to be specifically identified. The genera are as follows:

1. *Gryphæa*, sp.
2. *Ostrea*, sp.
3. *Lamna*, sp. (teeth).
4. *Galeocerdo*, sp. (teeth).

The strata have a slight dip (5°) northerly; and a little to the north, where the thin-bedded sandstone only is visible, the beds are horizontal or dip slightly to the south. A mile or two farther, *i. e.*, west, we meet several outcrops of a dark ocher-yellow sandstone, in which some pipe-stem calcareous fragments suggested those found at Hopley's Hole. A few indistinct vegetable remains were also obtained, but nothing characteristic. The slight dip is reversed in a subsequent exposure, showing an extremely low fold, the meaning of which will be explained later. Following these are a series of bluffs, sandstones, or sandy shales, some of which we were enabled to visit. None of them afforded us any fossils. Over these, we noticed a few washed exposures of white and cream-colored clays.

These doubtless all belong to the Upper Cretaceous, though, in view of their very slight dip, it would require more time than we had at our disposal to make out their exact stratigraphical relations. In general, it may be said of these sandstone bluffs that they are more tilted as we approach the mountains, and seem to owe their position to the forces which threw up this range of hills.

On reaching the Forks of the Musselshell, we come into a more attractive region. From the Judith Gap to this point, the prairie is almost a desert, dry and parched, and the grass very thin. Both branches of the Musselshell River, however, are fine running streams, and at their union the alluvial country is wide and susceptible of profitable cultivation. Just before reaching the Forks, we passed a ranch where a system of irrigation had produced excellent agricultural results.

From the Forks our road took us along the north branch of the Musselshell River, and two miles beyond we entered the Musselshell Cañon. The open country here is rough, and is characterized by many step-like ridges of sandstone, on one side steep, showing the edges of the strata, and on the other sloping off gradually, and covered over with grass.

MUSSELSHELL CAÑON TO CAMP BAKER.

The Musselshell Cañon divides the Little Belt Mountains from what is called the Elk Range. It is a narrow mountain-ravine, with steep hills on both sides, which sometimes approach very closely together, and again recede, giving room for a little strip of green meadow-land on the border of the stream. It is, throughout its length of eight miles, very picturesque, especially near the eastern end, where the abrupt walls and buttresses of white limestone contrast strongly with the dark-green foliage of the pines and spruces. All together, it was a most delightful relief from the parched alkaline prairie on which we had made our camps for the preceding fortnight. The waters of the stream are clear and cold, and abound in what is apparently a species of *Coregonus*. This fish rose readily to a fly, affording to some members of the party fair sport, and furnishing a very agreeable variety to the sameness of our daily fare.

On leaving the open country and entering the cañon, we came abruptly upon the Carboniferous rocks. A band of red clay a few feet wide is quite conspicuous at its eastern opening, followed by several others less striking and quite narrow, all red or ocher-yellow. These are interstratified with a sandstone which contains great numbers of *Ostrea congesta*, Con., as identified by Mr. Whitfield. These dip west 50°. Immediately following these are successive layers of limestones and slates, and then several hundred feet of limestone.

From the former beds the following fossils were obtained:

1. Bryozoan (undescribed).
2. *Aulopora*, or bases of *Syringopora*.
3. *Zaphrentis centralis*, Ev. & Shum.
4. *Productus semireticulatus*, Mart.
5. *Productus muricatus*, N. & P.
6. *Productus*, sp., probably young of *P. punctatus*.
7. *Productus*, sp., approaches forms referred to *P. Prattenanus*.
8. *Productus multistriatus*, Meek.
9. *Athyris*, sp.
10. *Pinna Ludlovi*, Whitfield (n. sp.).

The overlying limestone-beds all dip like the others, a little south of west, 50° to 60°. These limestones form a number of high vertical walls and isolated towers, which are worn out into a variety of fantastic forms which have already been alluded to. These are especially conspicuous on the north side of the stream, though similar walls are seen too on the other side in the line of the strike. This limestone is very cherty, the fragments of flint being numerous; and it is to their presence that the rock owes the peculiar forms in which it now appears. The walls show no evidence of structure or stratification. They abound in little cavities and holes, often partially filled with stalactitic masses of carbonate of lime, showing the extent to which the solvent action of water has worked upon them.

A similar relation of the rocks was observed on the upper slopes of the Bridger Mountains; that is, the series of bright-red indurated clays, with a little Cretaceous sandstone, followed by thin layers of limestone full of Carboniferous fossils, and then 500 feet or more of a firm cherty limestone, weathering out into walls showing no stratification and rarely containing fossils. The limestones are overlaid by (Jurassic and) Cretaceous and underlaid by Silurian. The similarity in the succession of the beds makes it quite certain that the *underlying* rocks at the entrance of the Musselshell Cañon are really the youngest, forming the upper part of the Carboniferous series, while the rocks which follow and overlie, apparently conformably, are older, and, in part at least, Lower Silurian.

The later layers of the limestone, going west through the cañon, have a somewhat different look from those seen farther to the east, being darker-colored and more uniform in appearance. Leaving the limestone, we passed over perhaps a quarter of a mile without finding any rock in place, though on the hill-slopes to the south masses of a hard, reddish quartzite indicate the presence of this as a member of the series. The next exposure reached was an argillitic slate, with veins of quartz, also dipping westerly. The hills for a considerable distance are rounded and covered with grass, exposing no rocks within the limits that we were able to cover.

The prevailing rock, as we continue up the cañon, following the course of this branch of the

Musselshell, is a clay-slate, of which there must be a very great thickness, interstratified with some sandstone-beds. The central portion of the range is trachyte, which is very abundant, forming a series of high hills and seriously interrupting our observations in the succession of the strata. Occasional outcrops of sedimentary rocks, principally slates and shales, appear; but as they contained no fossils, and as their succession was everywhere interrupted by the trachyte, their relations to what had preceded remain very uncertain. On the whole, the cañon gives a very fair exposure of the successive rocks, and to one who could do more than take passing notes in riding through it would no doubt yield some important facts.

Leaving the cañon, we emerge into an open rolling country, covered with grass, and with few exposures of the underlying rock. This, as far as could be observed, was a yellowish fragmentary slate, with occasional veins of quartz and calcite. A number of openings have been made by individuals prospecting for metal, but only faint indications of copper were observed. At Copperopolis, a mine has been sunk some 40 feet into this slate, and some very fair copper-ore and a little silver ore are being taken out. The mine is being worked on a very small scale indeed, only two men being engaged in it; but the ore obtained is sufficiently valuable to pay its way to the East, where (at Baltimore) it is smelted.

Near this point we pass the divide, and descend rapidly to the valley of Deep Creek, leaving the Musselshell behind us, and striking waters that flow into the Missouri near Sun River; that is above Fort Benton.

The valley of Deep Creek, though here somewhat narrow, becomes rapidly wider as we follow it down to Camp Baker. It is a fertile alluvial plain, and is no doubt susceptible of successful and profitable cultivation. There is as yet, however, no market for cereals in the vicinity, and the grassy meadows are given up to large herds of cattle, which range at will over the valleys and foot-hills. Every settler owns some cattle and horses, and these require little or no care, even in winter. The inhabitants state that they cut no hay for the winter-consumption of their stock, nor do they build stables or shelters for them at that season. The animals are said to run out all winter and to keep fat on the standing hay. Montana beef has quite a reputation for excellence west of the Missouri, so that the raising of cattle is likely to prove the most profitable pursuit for the settler until railroads shall have supplied him with a market for other products. Deep Creek, like most of the streams in this neighborhood, abounds in delicious trout and grayling (*Thymallus*), both of which attain a large size, sometimes weighing three pounds and more.

To our left, as we come down the valley of Deep Creek, we have the Elk Range high above us, the summits of which consist of trachyte. This has taken many curious forms, as pinnacles and towers, which rise above the timber, and give to the hills a very castellated appearance. An outcrop of purplish-red slate to the left of the road, and dipping 40° southerly, deserves to be mentioned, as its exact counterpart was seen at Camp Baker, sixteen miles distant, there overlying the Potsdam limestones. To the right, that is west, were a series of limestone ridges with masses of trachyte interstratified. These beds of trachyte have all the appearance of sedimentary rocks at a distance, so entirely do they conform to the uptilted beds of limestone. These latter have a dip of 40° to the southwest. They have the appearance of the Potsdam limestone beds just spoken of as occurring at Camp Baker, and since, if continuing, their strike would make them appear there, it is hardly to be doubted that they too are Silurian.

The Sulphur Springs are about 17 miles from Copperopolis, and lie at the point where the road to Camp Baker turns at a sharp angle to the west. The springs have a temperature of 150° or thereabouts, and are strongly impregnated with sulphureted hydrogen. They are quite well known through the Territory, and are believed to have the beneficial effects generally ascribed to similar springs, and to be especially valuable in cases of rheumatism, a complaint very common among miners. Considering the vast trachytic upheaval which has taken place in that vicinity, the presence of hot sulphur springs can hardly excite surprise.

From the Sulphur Springs, the road continues west, at the foot of the Big Belt Mountains, crossing a wide grassy plain, which has an even, uniform slope up to the edges of the hills. The stream, some ten miles from the springs, where Newland Creek joins it, runs through a gorge of porphyritic trachyte with a distinct columnar structure. This rock borders the creek for some distance, and the dike runs across the road, continuing on in a northerly direction. From here a march of seven miles took us to Camp Baker; the road passing along by bluffs of Miocene Tertiary, to be described later.

CAMP BAKER.

At Camp Baker, where we made a short stay, we were the recipients of most kind hospitalities from the officer at that time in command there, from whom also we received valuable information in regard to the surrounding country. During the time spent at this point, we were enabled to make an imperfect reconnaissance of the immediate vicinity. The descriptions given below may be better understood by reference to the following cut (fig. 9):

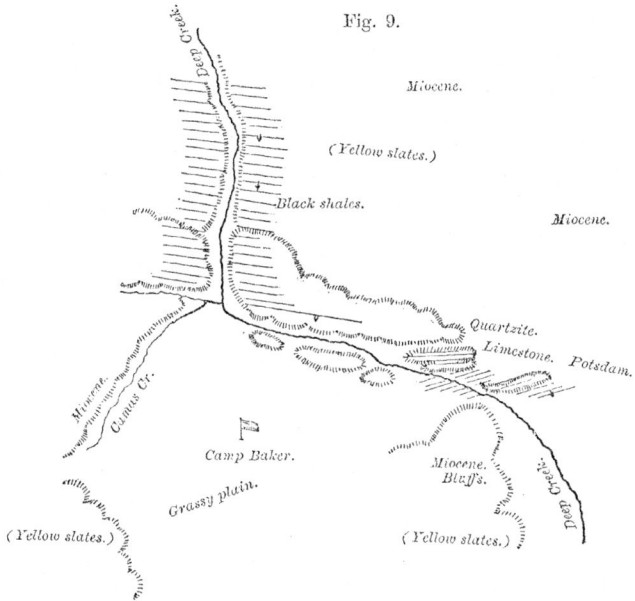

Camp Baker lies in a broad plain, which is surrounded on all sides by mountains, of which the Big Belt to the south are the most conspicuous and highest. We are here on the eastern border of the mountain-region, which extends far to the westward. The valleys of Deep Creek and its tributaries are filled with deposits of Miocene Tertiary. These consist for the most part of homogeneous cream-colored clays, so hard as to be with difficulty cut with a knife. The lower layers are generally more loose and homogeneous, while the upper beds are harder, firmer, and sometimes quite calcareous. Some of the upper beds are remarkable for the large number of white clay concretions which are found in them.

The beds are horizontal, and rest unconformably on the somewhat upturned yellow and red slates below; the clays of which they are formed resemble closely those of the Miocene beds at Scott's Bluffs near the North Platte River in Wyoming. The deposits at Camp Baker have been extensively denuded, and nowhere reach any very great thickness. At a point about three miles southeast of the post, some bluffs were noticed where the Miocene beds attained a thickness of 200 feet, and these were capped by 50 feet of Pliocene clays, both beds containing characteristic fossils.

We saw the first exposures of these beds a few miles west of the Sulphur Springs, just after crossing the high ridge of trachyte before referred to, through which Deep Creek flows. From here, the lake-bed was traced continuously along Deep Creek for a distance of fifteen miles. Beds of the same character, containing fossils, were found on Spring Creek to the east, on White-tailed Deer Creek, about seven miles to the north of Camp Baker, as well as on Camas Creek to the southwest. On Camas Creek, the beds are exposed for a mile or more in bluffs ranging from 20 to 25 feet in height. The exposures on White-tailed Deer Creek are much more extensive than those last mentioned. Those on Camas Creek are in thick, rather indistinct, layers, and contain more or less bluish sand in irregular layers, and sometimes a little coarse gravel. Traces of this deposit, containing what appear to be remains of *Rhinoceros*, were also observed two miles or more south of Moss Agate Springs (to be referred to later), and at a considerable elevation above the creek-bed. With more time than we had at command, they could, no doubt, have been traced much farther, although in many places the beds have been washed out, or have been covered by the later local drift.

In the Miocene beds were found a species of *Rhinoceros*; several species of *Oreodon*, Leidy, and *Eporeodon*, Marsh; a canine tooth apparently of *Elotherium*, Pomel; and remains of Turtles. In the Pliocene beds, the principal fossils were a species apparently of *Merychyus*, Leidy; remains of an equine smaller than the modern horse; and Pliocene Turtles. These fossils have not yet been carefully studied, and, for this reason, their relation to the remains found in the other lake-basins of similar age cannot here be stated. The line of separation between the Miocene and Pliocene beds is, in some places, well marked. It consists of about six feet of hard sands interstratified with layers of very small, water-worn pebbles, soldered together into a hard mass. Each of these layers is about 6 inches in thickness. Immediately above these strata, the Pliocene fossils were found.

It is known that in the neighborhood of Fort Shaw, and near Helena, Pliocene deposits exist; and near Fort Ellis, and in the valley of the Yellowstone, we saw, but were unable to examine, gray sands and marls, which Dr. Hayden refers to the same age. No Miocene beds, however, have been identified at any of these localities. It seems probable that, in Pliocene time at least, the Baker Lake may have extended north to the Missouri River, and perhaps up that stream to the "Three Forks", thus connecting with the lake which existed near Fort Ellis. Indeed, it would seem that we just touched upon the southern edge of this basin, which may have extended far to the north and west.

An interesting point in connection with these deposits is the fact that, with the exception of one deposit in Colorado, they are at a much greater elevation than any other beds of the same age now known on the continent. The elevation of the White River beds is about 3,000 feet, and that of the Oregon basin somewhat less; while that of the deposits near Camp Baker is over 5,000 feet.

On the east side of the plain on which Camp Baker stands, the Miocene has entirely disappeared. It is to be noticed that these Tertiary beds were deposited after the elevation of the older rocks, and that most of the denudation now visible in these rocks must have been accomplished before the deposit of the Tertiary, as it is repeatedly seen filling the depressions and unevennesses in the slates, as also covering over the ridges of trachyte. Underlying the Tertiary, and tilted up at a small angle, appear a series of yellow slates and shales, which are quite generally distributed in this region, though not seen elsewhere. They are seen generally as a fine-grained slaty rock, friable and weathering readily, so that exposures of the rock in place are rarely found. Occasionally, there are observed in them immense black concretions of remarkable structure. In the interior, these consist mostly of a calcareous clay, very hard, and showing distinctly what is called the cone-in-cone structure. Outside of this, the lime is purer, though lying in concentric layers, and the exterior shell is made up of fibrous calcite half an inch in thickness. The clay cones radiate from the center of the concretions.

The slates are destitute of fossils, and their age is only a matter for conjecture. The most remarkable feature connected with them is that they have, in spots, a bright brick-red color; thus, in riding over the country, a patch of intensely red-colored soil will be seen here and there, strongly suggestive of the burned lignite beds of the Missouri River. The slate has at such points the appearance of burned pottery; the material being harder and firmer than the surrounding rock. In some cases the red color was uniform in the rock; but generally it was distributed in successive bands, as though produced by the action of hot water. The red patches are quite local, and seldom cover more than a few square yards, though in one case they were seen extending along a range of hills for a hundred yards or more. That the effect produced has been caused by the action of heat cannot be questioned, though under what conditions no attempt is made to conjecture. As has been said, these shales and slates are tilted up unquestionably; but their exact relations to the underlying rocks could not be made out without more opportunity for investigation than we had.

The difficulty in settling the matter arose from the fact that the loose shale seldom showed its true position.

We find this formation in the immediate vicinity of Camp Baker, both to the east, where it forms high hills 250 feet above the plain, also to the south and west, where it is intersected by some dikes of porphyry, and quite extensively below in the valley of Deep Creek, as well as along the valley of White-tailed Deer Creek. Its general distribution seems to conform to a certain extent to that of the Miocene Tertiary that is filling the valleys between the older rocks.

The older rocks alluded to form the ranges of hills conspicuous about Camp Baker. Immediately north of the post lies a range of hills, having an east and west trend, through which Deep River takes its course by means of a cañon, which gives an excellent section of the rocks of which the hills are composed. The rocks all dip south, and this dip continues the same for a mile or two to the north. South of the range alluded to, and close to the post, are several minor hills, and, at a distance, a series of others all singularly alike in appearance. The section of rocks alluded to is as follows:

Quartzite	20 feet.
A series of colored shales, chiefly red, but also green and blue, with a bed of trachyte interstratified	150 feet.
Two ridges of limestone, in all	80 feet.

These limestones show abrupt bluffs to the north, and dip southerly. In the northernmost of the ridges were found—

1. *Crepicephalus (Loganellus) montanensis*, Whitf. (n. sp.);
2. *Obolella*, sp.?;

identifying the formation as Potsdam, according to Mr. Whitfield. Following this is a quartzite, which forms the south side of the hill alluded to. The section is continued through the cañon: quartzite 40 feet, firm and solid, with a reddish tinge of color, breaking into massive blocks; underneath is a series of bright green slates, followed by a variety of clay-slates, mostly dark-colored, with occasional beds of hard solid quartzite and some thin layers of limestone. After half a mile, the ridge is passed, and the stream comes out into the open country. The rocks, for a mile or two, however, are mostly the same in dip, and are conformable. They are chiefly dark blue shales.

The appearance of the quartzite hills in this neighborhood is peculiar, as they all have a gradual slope to the south, but are nearly vertical toward the north, on which side there is at their foot a talus of large cubical blocks of quartzite.

We were unfortunately not able to visit the Big Belt Mountains.

CAMP BAKER TO FORT ELLIS.

From Camp Baker, the party marched to Fort Ellis; the road for a short distance being the same as that before traveled. The road passes to the right of the Elk Range. Twenty miles from Camp Baker, we reached the extremity of this range. At this point, we passed immediately from the grassy meadow onto the older rocks. Here we found first a red shale similar to that at Camp Baker, and also to that observed higher up, four miles the other side of the Springs. This was followed by a heavy massive quartzite, a little reddish and very firm; and overlying this was a considerable thickness of limestone. This last is well exposed just above Moss Agate Springs, and in some of the layers we found an abundance of fragments of *Trilobites*. The limestone is much of it very cherty, and in many places it formed the same abrupt and peculiar shapes noticed elsewhere. Just above Moss Agate, there is a little superficial synclinal fold in the limestone, the axis of which has an approximately northeasterly direction. Moss Agate Springs takes its name from the fragments of flint, chalcedony, and agate, which are common on the adjoining hills, and many of which, from the presence of the arborescent forms of psilomelane, are popularly called "moss agates".

These fragments of silica are evidently from the limestone, and are quite characteristic of it. Similar fragments of chalcedony, though without the moss effect, were found abundantly in some of the little hills just by Camp Baker. The limestone is evidently the same as that, as is moreover proved by its association with the quartzite and by the few fossils found in it; these were all of one species, a new *Trilobite,—Arionellus tripunctatus*, Whitf. (n. sp.).

The road from Moss Agate passes, it is true, more or less at the end of the hills, but at such a distance from them as to afford but little opportunity for observation. From a distance, it is observed to how great an extent the hills are made up of limestone, with the conspicuous trachytic prominences before mentioned. From the limestone, we pass immediately to a dark, somber sandstone of granular texture and quite peculiar in appearance. This had a dip to the west, and contained some indistinct plant-remains.

On our return journey, we found time to touch at the southeastern extremity of the same hills near the source of Flathead Creek, and here we passed directly from sandstones resembling the one spoken of to the limestone exactly similar to those so often observed at various points in this range. It agreed in all respects with the other exposures. A few indistinct fossils were obtained from a loose block, which had evidently come from close at hand, and these show it to be Carboniferous. They were identified by Mr. Whitfield as *Spirifera centronata*, Winch.

The country near the branch of Deep Creek on the south side of the Elk Range is attractive and covered with good grass, supporting large herds of cattle; but, after passing the low divide which separates the above-named stream, a tributary of the Missouri, from Shields River, a branch of the Yellowstone, a more or less decided change is observed. The prairie is here dry and barren, especially to the south of Cottonwood Creek, and supports nothing but a thick growth of sage-brush. It is watered by several running streams beyond Sixteen-mile Creek, of which Cottonwood is one of the most important, in view of the fact that its banks are fringed with fine trees, from which it takes its name.

As we approach Bridger's Pass, the character of the country improves again, and the large numbers of cattle met with near this point indicate its capabilities in the way of grazing. Of the geological relations of this part of the road, we saw little on our way south. While returning, however, our opportunities for observation were better, and the results are presented immediately below. Bridger Pass is a high mountain-divide, thickly wooded, and with the high limestone cliffs of the Bridger Mountains overhanging it on the west side. The scenery is fine, and the change from the bare prairie to the grateful shade of the wooded mountain-side is gladly welcomed by the traveler Geologically speaking, the prevailing rock is the dark sandstone described later, and known to belong to the Upper Cretaceous. The position of the strata is nearly vertical. An occasional dike of igneous rock was observed, and one of these was conspicuous on the north side of the pass. It consists of a greenish basalt in spherical nodules, separating in the fracture into successive thin slabs. High above the road, as we approach Fort Ellis, we noticed the horizontal strata of the Pliocene Tertiary, which, according to Hayden, extends far away toward the west.

From Fort Ellis, the party extended their trip into the Yellowstone Park. We introduce here, however, the additional observations made on our return-trip through the country just mentioned.

BRIDGER MOUNTAINS.

On our return to Carroll from Fort Ellis, early in September, we encountered much trouble at first from the condition of the roads, which were almost impassable, owing to the unprecedented amount of rain that the country had recently received. We made use of the delay which this occasioned in the movements of the wagons, to make a little exploration of the Bridger Mountains, or East Gallatin Range, as it is sometimes called. These observations could not be extended beyond the east side of the range, and hence are only fragmentary. Considerable time was devoted to the same mountains by Dr. Hayden and his parties in 1871 and 1872, and reference may be made to his reports for those years for the facts observed by them.

This range of mountains is especially conspicuous as viewed from the east side, rising up steeply from the deep and narrow valley, and terminating in a nearly perpendicular white wall, with a sharp knife-edge for its summit. We ascended the ridge from two points: first, September 4, from a point in the valley below, about six miles from Fort Ellis; and, again, September 5, from our camp, a short distance to the north side of the divide in the Bridger Pass.

The rock of the valley, and indeed of the pass, as far as observed, is a sandstone of somber tints, gray, brownish, or greenish. The texture is generally granular and gritty, and the rock is more or less speckled with grains of quartz and feldspar. In general, it may be said to be a sandstone ma from poorly-assorted materials. It contains, in some layers, impressions, generally indistinct, of vegetable remains. It is referred, as a whole, to the "Coal Series", by Dr. Hayden; and he further estimates its thickness at 10,000 feet. This seems to us considerably to exceed the truth. We found the same series of sandstones extending in a number of wide folds over the prairie to the north; and this would make it probable that even if there be a thickness of 10,000 feet of vertical strata belonging here, it has been formed by the pressing together of an anticlinal fold parallel to the range of mountains. This is the more likely, as the strata of the beds all dip steeply, and are often overturned, the dip being reversed.

Ascending the hills from the point first mentioned, somewhat north of the Bridger Peak, we passed for a long distance through the timber, crossing, here and there, little open parks and valleys, up to the foot of the range proper. Up to this point, we had seen but few exposures of rock, and those similar to the sandstone already described. The section observed from this point to the summit is as follows: Red earth and clay, with occasional masses of indurated red clay, seldom showing any stratification; in all, 60 feet. Following this, and, in its present position, overlying, though, in fact, geologically, underlying it, is a thick-bedded sandstone, dipping 60° west; strike north 20° west. This rock was mostly yellow and ferruginous; its texture gritty, at times becoming a mass of coarse pebbles. Occasional layers were calcareous, and contained multitudes of indistinct Cretaceous shells (see list below). These often yielded to the weather, the rock becoming then rusty and cellular. The visible thickness of this deposit was 40 feet. Then, after a small interval, follows a firm, blue, compact limestone; the first layers containing a few Jurassic fossils, and those following the same in greater numbers (see list below). The thickness of this bed is about 60 feet. Following this is a sandy limestone; and then comes the Carboniferous limestone, which forms the remainder of the upper part of the hill for a distance of 700 or 800 feet, the total thickness of these strata being perhaps 500 feet. This limestone has the same massive and, on weathering, structureless character remarked elsewhere. Some layers seem to be a conglomerate of fragments cemented together by a calcareous paste. Thin layers of dark flint, two or more inches in thickness, are common, running irregularly through the limestone blocks, and also isolated masses of the same rock of greater or less size. At the summit, the dip is 70° east. Fossils were not common in this rock; those found were chiefly corals. Continuing along the narrow summit for some distance toward the north, all the time on the solid limestone, we found its dip varying considerably from east to west. On descending, a band of red clay was passed over at the foot of the compact limestone, and calcareous layers interstratified with it contained some Carboniferous fossils. The dip here was west. This is the same band noted on the succeeding day, and to be described farther on. In other respects, the return trip added nothing to what had been before observed.

On the following day, the ridge was ascended again from a point some eight miles beyond; but it did not yield us the complete section of the rocks that we had hoped for. The approach to the mountains was, for the most part, of necessity through the timber; the rock appearing but seldom, and this the dark-colored sandstone before noted. What was observed here would not enable us to do more than guess at its total thickness. Emerging into the open ground, high up on the range, we came upon a high ledge of a very massive, coarse sandstone, or rather a conglomerate. The strike was north and south, and the dip east 35°. The thickness actually exposed was small. Rising 500 feet from here, we found a series of limestone exposures mostly covered with grass. They yielded some Jurassic fossils, similar to those obtained the day before. The rock following was, as before, a white, sandy limestone, sparkling in the sun, and without fossils; then appeared the Carboniferous limestones.

The point we had now reached is conspicuous from all parts of the surrounding country, being marked by two lines of deep red, like bloody gashes, in the side of the mountain. These red bands, though narrow, may be traced along the east slope of the hills for a considerable distance north and south, and form quite a striking feature of the range. The lower bed, made up of an indurated red clay, was only 4 feet in thickness; but the color was very intense. Interstratified with these bands was a small thickness of variegated limestone, generally purplish, sometimes vermilion or greenish. This limestone abounded in Carboniferous fossils; not infrequently the shells occupied the center of little grayish circles in the reddish rock. These soft red bands have generally yielded to denuding influences, and the point where we stood was a narrow neck of land with a deep gulf opening below us to the south and southeast.

From here to the summit, we were on the massive Carboniferous limestone containing corals and crinoidal plates, with here and there a *Spirifera*. The summit of the ridge attained here was considerably higher than that previously ascended, and was evidently as high as, or higher than, any neighboring point north or south. The aneroid barometer indicated that the height was in the neighborhood of 10,000 feet. The higher points of the summit were thickly covered with snow, on which were lying thousands of dead grasshoppers; and in many places we saw the tracks of the grizzly bears which had ascended the range to feed on these insects.

The prospect from this point is exceedingly grand and extended. The ridge, as has been remarked, is, at its summit, extremely narrow, coming to a sharp knife-edge, and the view is unobstructed in all directions. Nearly north and south stretch the irregular summits of this rugged range, while on either side the eye sweeps over the open prairie till arrested by the mountains which rise above the plain. To the east, the Crazy Woman's Mountains are most conspicuous; to the south, the ranges near the Yellowstone River; and westward, the rich Gallatin Valley extends to the "Meeting of the Three Waters"; and far beyond were the Bitter Root Mountains. At the foot of the abrupt cliffs on which we stood was a little mountain lake, far below us, though seemingly at our very feet. With its deep-blue waters, it was prettily set off by the white limestone cliffs above and the dark pines inclosing it on the farther side.

The following cut (fig. 10) will give some idea of the general trend of the summit of the range. The points lettered (A, B, C, D) refer to the cuts which follow, showing roughly the dip of the

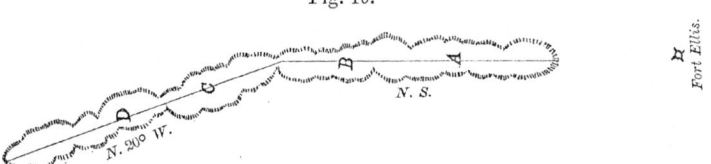

Fig. 10.

strata where indicated. No special importance is attached to these, except as showing the irregularity which exists at different points. The younger rocks lie on the east side, the Carboniferous

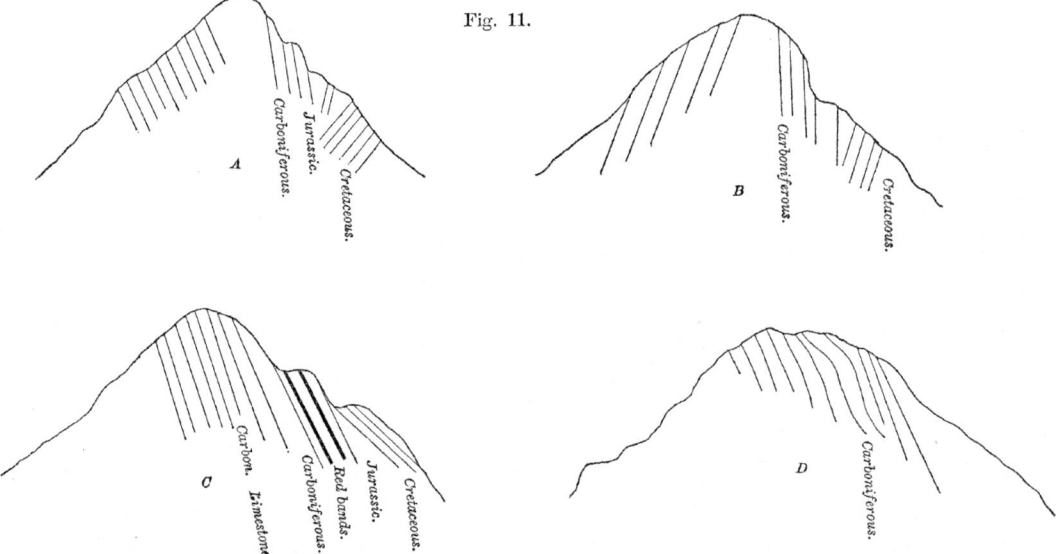

Fig. 11.

limestones form the summit, and the older rocks are on the west, with a reversed dip. We were unable to extend our observations below the summit, and hence have nothing to add in this relation to what is given in the reports already referred to.

The following is a list of the fossils obtained during our examination of these mountains, as identified by Mr. Whitfield:

Cretaceous, September 4 and 5.

Ostrea congesta, Con., associated with fragments of carbonized wood.

Jurassic, September 4 and 5.

1. *Camptonectes extenuatus*, Meek.
2. *Camptonectes bellistriata*, Meek.
3. *Myacites (Pleuromya) subcompressa*, Meek.
4. *Myalina (Gervillia) perplana*, Whitf. (n. sp.).
5. *Gervillia erecta*, M. & H.
6. *Gervillia sparsaradiata*, Whitf. (n. sp.).
7. *Gryphœa planoconvexa*, Whitf. (n. sp.).

Carboniferous, September 4.

Summit.

1. Cyathopylloid coral.
2. Crinoidal plates.
3. *Platycrinus*, sp. ?.
4. *Spirifera centronata*, Winch.

Limestone interstratified with the red bands.

5. *Productus nebrascensis*, Meek.
6. *Chonetes mesoloba*, Norwood & Pratten.
7. *Athyris*, sp. ?.

Carboniferous, September 5.

Summit.

1. *Cystiphyllum*, sp. ?.
2. *Campophyllum*, sp. ?.
3. *Campophyllum torquium*, Owen.
4. *Chœtetes*, sp. ?.
5. *Zaphrentis centralis*, Ev. & Shum. ?.
6. *Syringopora mult-attenuata*, McChes.
7. *Spirifera centronata*, Winch.

Limestone interstratified with the red bands.

8. *Spiriferina Kentuckensis*, Shum.
9. *Athyris planosulcata*, Phil. ?.
10. *Athyris subtilita*, (H.) Meek.
11. *Rhynchonella Osagensis*, Swall. ?.
12. *Streptorhynchus crassus*, M. & W.
13. *Productus punctatus*, Mart.
14. *Productus costatus*, Sow.
15. *Productus Prattenanus*, Norwood.
16. *Productus cora ?*, or perhaps *P. Prattenanus*, Norwood.
17. *Productus*, sp.; may be *P. nebrascensis*, Meek.
18. *Chonetes mesoloba*, N. & P.
19. *Chonetes granulifera*, Owen.
20. *Euomphalus*, sp.

FROM THE BRIDGER MOUNTAINS TO THE FORKS OF THE MUSSELSHELL.

We camped September 5 on Cottonwood Creek, and made from here a short excursion to the west of the road. The main valley of Shields River is a synclinal, lying between the Bridger Mountains and the Crazy Woman's Mountains, with an axis pointing in a direction about north 20° west. In the valley, the rocks are rarely exposed; but riding up the creek, two or three miles from the road-crossing, we find the rocks dipping 30° east, with the strike north 30° west. The exposures here show a friable sandstone, disintegrating readily. The rock has a dark, somber appearance, and is made up of a greenish or brownish base, with small grains of quartz and a little feldspar. For a distance of two miles, the inclination remains the same; the rock standing up in a series of wave-like ridges, all having an abrupt side toward the west, and a gradual slope to the east. Looking from the eastern side, the existence of the abrupt rock exposures would hardly be expected, so gradual is the rise of the grassy slopes. From the west, on the contrary, the eye is immediately struck by the remarkable series of hills with precipitous fronts.

Some five miles from the road-crossing, there is a sudden change of dip, and as sudden a return to the easterly direction: this is very probably a local change, occasioned possibly by a dike of igneous rock noticed at that point. The rock is here generally a sandstone, answering more or less closely to the description given above, sometimes a sandy slate, sometimes a whitish-gray sandstone. At the headwaters of Cottonwood Creek, about six miles from the road, we found an exposure of a brown sandy slate, full of fucoidal remains, and containing a few indistinct shells. As this rock is apparently one of the lowermost layers in the group of rocks being described, these fossils are of interest as furnishing a clue to the thickness of the strata. The fossils are very poorly preserved, but have been identified by Mr. Whitfield as follows:

1. *Crassatella*, sp.
2. *Crassatella*, near enough to *C. vadosa*, Morton, to have come from New Jersey.
3. *Inoceramus*, sp.
4. *Pholadomya*, sp.
5. *Gryphæa*, sp.
6. *Panopœa*, sp., very near *P. occidentalis*, M. & H.
7. *Scaphites larvæformis*, M. & H.

Scaphites larvæformis is regarded as characteristic of Dr. Hayden's No. 2. Above this bed there must be 5,000 feet of rock belonging to the Cretaceous, though referred in part by Dr. Hayden to the Coal Group.

At the point mentioned we pass a deep grassy valley a few hundred feet in width, and on the other side rises a long range of high bluffs 100 feet above, and extending for a mile or more (see fig. 12).

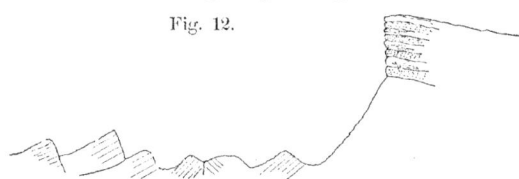

Fig. 12.

The rocks are exposed for a height of from 10 to 50 feet in the perpendicular eastern front of the bluffs, and form a feature of the country quite conspicuous even from a distance. The rock is a brown and gray sandstone in alternate layers, with occasional slaty bands. The dip is here westerly, it being the under part of a very long and low fold. From the summit, quite a good view is obtained to the west; the bluff has an abrupt front both to the east and northwest. The valley alluded to occupies the position of the axis of the anticlinal, and the fold itself is a continuation north of the folding which took place in the Bridger Range.

Turning north from here, we crossed the divide a mile beyond, and came into a long valley which trends a little west of north. The rock observed here was a brownish-yellow sandstone, with a clay-shale underlying it, and is undoubtedly Cretaceous, though containing no fossils. The valley alluded to drains into Sixteen-mile Creek. We followed it for a distance of ten miles, keeping along with the strike of the rocks, and found it abundantly covered with thick grass, or rather at this season with hay cured in the ground, which could afford grazing for multitudes of cattle. Turning again easterly, across the strike of the rocks, we cross a long series of wave-ridges dipping east as before, and much resembling those previously observed. A very white fine-grained sandstone forms a series of bluffs not much west of the road.

The valley of the south branch of Deep Creek is wide and level. On the northeastern side, where the road to the Forks of the Musselshell turns off to ascend the divide, there is quite a high ridge, extending from the end of the Elk Range across toward the Crazy Woman's Mountains. This valley is obviously, like its continuation below, a synclinal, for the strata dip sharply to the west 70°, the strike being the same northwest. The same dark-colored sandstone forms the first layer: this is underlaid by a sandy slate with large clay cannon-ball concretions. From here on for a mile, the dip is continuously westerly, there being the same series of wave-ridges observed before, only here the dip is reversed, and the abrupt side is toward the east. The strike remains the same, but the dip is gentler, averaging 40°. After some 5,000 feet of strata, the dip is reversed. An exposure of rock on the east side of the trail shows a laminated sandstone, generally soft and friable, but in some places very hard. The dip of the first layers is 30°, and this increases as we proceed to 45°, the inclination being here toward the east or northeast. A mile farther on, near the head of Flathead Creek, we notice another fold. The rock is here a soft yellowish sandstone, dipping west at a small angle, 15° to 20°. This contained many oval clayey concretions, and in the seams in the rock there was more or less calcite. Ripple-marks were noticed in one or two places. Still farther on, the opposite side of the fold is seen, and here it appears that the dark-green and gray rocks seen just after leaving the south branch of Deep Creek underlie the soft yellowish sandstone observed near Flathead Creek. For a mile or two more, we pass over the sandstones, chiefly the dark rock, but occasionally noting beds of the lighter-colored. This latter is much cracked and broken, scaling off into platter-like slabs, so that good exposures of it are seldom seen. Another fold is passed over just before reaching the broad valley of Norton's Creek. We have thus the indications of three great folds between South Deep Creek and Norton's Creek, a distance of ten miles in a straight line. The strike varies from north to west, the dip is generally as much as 40°, and sometimes much more. A mile or two before reaching Norton's Creek, we pass to the left of a high butte formed by three narrow dikes of eruptive rock, seemingly conformable to the sandstone.

At Norton's Creek, the country changes a little more, and we come upon a broad fertile synclinal valley. In this neighborhood, igneous rocks, before rare, become very common, and beds of trachyte and basalt are repeatedly seen interstratified with the sandstones. The most conspicuous example of this is just to the west side of the meadow through which Norton's Fork flows. Here is a bed of trachyte apparently conformable to the sandstone, and evidently having been erupted between two layers of that rock. It has a semi-columnar structure; the heads of the columns pointing toward the east, thus appearing as if it dipped west, though in reality the sedimentary rocks have an inclination in the opposite direction. In the broad meadow of Norton's Fork, a number of isolated buttes of trachyte may be seen; some of these having taken quite peculiar forms. In these folds, it is seldom possible to trace any single layer of rock, because the characters are not distinctive enough; occasionally, however, this may be done, as in the case mentioned above. A careful plotting of the successive exposures would doubtless show the continuity of the strata, and give an exact estimate of the thickness of the rocks involved, together with the width of each of the folds. This we were of course unable to undertake.

On the east side of Norton's Meadow, the dip is westerly, and the strike northwest. Here a brown sandstone is exposed, followed by a gray trachyte in beds, which, at a distance, look like a solid sandstone, and might easily be confounded with sedimentary rocks. Opposite where the South Fork of the Musselshell is joined by Flathead Creek, is the extremity of a little range of hills, trending northwest, and forming a sort of spur of the Elk Range, conforming in direction to the low folds we have been tracing, and seemingly like one of them, a little deeper, and having brought up lower strata. Following the sandstone, which is without fossils, we have, as we cross the east end of this hill, some beds of red clay, making a red soil, but not apparently very thick. Above on the hill is a hard, red quartzite, in massive blocks, which are scattered over the surface of the slope. On the east side of the hill, near the creek, we have several exposures of a gray and yellow sandstone dipping east, strike northwest, followed by a reversal of dip in the same beds. The rocks here observed are a dark ochery-yellow sandstone, firm, and in rather thick layers, and a whitish sandstone, sometimes in very thin, papery layers, sometimes massive, but not often very firm; much the same association as at Hopley's Hole.

The foldings here are not nearly so extensive as those described before; the thickness of rock involved being perhaps not more than 1,000 feet. Near the hill, the dip is steep; but a mile from it the inclination becomes very gradual, and insensibly the strata subside, becoming nearly horizontal. A slight eastward dip in the white sandstone is, however, reversed before reaching the Forks, where there is a broad alluvial country. This seems to be the dying out of the action which was more intense to the westward. Beyond the Forks, on the road to the Judith Gap (before traveled), the same brown sandstone and white sandstone are seen again, with a slight dip, which is once more reversed, forming apparently a final fold in our series, though the inclination is so slight that the direction remains uncertain.

Our course along Flathead Creek was very nearly at right angles to the prevailing direction of the strike, so that we had a very good opportunity to observe the relations of the successive folds.

FROM ARMELL'S CREEK TO THE MOUTH OF THE JUDITH.

From our camp on Armell's Creek, a short excursion was made to the mouth of the Judith River; the intention being to make such examination of the country at that point as our limited time would admit of.

The beds at the mouth of the Judith have been explored only once before (by Dr. Hayden), and their age has hitherto been in doubt. We were able to remain but two days in this interesting locality, and the results obtained were of course meager. Enough, however, was seen to establish the age of the beds at this point as beyond a doubt Cretaceous; three members of this division of Mesozoic time having been found there and identified by fossils.

The ravines, which occur so constantly along the Missouri, extend back from that stream but a few miles, except where a river enters it. Tributaries, however, carry the ravines and the accompanying Bad Lands back, sometimes to their sources. The country which may properly be considered as Bad Lands near the Judith is quite extensive, and is of the most rugged and barren character. Each little stream that flows into the Missouri is bordered by a strip of country more or less wide, that is gullied and washed out in deep and precipitous ravines, without vegetation, and generally utterly impassable, except for the bighorn or the wolf.

The Bad Lands on the Judith River extend along that stream for about twenty-five miles from its mouth, and run back from the river for about five miles on each side of the stream. Those on Arrow Creek, which flows into the Missouri a few miles west of the Judith, extend along it for ten or twelve miles back from its mouth, and have an average breadth of four miles on each side of the stream. Those on Dog Creek stretch back into the bluffs for about fifteen miles, running over to meet those of the Judith for about six miles of this distance, and reaching eastwardly nearly over to Armell's Creek, which also has an extensive system of Bad Lands.

The rocks are chiefly sandstone, quite pure, often quite hard, but occasionally so soft as not to cohere in blocks when removed from the beds. Occasionally, thin beds of an arenaceous limestone are seen, and from these a few fossils may generally be obtained. Yellowish sandy clays and marls also occur toward the base of the bluffs, but without fossils, as far as could be seen, and lacking any distinctive features. Much of the lower portion of the bluffs is concealed by deposits of the Fort Pierre beds, Cretaceous No. 4, which occurs all along the Judith River bottom and in many of the ravines, sometimes running far back into the bluffs. These beds agree in all respects with the deposits of that age seen near Carroll, Crooked Creek, and Box Elder. They were the same dark shales, containing the limestone concretions, with *Baculites*, &c., and abounding in the glittering selenite crystals that seem to be peculiar to these beds.

From our Camp on Armell's Creek, we followed the Helena road back toward Camp Lewis for five miles or more, and then, leaving it, took a course a little west of north, and, passing about ten miles to the eastward of the Moccasin Mountains, struck the divide between the Judith and Dog River, by which road alone our point of destination could be reached with the wagons. The time occupied in reaching our camp on the Judith was two days; the distance traveled being a little more than forty-five miles.

At a point two miles north of our camp, on Armell's Creek, an exposure of bare bluffs was noticed, which furnished the following section, from below upward:

	Feet.
Dark-gray horizontally-laminated shales	60
Laminated slightly ferruginous sandstone	12
Soft, whitish clays, about	100
Dark-gray clays, interstratified with layers of impure limestone concretions, about	100
Total	272

The laminated sandstone contains numerous irony concretions, from the size of a pea up to two inches in diameter. These are quite soft, and break readily, showing a concentric structure. The sandstone is much weather-worn. The limestone concretions, on exposure to the atmosphere, crack and break up so that the surface of the bluffs is strewn with their angular fragments. They do not particularly resemble the concretions of the Fort Pierre shales seen near Crooked Creek.

Later in the day, to the northeast of the Moccasin Mountains, we passed over a good exposure of the Fort Pierre clays; and about three miles beyond this, but at a much higher level, were seen about 100 feet of white and yellow sandy clays, capped by a thin layer of fine grained calcareous brown sandstone. This latter was found in place only on the tops of the highest hills. A few shells characteristic of No. 4 were found in the Fort Pierre beds, but none of the other exposures examined yielded any fossils. All the beds seen during the day were substantially horizontal.

The divide along which our road took us is for twenty-five miles a gently rolling prairie, covered with a fair growth of bunch-grass. It is a favorite feeding-ground for the buffalo; but, when we passed over it, only a few of these animals were seen, although signs of their recent presence were everywhere apparent. As we approach the Missouri River, the divide becomes less and less wide and the road more winding. Deep ravines and coulées from Dog Creek and the Judith River run back until they almost meet, so that the road becomes narrow and often difficult. About seven miles from the Missouri River there is a narrow pass, the only approach for wagons to the mouth of the Judith. Here the divide is only 10 feet wide, and on both sides steep and precipitous ravines run off to the east and west. This backbone continues for fifty or seventy-five yards, in which distance it turns and twists sharply every few feet. Sometimes the wagon on one side seems to hang over a precipice a hundred feet in height, while on the other it grinds along against the face of a sandstone bluff elevated a few feet above the level of the road, or it has to be lowered carefully down an almost vertical slope of 30 or 40 feet, and to be dragged painfully up another as high and steep. From this point, a march of four miles over a gently rolling plateau brings us to the final descent into the Judith River bottom. The road down into the valley is long and steep; the difference in height between the top of the bluffs and the level of the valley being 1,200 feet.

The upper 400 feet of the bluffs are composed almost wholly of beds of sand, white and yellow, nearly pure, interstratified with occasional fragmentary layers of a fine-grained, clayey, brown or red sandstone. The beds of white sand contains a few poorly-preserved Unios and the remains of Dinosaurs (*Hadrosaurus*) and Turtles (*Trionyx*). The yellow sands contain many concretions of hard, yellow clay, but are without fossils, so far as examined. All the beds are horizontal, and most of them are quite hard. The white sands in some places change into a laminated white sandstone, and seem to be always overlaid by the brown sandstone. At a lower level, these beds seem to pass into a white, firm, clayey sandstone, which is very hard; but we were unable, in the limited time at our command, to fix the point at which the change took place.

The character of the lowest portion of the beds on the Judith is much obscured by the presence of the Fort Pierre clays in the valley, and by the washing out of the base of the bluffs and consequent dropping down of the rocks above them. This has taken place almost everywhere along the Judith and the Missouri Rivers at this point; and, in consequence of this, the rocks dip at every conceivable angle, and in all directions. A careful examination, however, will serve to convince the observer that all the beds are really horizontal, and that the apparent bendings and twistings of the rocks referred to by Dr. Hayden are due simply to the action of running water. This element has here acted on a scale so enormous as to be almost inconceivable to one who is not familiar with the important part that is played by this agent in denudation in the West.

At a time in the past when the Judith carried much more water than it does at present, the undermining of the high bluffs was constantly going on, just as the higher alluvial banks of the Missouri River are being undermined at present; and, as the lowest beds were washed out, the superincumbent rocks slipped down in vast masses. The process, on a small scale, may be seen every day while ascending the Missouri. Besides this, the water, which in spring, from the melting snows and the early rains, is carried by each of the thousand ravines which we find here, not only washes down the sides of the ridges, but works under the bluffs, often boring for itself an underground passage from one *coulée* to another. Such passages increase in size annually, and finally become so large as not to be able to support the weight of the rocks above, which sink down and fill up the tunnel. It is to these causes, and to these alone, that the apparent irregularity in the strata at this point is owing, and not to any uplifting of the various mountain-ranges which exist in the vicinity. The beds at the mouth of the Judith have been very little, if at all, disturbed by this latter agency.

The Fort Pierre beds form what may be termed the lowest bench of the bluffs along the Judith near its mouth. They have been very much denuded; at one point reaching a height of 560 feet above the river's level, and at other places along the bluffs being apparently wanting. Deposits of this age are found, not only in the main valley of the Judith, but in many little ravines back in the bluffs as well. It is evident that they at some points have been covered by the younger rocks which have dropped down from above. From the facts above mentioned it is very difficult, if not quite impossible, to get at the lowermost strata of the bluffs; and we were unable to accomplish it satisfactorily at any point.

A considerable amount of surface-drift was noticed in the valley of the Judith and in the ravines running into it. This consists almost wholly of water-worn limestone pebbles, similar in appearance to the limestone observed at the western end of the Judith Mountains, in the Snowy Mountains, &c. One of these drift-pebbles contained *Spirifera centronata*, Winch.

About two miles below our camp, and just above the crossing of the Judith, the Fort Pierre beds extend up the foot of the bluffs to a height of about 100 feet. Above these, where the main bluffs become visible, we noted 40 feet of soft, washed, yellowish clays, and over these 18 inches of hard, blue to gray, impure limestone, containing:

    1. *Pholadomya subventricosa*, M. & H.
    2. *Liopistha (Cymella) undata*, M. & H.
    3. *Thracia Grinnelli*, Whitf. (n. sp.)

This was followed by 15 inches of soft, finely laminated sandstone, in color from white to yellowish-brown; next came 20 feet of soft yellow clays; and finally a layer of sandy limestone from 3 to 6 inches in thickness, and consisting almost wholly of the following shells, crowded closely together:

    1. *Tellina scitula*, M. & H.
    2. *Sphæriola Moreauensis*, M. & H.
    3. (?) *Callista Deweyi*, M. & H.
    4. *Lunatia concinna*, H. & M.
    5. *Narica crassa*, Whitf. (n. sp.)
    6. *Baculites ovatus*, Say.

At a point said to be about one-third of the way up the bluffs on Dog River, the following fossils were collected by two members of the party:

    1. *Mactra warreniana*, M. & H.
    2. *Cardium speciosum*, M. & H.
    3. *Tellina (Arcopagia) Utahensis*, M. & H.
    4. *Tellina (Arcopagia) subulata*, M. & H.

They are imbedded in a soft yellow sandstone. These fossils, most of which are characteristic, and which have been compared by Mr. Whitfield with typical fossils now in the Smithsonian Museum at Washington, indicate the lower portion at least of these beds to belong to Cretaceous No. 5.

At a point a little south of where the road descends into the valley, and about 300 feet above the level of the river, the following section was taken, from below upward:

	Feet.
Hard, gray, laminated sandstone, passing near the top into a softer, yellowish rock	50
Yellow clayey sands	30
Soft yellow clays	50
Total	130

Where the road comes into the valley, a bed of hard white sandstone, interstratified with layers of yellowish laminated sandstone, is seen, the whole about 50 feet in thickness. No fossils were found in either of the above.

It may be stated in general terms that the lower two-thirds (or 800 feet) of these bluffs consist of yellowish clays, interstratified with thin layers of sandstone and limestone, and that the upper 400 feet is almost wholly sandstone, more or less hard, generally white, but sometimes varying from that to a dark brown. Lignite occurs in the upper sandstone. A few hundred yards from our camp we noticed a bed of sand 15 feet thick, with several layers of impure lignite from 1 to 2 inches in thickness running through it. This bed had slipped down from some point high up on the bluffs, as it had no connection with the neighboring rocks, and had quite a steep dip. From the fossils obtained, it seems that the upper beds of sands and sandstones must be referred to what have been called the Fort Union Beds, or No. 6 of the Cretaceous.

It is a matter of regret to the writers that the observations at this point were so few and so disconnected as to give but little idea of the structure of the bluffs and the relations of the beds. The extent of country to be covered by our observations was very large; and patient study and observation, extended over a considerable time, would have been required to do justice to the locality.

LITTLE ROCKY MOUNTAINS.

A delay of a few days at Carroll on our return journey was in part utilized by a short excursion to the Little Rocky Mountains, which lie about twenty-five miles from the Missouri River, almost due north of that settlement. The starting-point was a short distance below Carroll; and, on reaching the north bank of the stream, we took a trail leading to Milk River, which we were able to follow for some distance. The road rises quite steeply on first leaving the alluvial plain of the river, and attains 400 feet of its final height within a very short distance. From here the rise is more gradual, the road winding to and fro, keeping on the summit of a narrow ridge, whose sides are washed down steeply on either hand. The washing-out of the bluffs was here even more striking than where observed on the south side of the Missouri; and the continually dividing and subdividing *coulées* form a labyrinth of little ridges and valleys, which would present a peculiar appearance could they be viewed from a point a few hundred feet directly above. The course for the road, however, has been so well chosen that the ascent is continuous; no descent into any minor ravines being necessary. The final rise is a matter of time, and the high plateau which forms the true bank of the river is only reached after a ride of several miles. The height at this point, as given by an aneroid, was 680 feet above Carroll, which corresponds closely with the similar measurements taken on the other side. After a little comparatively level prairie, the gradual rise is continued, and at the foot of the hills the height is 1,250 feet above the river. A section from Carroll to the mountains is given in figure 13, which it is interesting to compare with figure 4; the scale is the same.

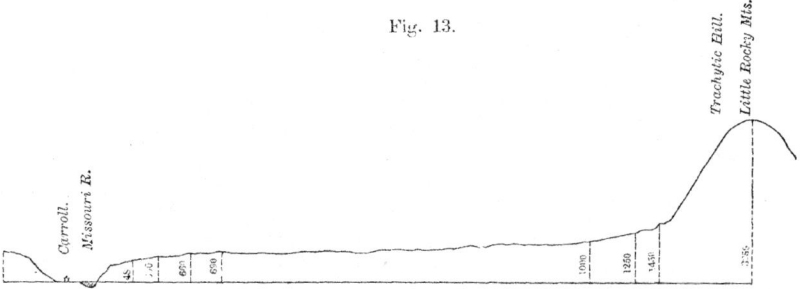

Profile section from Carroll to the Little Rocky Mountains. Course North and South. Distance direct about 25 miles.

The bluffs on the north bank are made up entirely of Fort Pierre shales, and these were observed from time to time nearly up to the mountains. In general character, they do not differ from those before described. The surface of the prairie as we pass from the river is covered far and wide with drift, very similar to that observed on the south side of the stream; though here the quartzite pebbles are even more numerous, and cover the surface of the ground so thickly as almost to have crowded out the scanty vegetation. Grass is hardly present at all, and even the few weeds have a hard struggle for existence. This is true for fifteen miles from the river. Approaching the hills, however, the grass is more abundant; and occasionally in the more favored spots it is sufficiently thick to make it worth the while of citizens of Carroll to come here for hay. In addition to the small, smooth pebbles, the same masses of red and gray syenite found on the Crooked Creek road were seen here. The relations of these will be spoken of more particularly hereafter (p. 135). The quartzite pebbles are most numerous within ten miles of the river-bank, and hardly extend much beyond twenty miles. The same is true of the blocks of crystalline rocks to some extent, though they were seen occasionally quite near to the Little Rockies. It is to be remarked that here also there are no deposits of drift, the pebbles being merely sprinkled over the surface. The nearer we approached the mountains, the more numerous became the slightly washed and rounded fragments of trachyte, containing large, clear crystals of orthoclase. Some fragments of the same rock, by the way, had been seen near Carroll, on the south side of the river. The source of these fragments was obviously to be found in the hills we were approaching, and subsequent exploration proved the truth of this conjecture.

The old trail was left after a time, and we continued on our way, striking across the prairie toward the hills. The country was very dry and barren; the only water seen being in some holes, and that was intensely alkaline. In general, it may be stated here that these hills are very dry, and do not give rise to the numerous running streams, which make the region near the Judith Mountains attractive. The level character of the prairie was favorable to the progress of the ambulance, but not at all so for geological investigation; an occasional wash of black shales being the sum-total of all that was observed during a march of twenty-five miles. As we approached the hills, we passed near to the edge of the high bluffs, which pitched steeply down to the valley of Little Rocky Mountain Creek. The view which was opened out to us was extended and striking, looking down on the Bad Lands of the creek at hand, and those which extended on indefinitely westward. The bed of the stream offered attractions for geological work; but the descent promised so badly for the mules and their load that it was decided to turn away, and keep on the high land.

We made our camp in a meadow some two miles south of the mountains at a spot which furnished a little stagnant water. Here we had the hills in front of us, and on either hand a terrace about four miles apart, which stretched southward till they blended with the general level of the prairie. These high terraces two hundred feet above the level of the adjoining plain, are conspicuous features of the landscape, and are important as bearing on the general question of the circumstances under which this country has been denuded. The results of the observations of the following day are contained for the most part in the accompanying sketch. We first examined the strata at the most easterly point (*a*). The intervening prairie was doubtless once covered with the upturned strata, but now only isolated patches are to be seen. At *a*, we found a brown massive sandstone, cellular and remarkably honey combed on the surface as if worn by water washing against it. Its texture was even, with the exception of numerous rusty iron pellets. It dipped strongly (60°) southerly, strike north 80° east; and, standing up as a high wall or rampart, it had survived the denuding influences which had been too severe for the overlying strata. The outer layer of this sandstone was 12 feet in thickness, and more compact than those that followed; the total thickness being 40 feet. The next exposure was in the *coulée* 400 yards behind this wall, where followed a series of blue and yellow shales 500 feet in thickness. These had the same direction of strike as the sandstone, but the dip was steeper, becoming nearly vertical, then changing to north. The observations in this direction were cut off by the high hill of trachyte at *b*. The talus from this hill extends out for some distance from it, covering up all sedimentary strata beneath it. At *c* rises a second complementary hill of trachyte, and lying between these two and limiting the prairie in this direction is an imposing limestone wall. This is worth mentioning, for it is so conspicuous an object as to be distinctly visible in clear weather at a distance of fifty miles to the south. The mountains seem from such a point to have a continuous white girdle running around them. This is due to the limestone and to its continuation east and west in the range; the abrupt wall of trachyte also continues this girdle where the limestone is interrupted. The limestone wall shows no stratification, but its face has a steep dip south 70°, and, in character as well as in result of weathering, resembles the Carboniferous limestone so often described.

Fig. 14.

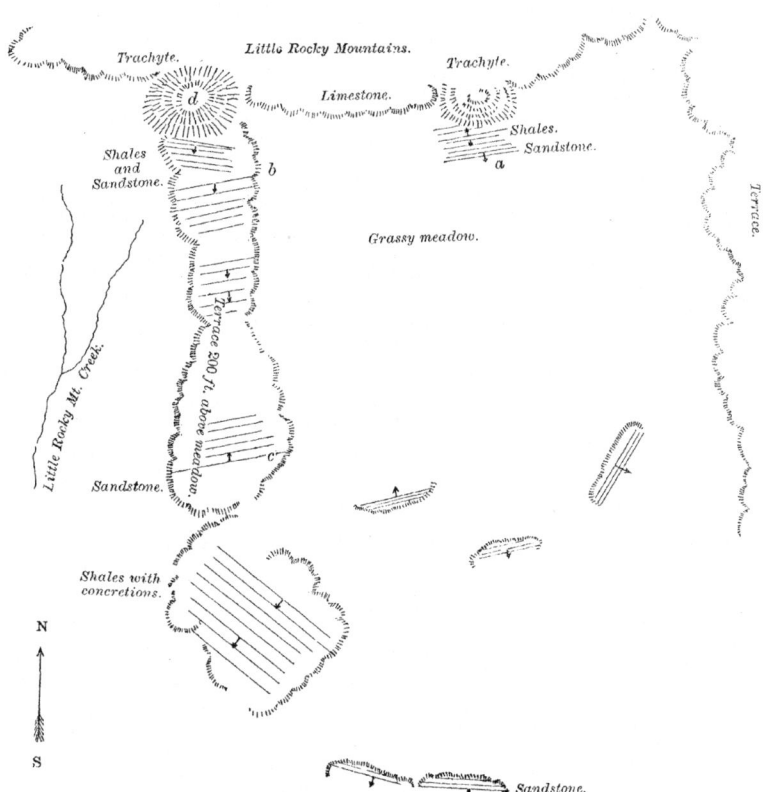

At the west end of this limestone wall, a little cañon opens out, showing the considerable thickness of the limestone. Lower layers afforded the following fossils, of which a list is here given, with remarks made upon them by Mr. Whitfield:

1. *Glauconome*, sp. ?.—"Too indistinct for specific determination."
2. *Productus*, sp. ?.—"This has a feature (elongated depressions) which is seldom seen in rocks above the Chemung of New York or Waverly sandstone of Burlington, Iowa."
3. *Chonetes*, sp. ?.—Resembles *C. granulifera*, Owen; also very like *C. subumbona*, M. & W.
4. *Chonetes*, sp.—"This may possibly be only a variety of the preceding, with which it was associated; but had I seen only this fossil, I should have thought it Lower Silurian."
5. *Spirifera centronata*, Winch.

In regard to these fossils, Mr. Whitfield says:

"The general expression of these fossils is that of Lower Carboniferous or perhaps Waverly. The locality and formation is worth further exploration in view of the rocks being Lower Carboniferous, or possibly even lower."

We ascended the hill at *d* with some little labor, owing to the thick growth of scrub-pines, with which it was covered, and from it obtained a fine view of the surrounding prairie and the desert country far to the west. The various ranges of hills were distinctly visible: the Judith Mountains with Cone Butte, to the south fifty miles distant in an air-line; the Moccasin Mountains; Bear's Paw Mountains, and so on. The height of this hill was 3,500 feet above Carroll, or 2,000 feet above the surrounding prairie. Of the general geology of these hills, little can be said from such a survey, except so far as the wide extrusion of the trachyte was noted. The hill in question was made up of the trachyte which had been found in such large quantities over the prairie to the south. This rock is remarkable for its very porphyritic character; the crystals of orthoclase being very numerous and of considerable size, a quarter to half an inch in length. They are usually more or less altered, and under the microscope prove to be made up of minute crystals apparently of a triclinic feldspar, the base consisting of the same material. The whole rock is very white on the fresh fracture; but the little iron it contains oxidizes on exposure, and the surface becomes rusty.

Descending the hill, we pass south over the terrace mentioned before, which would give a good section of the rocks to one who had the time to examine it with care. The lower portion of the southern face of the hill is precipitous; the trachyte showing a bold front. Passing from the talus of the mountain, we came upon a series of variegated shales, mostly bright-red, also greenish and blue, evidently baked by the eruption of igneous rock close by; occasional beds of red sand-rock and mud-shales occur with the others. The general strike is shown on the map. The total thickness of these shales was some 800 feet; no fossils were found, only a few indistinct vegetable remains. Overlying these shales, with a slight change of strike, was a thick-bedded sandstone honeycombed, and in other respects so similar to that described as occurring at a, that the identity of the two can hardly be doubted; the underlying shales also correspond. From this point south, the dip became more and more gradual, the terraced hill more grassy, and at d, perhaps two miles from the hills, the dip is reversed, and the sandstone of a and e appears with a slight northerly dip. Still farther south and west, the hills are more broken, and we passed over a series having a somewhat different strike, consisting of a sandstone, then black shales containing large concretions with selenite plates; and, overlying this, other sandstone layers. This shale suggests strongly the Fort Pierre Group, which is seen horizontal only a few miles distant on the prairie. Other exposures of sandstone, yellow and granular, were noted at points to the south (see figure); they had a strike and dip as shown in the sketch. These latter are exceedingly similar to those which yielded No. 5 fossils at Box Elder. No fossils were found, however; though it cannot be doubted that the series of rocks belongs mostly to the Upper Cretaceous. Enough has been said to show, with the help of the sketch, that the relations are by no means simple. In general, it may be said that the hills, at least at this point, give evidence of folding; the axis lying east and west, so that the uplifting force must have been from the south. Our return trip was made by the same trail, and admitted of no further observations.

THE GEYSERS OF THE YELLOWSTONE PARK.

The route followed by the party in going from Fort Ellis to the Yellowstone Lake and Geyser Basins and returning was that generally taken from this point: through the cañon of the East Gallatin River and down the valley of Trail Creek to the Yellowstone River, thence up its valley to the Mammoth Hot Springs, and hence to the falls, the lake, and the geysers. This route has been twice explored by Dr. Hayden and his parties in 1871 and 1872, and the objects of interest in the park have been described in addition in the valuable report of Captain Jones and Prof. Comstock, who visited it in 1873. It was not to be expected, therefore, that our hurried trip of nineteen days from Fort Ellis and return would give us any opportunity to collect any important additional facts.

It therefore does not seem to us desirable to attempt here an account of the somewhat disconnected observations we were able to make on our very rapid journey from Fort Ellis to the Geyser Basins, as they must be, in a great measure, repetitions of what has been already published. We may remark, in passing, upon the very great beauty and interest of the whole region, and the wonderful field that it offers for the study of all kinds of modern volcanic rocks.

It seems, however, that it may be of some little interest to record the action of the more important geysers as observed by us during the day or two which we spent in the basins. We do this, not imagining that the facts in themselves have any especial importance, except so far as this: that the more the facts in regard to the geysers and their operations are accumulated and recorded, the better will ultimately be the understanding of the phenomena involved.

We reached the Lower Geyser Basin the evening of August 20, and, having at that time and during the following morning but a few hours of daylight in all, we saw no display from the more prominent of the geysers of this basin. The only particularly noticeable eruption observed by us was from the "Architectural" Geyser. The discharge took place in the evening, and was repeated again in the morning, lasting each time about 45 minutes. There was no single stream thrown to a great height; but a continued, confused mass of jets was thrown in all directions, with occasional spirts, to a height of 30 or 40 feet. From its very irregularity, it seemed to us one of the most attractive of the small geysers. The various other interesting points in the basin, the "Mud Puffs," "Paint Pots," etc., were duly examined, but do not need special mention here.

We arrived at the Upper Geyser Basin August 21, and remained there until the morning of August 24, or about 60 hours. Our note-book gives the following facts in regard to the eruptions of the more important geysers:

Old Faithful, the guardian of the valley, showed a very high degree of regularity during the whole period of our stay. The interval between the commencement of the discharges was 65 or 66 minutes; and, as timed by us for nearly 24 successive eruptions, varied very slightly from this interval. The eruptions were of a very uniform character, differing but slightly in manner or duration (about three minutes) or in the amount of water thrown out. During the night, we were roused each hour by the first rush of the water and steam, and certainly nothing could be more beautiful than this grand fountain in action, illuminated by the light of the full moon. The average height of the column of water, as determined by Mr. Wood, was 115 feet.

The solid portion of the geyser, that is, its ornamented crater, has been much injured by the depredations of selfish visitors, who do not realize that the injury to the crater done by them in a few minutes can never be repaired. One of the most interesting features of this geyser, to one who has recently visited the Mammoth Springs, is the great similarity between the step or basin formation here and that of the calcareous springs, the same cause working here, but under quite different conditions.

Bee Hive.—Our camp was situated in a grove of trees on the Fire Hole River, just opposite the Bee Hive Geyser, so that we were able to observe it under very favorable circumstances. During a period of 60 hours, there were three eruptions; the interval between the first and second being 26 hours, and that between the second and third 25 hours. The duration of the action was four or five minutes, and the measured height 200 feet. The amount of water ejected is comparatively very small; the apparent discharge being greater than the real. This discharge consists largely of steam, which is swayed in one direction and another by the wind; the gracefully-waving column of steam and water producing a beautiful effect. Its charms are considerably enhanced when the sun strikes the jet so as to produce a rainbow near the top of the column. This geyser has a crater alone; there being no step formation at its foot in consequence of the small amount of water which it throws out. The force of the escaping steam and water is very great, and seems almost to shake the crust in the vicinity. A little attendant geyser at the foot of the Bee Hive acts as a sort of forerunner to it, giving notice by its little stream when its larger companion is about to move.

Grand Geyser.—We were fortunate enough to see one very fine display of the action of this geyser. It is especially impressive, because of the absence of any elevated crater; the water rising from the very level of the ground. The height of the first discharge did not much exceed 100 feet. It rose to this point in a series of violent pulsations, remained at this altitude for three or four minutes, and then sank back into the pool, which became quite still. A moment later it had commenced again, the water rising certainly 150 feet by estimate. This again sank down and again rose to its maximum height, and this was twice repeated.

Giantess.—The accounts of the eruptions of the Giantess have been so glowing that we were especially anxious to have an opportunity of observing it ourselves. When we arrived, August 21, the crater was quite full and bubbling, seeming to promise a speedy eruption. The following day at 6.30 a. m., it boiled up vigorously, throwing up jets a few feet into the air, exciting hopes that it was about to perform, and bringing those who were in camp somewhat hastily across the stream. At 9 o'clock it boiled up again, at times throwing out considerable water, so that it was nearly empty as far as we could see, looking far down into the crater. It rapidly filled, however, and a second outburst on a small scale took place. Two hours later a more vigorous display commenced, the hot water being thrown to a height of 100 feet, by a series of successive irregular throbs, like the beats of a pump; the heavy thumping going on below in a startling manner. This irregular display, extremely interesting and beautiful, yet nothing compared with what the Giantess is said to do, lasted for an hour; the entire volume of water thrown out being very great. At length, with a sudden burst, the steam drove up the water to a much greater height than before seen; the noise and concussions accompanying the outburst being very violent. The water was kept at its greatest height for two or three minutes, and for this time we found the Giantess all that had been claimed for it. But the reservoir was almost exhausted, and in a short time the only escape was a mass of steam, which rushed out of the crater with a force which no words could describe.

After we had become somewhat accustomed to the noise of the eruption, and the awe inspired by the vast outburst of steam had in a measure subsided, we experimented upon the violence with which the vapor was ejected by throwing into the crater trunks of trees, logs, and other objects which could be found near at hand, and the height to which these were thrown by the escaping steam was a good indication of the force which was being expended. The heavier of these objects sank nearly to the narrowest part of the crater, and after being held for a moment suspended at this point, rising and falling, according to the violence of the jet which they met, were swiftly shot forth, often rising to a very great height.

This steam escape lasted for an hour without any sensible diminution in violence, and we could not help regretting that all the water had been ejected before the most powerful burst of steam had begun, so that we might have had a full display of the power that was at hand acting on the water. The conception of force given by this great steam escape was perhaps even greater than if it had taken merely the form of a fountain. Six hours later the steam was still escaping, though with somewhat diminished energy, and an occasional liquid jet seemed to show that a little water was draining into the reservoir, only to be immediately ejected.

This great steam escape is important as bearing upon the general subject of geysers, showing the vast amount of steam which must be accumulated before the discharge can take place, and the high tension under which it must be.

The *Castle Geyser* was active most of the time during our stay, though with varying force. The amount of water discharged was never very large, and the highest jets did not exceed 50 feet.

The *Grotto* was also almost continuously active, and after seeing the injury done to its crater by visitors, the large majority of whom are residents of the Territory, we could not help wishing that the discharge of boiling water were absolutely continuous, so that the depredators might be kept at a respectful distance.

The *Saw-mill Geyser* played frequently at short intervals, but quite irregularly.

The *Giant* was quiet, occasional spirts of water to the top of the crater being the only sign of latent energy.

GENERAL CONCLUSIONS.
DISTRIBUTION OF THE FORMATIONS.

Pre-Silurian rocks.—Up to the time when we reached the second Yellowstone Cañon, we had seen absolutely nothing of any rocks older than the Primordial series. This is true, not only with respect to our observations, made in the several minor ranges of mountains, but also includes the inferences to be drawn in regard to the elevated points not reached, from the absence of any crystalline rocks in the local drift. The only exception to this was at Camp Baker, where the drift contained such masses, doubtless from the neighboring Big Belt Range, which we were unable to visit, but in which we should expect to find a considerable development of the Pre-Silurian series.

Granitic rocks have been observed by others on the east side of Gallatin River, but they did not appear within the limits of our observations. The inferred absence of crystalline rocks from the minor ranges of hills, which break through the prairie at different points in this part of Montana, for example, the Judith Mountains, the Snow Mountains, Little Rocky Mountains, etc., if correct, would make it improbable that ore deposits of any economic value should be found in them.

Silurian.—Primordial series.—We observed strata, proved by fossils to belong to the Potsdam, at two localities, and the relations of the rocks at these points as far as made out have been described; they may, however, conveniently be recapitulated here.

At Camp Baker, Primordial fossils were found in a limestone hill to the northwest of the Post; the series and the estimated thickness are as follows: Quartzite, 20 feet; variegated shales, mostly bright-red, also green and blue, 150 feet; limestone, in a double series of ledges, 80 feet; quartzite, reddish, slightly micaceous, then a series of colored slates, mostly green, followed by shales and thin beds of sandstones and limestones, in all probably 1,500 feet; still further conformable shales, 1,000 feet. These extend toward the north farther than we could follow them It is enough to say that the total thickness of the conformable strata underlying the fossil-bearing limestone cannot be less than 3,000 feet, and is probably much more. All the facts point to a *very great* development of Lower Silurian rocks.

The same rocks were identified at Moss Agate Springs at the south extremity of the Elk Range of Mountains; we found here red shales like those at Camp Baker, quartzite and limestone, the latter containing many fragments of *Trilobites*. We were able only to glance at this locality, and consequently the observations stand out isolated. To the Primordial we refer also the rocks underlying (in position overlying, in consequence of an overturn) the Carboniferous limestone of the Musselshell Cañon, of which there must be a thickness exposed of some 1,000 feet. It is also very probable that the limestone and red shales of the east bank of Deep Creek observed in isolated patches belong to the same time. With the exception of the above, no rocks older than the Carboniferous were seen by us anywhere from Carroll to Fort Ellis. It is certainly not to be affirmed positively that they do not exist in the mountains touched at; the contrary is probable, but it is quite certain that, if present, they are in all cases subordinate.

Carboniferous.—Carboniferous rocks are largely and very uniformly developed over this part of the Northwest, as has been remarked by Dr. Hayden. All of the minor ranges of hills, repeatedly referred to, contain Carboniferous limestone to a large extent. In fact, the most striking and characteristic features of all these minor ranges are the walls of white limestone, which stand up conspicuously above the timber, and attract the attention even from a great distance. The very uniform nature of this limestone has been noted, and to its character in weathering out into steep walls and isolated towers is due the conspicuous appearance mentioned. The general facts in regard to this formation, collating those obtained at different places, may be summed up as follows: The upper portion consists of limestone in thin beds, with layers of shale and a little sandy slate. These upper layers contain fossils more abundantly than the following beds. *Productus, Chonetes, Spirifera, Athyris, Rhynchonella,* and *Streptorhynchus* are abundant forms. At the Bridger Mountains, some bands of red clay in the upper part of the formation were very conspicuous and persistent, and suggestions of them were seen elsewhere. At Cinnabar Mountain, in the Yellowstone Valley, the intensely red clays and shale, from which the mountain derives its name, immediately overlie Carboniferous limestone, and belong, as elsewhere, to the upper part of the formation. Below these irregular, thin beds, showing a somewhat different character at different localities, comes the mass of the limestone already many times described. It is firm, bluish white, and always cherty. The flint is sometimes in uniformly-distributed particles of small size, sometimes in broad bands. When acted upon by the weather, the rock takes the form of vertical walls and steep towers, showing no trace of stratification. Reference must also be made to the remarks of Mr. Whitfield upon the fossils found by us at the Little Rocky Mountains. He says: "The general expression of these fossils is that of Low Carboniferous, or perhaps Waverley." To this, we can add nothing, except that the fossils came from a limestone underlying the massive blue limestone before spoken of, containing *Zaphrentis* and other corals in considerable abundance. Except at this point, we found nothing to suggest the possible occurrence of any rocks between the Primordial and the usual Carboniferous.

As to the total thickness of the Carboniferous formation as here developed, we can only hazard a conjecture, which cannot be of very great value. The compact limestone spoken of must be at least 500 feet in thickness, and the total may be 600 feet. At any rate, it is certain that the deposits point to a uniform condition of things at the time when the formation was laid down.

Jurassic.—Jurassic fossils were found on the east slope of the Bridger Mountains at both points where the ascent was made. The only rock observed was limestone, and the fossils were quite abundant, in some layers, at least. The thickness seen was small, and on the one side was a Cretaceous fossil-bearing sandstone, and on the other the undoubted Carboniferous limestone. The interval on both sides was small, and we should regard an estimate of 100 feet for the total thickness as a large one. In regard to this, Dr. Hayden says: "The Jurassic rocks are crushed together in the uplift to such an extent that they are quite obscure, and do not appear to much advantage; but, in Union and Flathead Passes, they are much better exposed." His final estimate of their thickness is not clearly stated; but elsewhere, in the same vicinity, he speaks of them as 1,200 feet thick. Whatever may be the facts at this point, we can safely affirm that the development of Jurassic rocks to the north and east is very limited. We had several opportunities for examining beds possibly Jurassic, in search of fossils; but in no case were we successful in our efforts to find such remains. On the contrary, in two distinct localities we passed from undoubted Cretaceous to undoubted Carboniferous, with a very small interval between of non-fossil-bearing strata. These intervening strata may very possibly belong to Jurassic time, and their apparent absence elsewhere may be due to the disturbing influences of the uplifts; but their relative insignificance seems to us quite certain. Banks of red soil were conspicuous at several points, and in appearance suggested, to a certain extent, the "Red Beds" referred to the Triassic in other localities. In three distinct cases, however, we found such layers immediately underlaid by Cretaceous sandstones; so that we think that the beds in question must belong in all cases to the latter horizon.

Cretaceous.—To the Cretaceous formation belongs the rock underlying the prairie over nearly all of the route traversed by us. We were unable, however, to obtain any satisfactory results as to the succession of the various beds. The sandstones, of which these rocks for the most part consist, are quite different at the various localities at which they were seen. They are generally without fossils, though frequently containing indistinct vegetable remains, and seem to lack any particularly distinctive or characteristic features. They have been so often described in the preceding pages that it is needless here to enlarge upon them. The lower part of the formation must be that visible on the Bridger Mountains, directly overlying the Jurassic. Very little is in sight, however, and the fossils obtained were very poor. When the rocks appear again in the valley, they are mostly the constantly-recurring "somber" sandstones. At the headwaters of Cottonwood Creek (see p. 122), we obtained a few poor fossils in a bed which stratigraphically was the lowest in a series of 5,000 feet involved in a gigantic fold. One of these fossils is credited to Cretaceous No. 2 of Meek and Hayden. From here up, in the order of their time, the rocks have been briefly mentioned. They are mostly dark-colored sandstones, occasionally shales, and all nearly destitute of remains of life. The only suggestions of fossils are the indistinct vegetable remains before mentioned, which were found best preserved in the upper strata. The thickness of this Cretaceous series has been estimated at 5,000 feet. Most of it is referred by Hayden, though without facts, to the doubtful "Coal Group, forming the transition from the Cretaceous to the Tertiary". We regard them all as properly Cretaceous; in fact, in some of the upper strata, fossils belonging to No. 5 were found. As has already been stated, beds of red clay immediately overlie some of the lowest Cretaceous strata; and, though their character is probably local and changeable, they are so noticeable where they occur that they deserve mention here.

Cretaceous No. 4.—The most distinctly-marked and characteristic member of the Cretaceous is No. 4, or the Fort Pierre clays, which have already been fully described. Their thickness was estimated at 700 to 1,000 feet. They extend from Carroll north and south for a distance of twenty-five miles from the Missouri. Further than this, they were observed below on the river one hundred and fifty miles from Carroll, and from here to the Judith River a distance of two hundred miles. Beds referred to these take part in the uplifted strata, both at the Judith Mountains and the Little Rocky Mountains, overlaid by Cretaceous No. 5. The Fort Pierre clays were not observed at any greater distance from the river than the points mentioned; and this is true, although beds both below and above them have shared in the folding near the Bridger Mountains. From this, it is concluded that the Fort Pierre clays are limited to the immediate valley of the Missouri at this point. In other words, while the conditions were such as to cause an immense accumulation of mud in what s now the immediate valley of the Missouri, different conditions prevailed at a greater distance from the river, and deposits of sandstone were going on.

Cretaceous No. 5.—The Fox Hills Group was determined beyond all question at three points: at Box Elder Creek, near the Judith Mountains; at Haymaker's Creek, near the Forks of the Musselshell; and at the mouth of the Judith River. The rock in each case was a sandstone, which is characteristic of the formation. Upper layers are very yellow and ferruginous, and lower beds white and gray. The local changes are very great. At the Judith Mountains, the thickness of the sandstone, at a point where some estimate of its relation to the underlying clays could be made, was thought to be about 300 feet. North of the Missouri, at the Little Rocky Mountains, sandstones similar to those of No. 5 were seen overlying concretions, and selenite-bearing shales, presumably No. 4; and hence their existence here may be considered probable. If now Cretaceous No. 5 is found at two points, on either side of the river, at a minimum distance of twenty-five miles, while between is No. 4, and no trace of No. 5, what has become of the latter? One fact observed may be mentioned in this connection: the dark clays are carried from Carroll one hundred miles and more down the river; and, at some of the lower points, these clays, which appear alone in the immediate river-bank, have a capping at a little distance of white and yellow sandstone. This observation, made from the deck of the steamboat, is of little value; but it suggests that the No. 5 may be here, where it belongs, directly overlying No. 4, while farther west, in the neighborhood of Carroll, it has been removed by the glacial flood, to be mentioned later.

A more thorough study of the Cretaceous beds at the mouth of the Judith would no doubt have assisted us materially in deciding the point in doubt had we been able to give the requisite time to their examination. As it was, the relations of the beds were, as has been said, somewhat complicated; and we were able to do no more than to identify by fossils the several members of the group exposed at that point. We found here the Fort Pierre clays in close apposition with rocks containing No. 5 fossils.

No. 6. *Fort Union Group.*—Beds of white sandstone, containing occasional layers of a clayey brown sand-rock, were found at the mouth of the Judith River, evidently overlying the beds of No. 5, before referred to. From these deposits of sand, we obtained the vertebræ and long bones of Dinosaurs, identified by Professor Marsh as belonging very near the genus *Hadrosaurus* of Leidy. With these remains were found Unios, and, in some layers, a little lignite; the general association seeming to refer the deposits to the Fort Union beds. Their thickness was estimated at 400 feet, though no sufficient data were collected to warrant any great confidence in this estimate.

Tertiary.—Distinct tertiary strata were observed in the neighborhood of Camp Baker, and their relations have been so fully described that a repetition is unnecessary. It may be mentioned, however, that the occurrence of a Miocene lake at this point, with beds 250 feet thick, is a matter of no little interest, and opens many interesting questions as to the relations of this with the other well-known Miocene lakes, as also to the Pliocene beds of the Upper Missouri and the Yellowstone Valley. The red and yellow slates, which seem to accompany the Miocene beds of Camp Baker, may possibly be Lower Tertiary, although, as has been remarked, they are not conformable with the overlying beds. In the absence of any decisive facts, however, we must leave this point undecided.

Quaternary.—More or less distinct evidence of Quaternary action was obtained at several points. True traveled drift was observed in the Missouri Valley alone. In Upper Yellowstone region, the amount of material transported has been immense; but the action is, comparatively speaking, local. Fine striæ, presumably glacial, were seen in the cañon above the mouth of Work Creek, and also in the granitic rocks near the bridge. At the latter point, the amount of transported blocks was very large. It may be of interest to note that the blocks apparently from this spot were traced south; and some few scattered bowlders were seen within 1,500 feet of the top of Mount Washburne, as if the action had been in that direction. This matter has been discussed for this locality by others, and we refrain from carrying it further.

The drift at the foot of the Bridger Mountains, the Elk Range, Little Belt Mountains, Snow Mountains, and Judith Mountains, in many cases exceedingly abundant, is in all cases purely local; almost exclusively Carboniferous limestone or trachyte. The masses and pebbles were distributed in the time of glacial flood, when the flow of water from these hills was very great. The action of this flow of water, in washing out deep valleys, has already been noticed. The special interest attaching to Quaternary phenomena is connected with the facts observed in the Missouri Valley, which have been alluded to, though not described in detail. North and south of the river from Carroll, the prairie is more or less covered with drift-pebbles and masses, whose source is not to be found in the neighboring ranges of hills. On the contrary, the southern limit of this drift is reached twenty-five miles from the river and about ten miles from the north limit of the Judith Mountains, where the surface-drift changes its character and commences to be made up entirely of trachyte from Cone Butte and the neighboring hills. To the north, the limit is not so distinctly marked; but it is reached within twenty miles of the river, where the trachyte of the Little Rocky Mountains takes its place. This drift is divided into two classes quite distinct from each other: first, we have the rounded pebbles, very uniformly scattered over the surface of the prairie; and, second, the large, angular blocks distributed here and there at random. The pebbles are generally small, sometimes several inches in diameter, but more frequently much less. They are flattened, quite smooth, and in fact bear much the appearance of common stream-pebbles; they are almost never glaciated. They show, however, the marks of the force of attrition by which they have been smoothed into shape, for the surface-layer of those of uniform texture is curiously marked with semicircular cracks, due to the constant blows which they have received against each other, giving them often quite an ornamented appearance. The material of the pebbles is 90 per cent. quartzite, generally yellow, sometimes dull red (jasper), and also rarely dark-colored. The remaining 10 per cent. is made up of material so heterogeneous that a catalogue of the varieties would be more curious than valuable; pieces of fossil wood, however, must be mentioned. As has been stated, the deposits are superficial in all cases. The material composing the drift of the second class is very generally a bright-red syenite; this forms masses sometimes three or four feet in thickness, but averaging about 18 inches. Next in importance is a similar rock, in which the place of the hornblende is taken mostly by black mica; still again, there are masses of black hornblende rock, a grayish syenite, but very little true granite. All these have a very Archæan look. Masses of semi-crystalline limestone also occur, though not frequently. These blocks, as has been stated, are uniformly angular, showing little trace of wear. They are less uniformly distributed than the pebbles.

The source of these drift masses can hardly be held in doubt. Confined, as they are, to the Missouri Valley, they make it almost certain that they have been brought by running water in the direction of the present stream. In the flood which followed the melting of the ice, which, to a greater or less extent, doubtless covered the higher mountains, and at a time when the land is supposed to have been depressed, the waters may well have spread over a width of forty miles, covering the now so nearly level prairie, and could readily have transported the smaller washed pebbles. The large blocks evidently demand stronger agencies, and it is difficult to make any other supposition than that they have been carried by floating ice brought from the westward, from the high mountains which form the main divide of the Rocky Mountains, in which the red feldspar-syenites and the quartzites must have a large development. This would account for their not being rolled bowlders. To the same time of glacial floods belong the formations of the terraces seen; especially those at the Little Rocky Mountains and Judith Mountains.

Our opportunities for making observations above and below Carroll on the river were exceedingly limited. Masses of a syenitic rock were observed, here and there, down the river, prominent at the mouth of the Musselshell River, and again at Fort Peck. Running notes from the steamboat-deck have little value, and not much can be based upon them. Far down the Missouri, near Bismarck, eight hundred miles from Carroll, the drift bowlders are numerous, and the quaternary sands form deep stratified deposits. These phenomena, however, join on to those which are observed more and more decidedly to the eastward, and the source of which is to be found to the northeast. West of Carroll, near the mouth of the Judith River, the drift just described was not observed. This evidence is negative merely, since, if once deposited as below, it can easily be imagined that subsequent denudation has obscured it.

It is interesting to note, in connection with the facts stated in regard to the drift from the westward, the extended and careful observations of a similar character, made at many different points, by Mr. G. M. Dawson, F. G. S., and described in the "Geology and Resources of the Region in the Vicinity of the Forty-ninth Parallel," Montreal, 1875.

If the report in question be consulted, a full description of these interesting facts will be found. It is sufficient for our purposes to call attention to the great prevalence of the quartzite drift over the prairie far to the north of the Missouri. The general character of this drift was much the same as that found by us, and it was also referred to the Rocky Mountains as its source.

PERIOD OF MOUNTAIN-ELEVATION.

Much of the country covered by our reconnaissance is, in some respects, a unique one, as may be gathered from the remarks previously made. The prairie, deeply gullied, as it is, by the Missouri and other minor streams, is, in general, of a pretty level character. The strata are horizontal, and there is little evidence of any elevation since those Cretaceous beds were laid down. Above the prairie, at a number of points, rise ranges of hills of no very great extent, and with an altitude averaging about 2,000 feet. They are seen far and near; and, rising blue and misty in the distance, from the dry, parched level, they are a most agreeable relief to the otherwise unbroken monotony of the landscape. They are important as serving to redeem the country from utter worthlessness, since they give rise to numbers of clear, flowing streams. The Judith Mountains, Moccasin, Highwood, Snow, Little Belt, and, north of the Missouri, the Little Rocky and Bear's Paw Mountains, are the most prominent of these ranges.

Rising, as described, from the level prairie, it is to be expected that they would give good sections of the rocks which once lay horizontal over the whole of this part of the country. This would doubtless be true, could the relations be studied in detail in each case. In fact, however, the extensive denudation has left only remnants of once extensive formations, so that in a given spot the continuity has been much interrupted. Furthermore, the commonly occurring ejection of masses of igneous rocks has served as a decidedly disturbing element.

As to the time when the elevation of our numerous mountain-ridges took place, the evidence, where decisive, points to the same conclusion reached elsewhere in the West, which indeed was to be expected. The time of elevation followed the close of the Cretaceous era. This is clearly seen at the Judith Mountains, where Cretaceous No. 5 has been involved in the general disturbance. The same cannot be questioned for the Little Rocky Mountains. The elevation of the Snow Mountains and the Little Belt Range embraced Cretaceous deposits; and, though it cannot be positively stated that the upper members of the formation came in at these points, this cannot be doubted, in view of the evidence.

The Bridger Mountains are the most interesting and satisfactory. They include strata from the Primordial to the top of the Cretaceous; all apparently conformable, and all elevated at one time. The junction of the Lower Silurian with the Carboniferous did not appear in that portion of the range examined by us.

At the other points where the Silurian was found, we unfortunately could not observe its relations to the overlying Carboniferous. At the Musselshell Cañon, the evidence is not conclusive; but the relations seem to imply conformability from the Cretaceous down to the Primordial. At Camp Baker, the Primordial stands alone; and we saw no evidence of the Carboniferous following it in the sequence of the strata, as would be expected. This fact strongly suggested to us, while on the ground, an earlier elevation of the Silurian; but this cannot be regarded as of much weight, in view of the fact that the extensive deposits of Miocene Tertiary may well cover up what follows and would otherwise be exposed.

RECONNAISSANCE FROM CARROLL, MONTANA, TO YELLOWSTONE NATIONAL PARK.

DESCRIPTIONS

OF

NEW SPECIES OF FOSSILS.

BY

R. P. WHITFIELD.

DESCRIPTIONS OF NEW SPECIES OF FOSSILS.

By R. P. WHITFIELD.

Genus CREPICEPHALUS, *Owen*.

CREPICEPHALUS (LOGANELLUS) MONTANENSIS, n. sp.

Plate 1, figs. 1 and 2.

Glabella and fixed cheeks, when united, subquadrangular in outline, contracted across the eyes, and abruptly expanding in front. Glabella narrowly conical, moderately tapering anteriorly, somewhat squarely truncate in front, strongly elevated, and gibbous in the middle and along the central line, marked by three pairs of lateral furrows, which are directed obliquely backward at their inner ends; anterior pair very short, and placed near the anterior end of the glabella. Occipital furrow only moderately strong. Fixed cheek rather narrow, not exceeding one-third the width of the glabella. Eye-lobes proportionally large. Frontal limb long, equaling half the length of the glabella. No perceptible anterior rim can be detected on the part preserved. Ocular ridges distinct. Posterior lateral limbs long and narrow, their lateral extension about equal to the width of the glabella.

The species is known only by the glabella and fixed cheeks, the latter imperfect; but the form is so unlike any other of the genus described that there can be no difficulty in recognizing it. The extreme elevation of the glabella is a marked feature.

Locality and formation.—In limestone of the Potsdam Group overlying quartzite near Camp Baker, Montana.

Genus ARIONELLUS, *Barrande*.

ARIONELLUS TRIPUNCTATUS, n. sp.

Plate 1, figs. 3-5.

Specimens consisting only of the central parts of the head and separated movable cheeks.

Glabella conical, the height above the occipital furrow equal to the greatest width at the furrow; anterior end rounded, as wide as two-thirds of the length above the occipital furrow; margins defined by strong, well-defined dorsal furrows; surface moderately convex, and very faintly angular along the median line; marked by three pairs of very faint lateral furrows, which are directed obliquely backward at their inner ends; occipital furrow deep, extending entirely across the base of the head; occipital ring moderately strong, and projecting backward in a central spine of undetermined length.

Fixed cheeks narrow and prominent, but rapidly sloping to the margins in front of the small, prominent and somewhat pointed palpebral lobes. Frontal limb short, rapidly narrowing at the sides, in front of the eyes, to the anterior furrow, which is deep and strong; anterior to the furrow the limb is suddenly contracted and subangular in the middle; bottom of the furrow marked between the sutural margins by three deep well-marked pits. Postero-lateral limbs narrow at their origin, beyond which they are unknown.

*The types of all the species here described are in the Peabody Museum of Yale College, New Haven, Conn.

Facial sutures directed forward on a line with the eye for a short distance, when they are directed inward with a strong curvature to the anterior furrow, in front of which they converge more rapidly, and, meeting in the median line, give an angular form to the frontal limb when the movable cheeks are absent. Movable cheeks subtriangular, exclusive of the posterior spine; central area convex; marginal rim strongly rounded and gradually widening from the front, posteriorly to the origin of the spine, which is of moderate strength, and as long as the glabella and frontal limb of the head. Surface of the movable cheeks covered with strong granules. The glabella and fixed cheeks have been similarly marked, judging from the pustulose surface of the cast of these parts. Thorax and pygidium unknown. The surface-structure, together with the well-marked pits in the frontal furrow, will serve to distinguish this from any other known species.

Formation and locality.—In limestones of the Potsdam Group; at Moss Agate Springs near Camp Baker, Montana.

Genus GRYPHÆA, *Lam.*

GRYPHÆA PLANOCONVEXA, n. sp.

Plate 2, figs. 9 & 10.

Shell of medium size; general outline more or less orbicular, or with a straightened cardinal margin; transverse section planoconvex. Lower valve more or less rounded, often quite ventricose, but sometimes depressed-convex; beak small and narrow-pointed or truncate, usually somewhat twisted, projecting slightly beyond the line of the hinge, and often incurved close to the cardinal border. Upper valve flat or slightly concave, smaller than the other. Ligamental area of the lower valve small; cartilage-groove narrow. Muscular imprints reniform, eccentric. Substance of the shell rather thin and nacreous; surface roughly lamellose.

The form of the shell as seen in several individuals strongly resembles that of an *Anomia*; but on splitting open one of the specimens, it revealed the features of a *Gryphæa*. The general form and characters are so distinct from any known species from rocks of Jurassic age that it may be readily recognized.

Formation and locality.—In rocks of Jurassic age in the Bridger Mountains, Montana; associated with *Camptonectes bellitriata. C. extenuatus, Gervillia erecta* M. & H., and *Pleuromya subcompressa = Myacites (Pleuromya) subcompressa* Meek.

Genus GERVILLIA, *Defrance.*

GERVILLIA SPARSALIRATA, n. sp.

Plate 2, fig. 8.

Shell small, much below a medium size, very oblique, and rather slender; the axis of the body of the shell forming an angle of not more than twenty to twenty-two degrees with the cardinal line. Anterior wing not determined, but apparently very small or obsolete; posterior wing proportionally long and narrow, the surface flattened and the outer angle very obtuse; body of the shell convex, the left valve much the most rotund, scarcely or not at all curved in its direction. Anterior margin slightly convex; basal margin rounded. Surface of the left valve marked by about five comparatively strong radii, with wider interspaces, those along the middle of the valve strongest and most distant; also by well marked, crowded, concentric lines, which are more distinct in crossing the radii than between, and on the posterior wing are directed toward the hinge in an almost direct line. Right valve less convex than the left and the markings less distinct.

This species somewhat closely resembles *G. montanensis* Meek (Geol. Surv. of the Territ's, 1872, p. 472), but differs very materially in the smaller angle formed by the body of the shell with the hinge-line, and also in the greater length of the hinge. It is possible it may be only a strongly marked variety of that species, but this can only be satisfactorily determined by more and better specimens. At present, however, it seems impossible to identify it with that one.

Formation and locality.—In rock of Jurassic age at Bridger Mountains, Montana; associated with characteristic fossils of that formation.

Genus MYALINA, *De Koninck.*

MYALINA? (GERVILLIA) PERPLANA, n. sp.

Plate 1, fig. 8.

Shell rather above a medium size and erect, elongate quadrangular in outline, with a rounded basal margin; anterior and posterior borders subparallel, slightly diverging from the cardinal margin toward the basal line, which is rather sharply rounded; height of the shell nearly or twice as great as the greatest length in an anterior and posterior direction, and the cardinal border nearly two-thirds as long as the greatest length of the shell. Surface of the left valve very depressed-convex, the anterior umbonal ridge being low and rounded a little within the anterior margin of the shell; beak small, compressed, not projecting beyond the hinge-line. Surface marked by low rounded undulations, on the body of the shell, parallel with the lines of growth, which become sharper thread-like lines along the postero-cardinal border.

The depressed and flattened shell, with the subparallel margins and erect form, will readily serve to identify the species. It is possible that the species may prove to be more nearly related to the genus *Gervillia* than to *Myalina* on the examination of other and better specimens; the surface-lining of the shell very closely resembles species of that genus, and the posterior wing is somewhat unlike *Myalina*, while its erect form is quite unlike *Gervillia*.

Formation and locality.—In rocks of Jurassic age at Bridger Mountains, Montana; associated with well-known Jurassic fossils.

Genus PINNA, *Linn.*

PINNA LUDLOVI, n. sp.

Plate 1, figs. 6 and 7.

Shell elongate-triangular, very gradually increasing in width from the beaks toward the base; the dorsal and byssal margins diverging at an angle of but little more than twenty degrees. Dorsal margin straight, as long as, or longer than the body of the shell; basal margin, judging from the lines of growth, nearly at right angles to the dorsal margin for a short distance, then directed, with a rapidly increasing curvature, to the byssal border. Apex and umbones unknown. Surface of the valves angularly convex, the left one the most ventricose, and the angularity quite perceptible. Both valves are marked, except for a narrow space along the byssal margin, by numerous, very distinct, and somewhat flexuous radiating ribs, strongest in the middle of the shell, and decreasing in strength toward each margin; about twenty-two to twenty-four of the ribs may be counted across the middle of the shell on the specimen figured, most of which are marked along the middle by a distinctly-depressed line. Concentric lines distinctly marked and often forming undulations in crossing the radii. Evidence of minute, scattered, spine-like projections exists upon the surface of the radii. Transverse section across the closed valves angularly elliptical; the relative diameters about as one and two.

The strongly-radiated surface and duplicated ribs are features that will readily distinguish this from other described species.

Formation and locality.—In limestones of the Coal Measures, in the cañon of the Musselshell, Montana.

Genus TAPES, *Mühlf.*

TAPES MONTANENSIS, n. sp.

Plate 2, figs. 1 and 2.

Shell small, transversely elongate-elliptical, the length being a little more than twice as great as the height; valves very depressed-convex; beaks subcentral, a little nearer the anterior end, very depressed and inconspicuous, scarcely rising above the general slope of the cardinal border; extremities sharply rounded, the anterior end broadest; basal margin broadly rounded, but a little more arcuate than the cardinal border. Surface of the shell smooth, and presenting the appearance of having been polished, with scarcely perceptible lines of growth.

We know of no described fossil shell very closely resembling this one. *T. Wyomingensis* Meek is perhaps the most closely related, but differs conspicuously in the position of the beaks, which, in that one, are situated only about one-fourth of the length from the anterior end, while in this they are nearly central.

Locality and formation.—In Cretaceous strata near the mouth of the Judith River, Montana, in beds apparently overlying the Fort Pierre shales.

Genus MACTRA, *Linn.*

MACTRA MAIA, n. sp.

Plate 2, fig. 5.

Shell small, subtriangular in outline, with moderately convex valves. Anterior and posterior cardinal slopes nearly equal, the anterior side a little the longest and less abrupt; concave between the beak and the anterior end, while the posterior margin is convex. Anterior extremity narrow, rather strongly rounding upward from the basal margin; posterior extremity subangular; basal line very convex, slightly emarginate just within the posterior angle; beak short, broad, and obtusely pointed, the apex minute, curving, and closely appressed. Body of the shell somewhat regularly convex from beak to base, marked by a strong, subangular, posterior umbonal ridge, behind which the shell slopes abruptly to the margin, and just within which there is a very faintly depressed sulcus extending from below the umbo to the basal line. Anterior umbonal ridge rounded and abrupt.

The specimen from which the description is taken is a partial cast, so that the surface is not perfectly seen; it appears, however, to have been nearly smooth, or with only fine lines of growth. The hinge characters are not clearly made out; the posterior lateral tooth, however, is seen to be long and slender, reaching nearly one-half of the distance between the beak and postero-basal angle. The pallial sinus is somewhat rounded, slightly directed upward, and extends nearly to, or more than one-third of the length of the shell from the posterior end.

This species is very similar in general expression to *M. incompta* White, MS., but differs in being longest anterior to the beaks, while the reverse is the case with that species.

Formation and locality.—In beds of the Cretaceous formation believed to overlie the Fort Pierre shales near the mouth of the Judith River.

Genus SANGUINOLARIA, *Lam.*

SANGUINOLARIA OBLATA, n. sp.

Plate 2, figs. 3 and 4.

Shell small, transversely broad-elliptical or suboval, widest anterior to the middle of the length, where the width is equal to about two-thirds of the length; extremities broadly rounded, the posterior one most sharply curved; basal margin strongly rounded, most abruptly so anterior to the middle of its length; cardinal margin much less strongly rounded than the basal border, slightly contracted posterior to the beaks, which are small, compressed, and but slightly projecting beyond the cardinal border. Surface of the left valve very depressed-convex, most strongly curved across the shell from beak to base, and, judging from the form, has been more convex than the right valve; posterior end marked by a very faint sulcus passing from behind the beaks to the postero-cardinal margin.

Surface of the shell marked by fine concentric undulations and finer lines of growth.

Formation and locality.—In sandy limestone of Cretaceous age near the mouth of the Judith River, overlying the Fort Pierre shales.

Genus THRACIA, *Leach*.

THRACIA (CORIMYA) GRINNELLI, n. sp.

Plate 2, figs. 6 and 7.

Shell of medium size, transversely broad suboval, nearly equilateral, slightly inequivalve, and apparently a little gaping posteriorly. Basal margin of the shell forming a regular elliptical curve between the points of greatest length; dorsal margin less regular than the basal, slightly contracted behind the beaks; anterior side somewhat rapidly sloping for two-thirds of the distance between the beaks and anterior extremity; extremities sharply rounded, a little less abruptly above than below the middle of the height. Beaks of moderate size, rather broad, slightly projecting above the cardinal line, that of the right valve the largest and extending beyond the left. External ligament small, prominent, and situated close behind the beaks.

Surface of the valves moderately convex, and apparently a little bent in an anterior and posterior direction; the left valve being the most convex. (This is the opposite from what is usually the case.) Valves marked by distinct but irregular and somewhat crowded concentric undulations, and also by a slightly depressed, oblique, somewhat curving sulcus extending from behind the beaks to the postero-basal border, which it scarcely modifies. Internal features and hinge-structure unknown.

The shell bears considerable resemblance to *Thracia Prouti* Meek and Hayden (= *Tellina Prout* M. & H., Proc. A. N. S. Phil., vol. 8, p. 82), but is less contracted posterior to the beaks, and the dorsal margin slopes more rapidly anteriorly, the shell being less full and rounded on this part; the beaks are also larger, and project above the cardinal line more than in that one; the basal line is also more regularly curved, that one rounding upward more strongly in front and less so behind, giving a straighter postero-basal margin.

Formation and locality.—In rocks of Cretaceous age at the mouth of the Judith River, Montana, which overlie the Fort Pierre shales of that locality.

Genus VANIKOROPSIS, Meek.

VANIKOROPSIS TOUMEYANA.

Plate 2, figs. 11-13.

Natica Toumeyana, M. & H., Proc. A. N. S. Phil., vol. viii, p. 270, 1856.
Naticopsis? Toumeyana, M. & H., ib., vol. xii, p. 423.—Meek, Smithsonian Check-List, Invert. Foss., p. 18, 1864.
Vanikoropsis Toumeyana, Meek, Pal. U. S. Geol. Surv. Territ., p. 332, pl. 39, fig. 2.

Shell rather large, naticoid in form, subglobose and a little oblique, composed of about four very ventricose, but not inflated volutions; spire short, depressed, conical, the slope of the spire inclosing an angle of about one hundred and five degrees; suture-line deep and well pronounced; body-volution forming more than two-thirds of the entire height of the shell; aperture broadly oval, rounded, and very slightly extended below, a little straightened on the columellar side, and slightly modified above by the preceding volution; columellar lip thickened and spreading on the body of the preceding volution, and covering but not concealing the umbilicus, or forming a true callus. Umbilicus small and deep.

Surface of the two outer volutions marked by strong, transverse undulations, or ridges, parallel to the margin of the aperture, and numbering about fifteen on the outer whorl; also, by coarse, revolving bands which cross the undulations and have slightly flattened interspaces; four of the bands occupying the space of about one-fourth of an inch on the middle of the outer volution. Substance of the shell very thick and solid.

When describing this species, we had supposed it to be entirely new, not having recognized it in the description of the imperfect individual used by Mr. Meek; but, on seeing his figure above cited, we suspect it may only be a more strongly marked individual of that species, and, although no direct comparison has been made, we do not hesitate to consider it in that light. It differs, however, in being more elevated and in the stronger vertical folds.

Formation and locality.—In beds of Cretaceous age overlying the Fort Pierre shales near the mouth of the Judith River, Montana.

EXPLANATION OF PLATE I.

Crepicephalus (Loganellus) montanensis.

	Page.
Fig. 1. View of the glabella and fixed cheeks partly restored in outline	141
Fig. 2. Profile of the same, showing the elevation of the middle portion	141

Arionellus tripunctatus.

Fig. 3. View of the glabella and fixed cheeks, showing the form and surface-markings	141
Figs. 4 and 5. Left and right movable cheeks of the species	141

Pinna Ludlovi.

Fig. 6. View of the right side of the specimen described, showing the radii, with their characteristic duplications	143
Fig. 7. View of the specimen looking upon the cardinal line, showing the convexity of the shell	143

Myalina (Gervillia) perplana.

Fig. 8. View of the specimen, with the basal portion restored, according to the lines of growth	143

Gryphæa planoconvexa.

Fig. 9. View of a lower valve, retaining a portion of the shell and showing the beak. The lower part of the specimen is wholly an internal cast, and shows the form and position of the muscular impression	142
Fig. 10. View of the under surface of the specimen as seen when separated from the shell of the smaller valve, showing the cartilage-area of the lower valve and the muscular imprint of the smaller one	142

NEW SPECIES OF FOSSILS

Capt. Wm. Ludlow's Exp. to Yellowstone Park, 1875. Plate I.

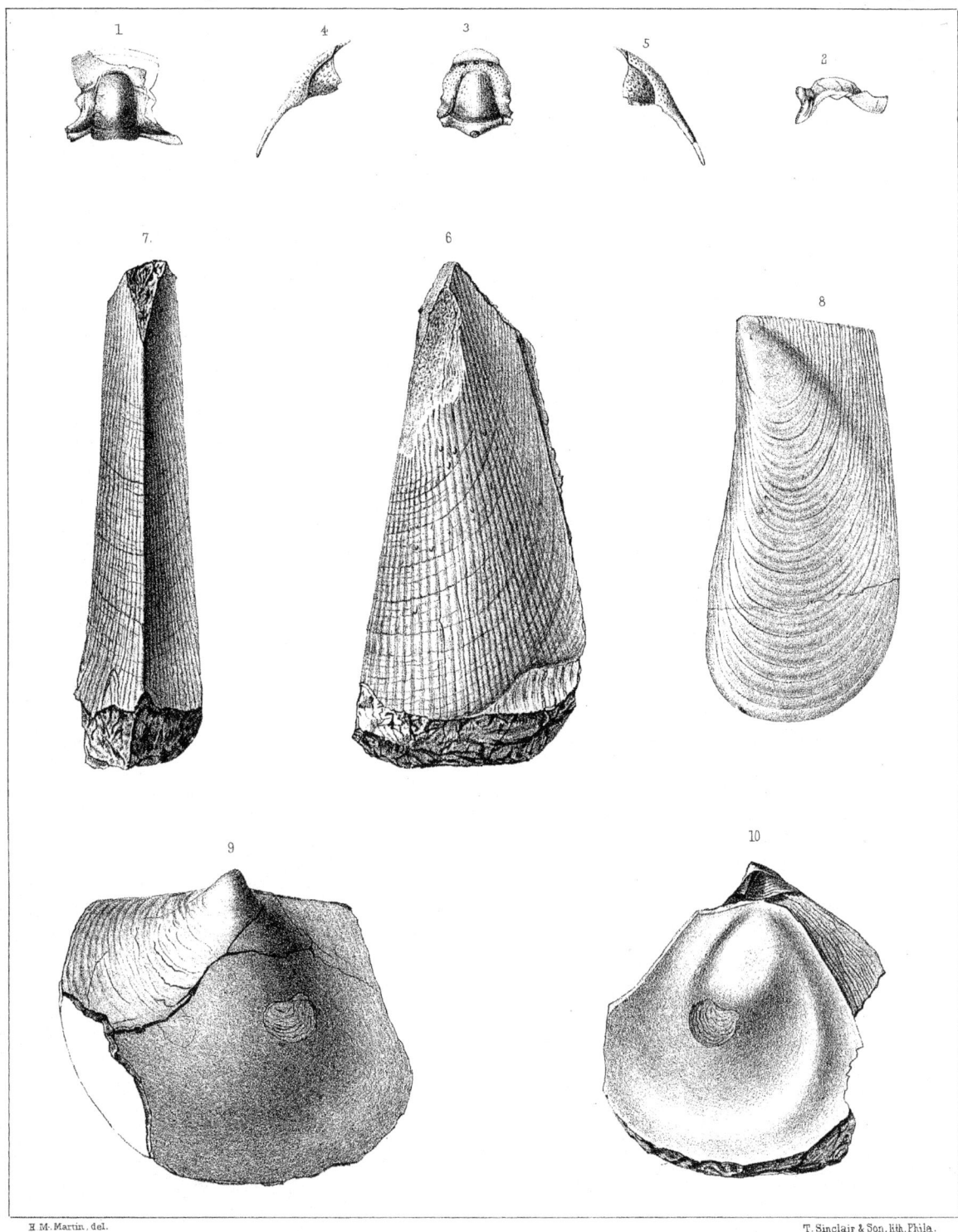

H. M. Martin, del. T. Sinclair & Son, lith. Phila.

EXPLANATION OF PLATE II.

TAPES MONTANENSIS.

	Page.
Fig. 1. View of the left valve, natural size	143
Fig. 2. The same enlarged, showing the nearly obsolete striæ	143

SANGUINOLARIA OBLATA.

Fig. 3. View of a left valve, natural size	144
Fig. 4. View of the same, enlarged to show more distinctly the form	144

MACTRA MAIA.

Fig. 5. View of a left valve, enlarged, showing the general form of the shell, the impression left by the removal of the posterior lateral tooth, and the sinus of the pallial line	144

THRACIA (CORIMYA) GRINNELLI.

Fig. 6. View of the right side of the specimen	144
Fig. 7. Cardinal view of the same, showing the bending of the valves	144

GERVILLIA SPARSILIRATA.

Fig. 8. View of the left side of the specimen described; the posterior end restored in outline	142

GRYPHÆA PLANOCONVEXA.

Fig. 9. Cardinal view of a very convex lower valve, showing the curved beak, which is truncated by attachment to some foreign substance	142
Fig. 10. View of the exterior of same, showing the general form	142

VANIKOROPSIS TOUMEYANA.

Figs. 11 and 12. Views of the opposite sides of the specimen described, showing the characters of the shell; the latter figure showing the aperture as seen on the specimen broken and imperfect	145
Fig. 13. A restored figure, showing what would appear to be the form of the aperture when complete. The umbilicus is shown as seen in the specimen when turned more to the right than in fig. 12	145

NEW SPECIES OF FOSSILS

Capt. Wm. Ludlow's Exp. to Yellowstone Park, 1875.   Plate II

INDEX.

A.

	Page.
Actiturus bartramius	87
Ægialitis montanus	86
vociferus	85, 92
Agelæus phœniceus	78
Alaudidæ	74
Alce americana	69, 91
Alcedinidæ	80
Alcedo alcyon	80
Alkaline deposits	99
Alluvial clays	97
Alluvial deposits	97
Alum Creek	23, 62
American Fork, (Musselshell)	57
American Lanner Falcon	82
American Widgeon	88
Amethyst Mountain	30
Ammonites Halli	101
Ampelidæ	76
Ampelis cedrorum	76
garrulus	76
Analysis of alkali	100
Anas boschas	88
Anatidæ	88
Anchura	101
Anser hyperboreus	88, 92
Antelope	70
Anthus Ludovicianus	74, 91
Antilocapra americana	70, 91
Appearance of country near Carroll	100
Aquila chrysaëtos	83
Archibuteo ferrugineus	83
lagopus sancti-johannis	83, 92
Architectural Geyser	131
Arctic Bluebird	73
Arctic Towhee	78
Arctomys flaviventer	67, 91
Ardea Herodias	87
Ardeidæ	87
Argillitic slate	113
Arionellus tri-punctatus	117, 141
Arkansas Flycatcher	80
Armell's Creek	33, 79
Arrow Creek	124
Artemisia	100
Arvicola riparia	68, 91
Assinaboines	11, 64
Astronomical observations	38–52
Athyris	113, 121, 133
planosulcata	121
subtilita	121
Audubon's Warbler	74
Aulopora	113
Avocet	86

B.

	Page.
Baculites ovatus	101, 126
Badger	66
Bad Lands	13, 73
Baird's Sandpiper	86
Baker, Camp	67, 69, 74, 114
Baker Lake Basin	116
Bald Butte	107
Bank Swallow	75
Barn Swallow	75
Bartramian Sandpiper	87
Bay Lynx	63
Bay-winged Bunting	77
Bear, Black	66
Cinnamon	66
Grizzly	66
Bear's Paw Mountains	55
Beaver	67
Creek	57
Beehive Geyser	26, 131
Benson's Ferry	57
Benton, Fort	9, 12
Berthold, Fort	11, 71
Big Belt Mountains	114
Elk Creek	57
Spring Creek	14, 107
Timber Creek	57
Bighorn	70
Birds	72
Bismarck, Dak	11, 32
Bison	71
Bitter Root Mountains	120
Black Bear	66
Butte	106
Black Hills, Dakota	85
Black-billed Cuckoo	80
Blackbird, White-winged	78
Red-winged	78
Black breasted Woodpecker	80
Blackhead, Lesser	89
Black-tailed Deer	70
Creek	19
Black-throated Bunting	78
Bluebird, Arctic	73
Western	73
Blue Grouse	84
Blue Heron, Great	87
Blue-headed Grakle	78
Blue-winged Teal	89
Bobolink	78
Bohemian Waxwing	76
Bonasa umbellus umbelloides	85, 92
Bos americanus	71, 91
Bottler's ranch	17

INDEX.

	Page.
Bovidæ	71
Box Elder Creek	13, 76, 79
station	13
Bozeman	17, 65, 67
Brackett's Creek	16
Branta canadensis	88, 92
Brewer's Sulphur Spring	114
Bridger Creek	65
Mountains	16, 68, 79
Pass	16, 83, 118
Bridge over Yellowstone	19, 66, 74
Broken Horn	26
Brook, Meadow	19
Browning, Captain	14
Brown Rat	68
Thrush	72
Bryozoan	113
Bubo Virginianus	81
Bucephala albeola	89, 92
Buffalo	63, 71
Creek	109
Heart Mountain	106
Mountain	71
Rapids	35
Bufflehead	89
Buford, Fort	81
Bunting, Black-throated	78
Burrowing Owl	86
Burnt Creek	57
Buteo borealis	82
calurus	82, 92
swainsoni	82, 92
Buzzard, Turkey	83

C.

Calamospiza bicolor	78
Callista Deweyi	126
Camas Creek	114, 115
Camp Baker	15, 115
Cooke	33, 56
Lewis	14, 107
Campophyllum torquium	110, 121
Camptonectes bellistriata	121
extenuatus	121
Canada Goose	88
Lynx	63
Canidæ	63
Canis latrans	64, 90
occidentalis	63, 90
Cañon of Coal Creek	17
Musselshell	84
Yellowstone, Grand	22
Second	18
Caprimulgidæ	80
Carboniferous fossils	119
limestone	107, 110
rocks	133
Carcajou	65
Cardium speciosum	126
Carpodacus cassini	76, 91
Carroll	12, 14, 101
road	11, 15
Cascade Creek	21

	Page.
Cassin's Purple Finch	76
Castle Geyser	26, 132
Castor canadensis	67, 91
Catbird	72
Catamount	63
Cathartes aura	83
Cathartidæ	83
Cedar-bird	76
Centrocercus urophasianus	85
Cervidæ	69
Cervus canadensis	69, 91
macrotis	70, 91
virginianus	70
Ceryle alcyon	92
Chætetes	121
Character of Hopley's Hole	111
Charadriidæ	85
Chaulelasmus streperus	88
Cherry Creek	57
Chestnut-collared Longspur	76
Chickadee, Long-tailed	73
Mountain	73
Chippy Western	77
Chondestes grammaca	78, 91
Chonetes	129, 133
granulifera	121, 129
mesoloba	121
subumbona	129
Chordeiles virginianus henryi	80
Chrysomitris pinus	76
tristis	76
Cinclidæ	72
Cinclus mexicanus	72, 91
Cinnabar Mountain	18
Cinnamon Bear	66
Circus cyaneus hudsonius	81, 92
Cistothorus palustris	74, 91
Claggett's	33, 56
Clark's Crow	79
Clay-colored Sparrow	77
Cliff Swallow	75
Coal Creek	17
"Coal Group"	122, 134
Series"	119
Coccygus erythropthalmus	80
Colaptes	80
auratus	81
mexicanus	81, 92
Cold Spring Creek	57
Collurio ludovicianus excubitoroides	76
Columbidæ	83
Colymbidæ	90
Colymbus torquatus	90
Common Dove	83
Common Wild Goose	88
Concretions at Crooked Creek	101
Cone Butte	71, 82, 104
Contopus borealis	92
virens richardsonii	80, 92
Cooper, Dr	84
Cooper's Hawk	82
Coot	88
Copperopolis	15, 113

INDEX.

	Page.
Copper-ore	114
Corals	133
Corvidæ	79
Corvus americanus	79
corax	79
Cottonwood Creek	16, 109
Coturniculus passerinus perpallidus	77
Cotyle riparia	75
Cow Bunting	78
Coyote	64
Crane, Sandhill	87
Crassatella	122
vadosa	122
Crater of Old Faithful	26
Crazy Woman's Mountains	57
Crepicephalus (Loganellus) montanensis	117, 141
Cretaceous clays	97
No. 4	99, 134
No. 5	103, 134
No. 6	127, 135
Crooked Creek	13, 64, 101
Crossbill, Red	76
Crow	79
agency, old	57
Crow, Clark's	79
Crows	14, 15, 64
Cryptonella	107
Crystals of gypsum	99
Cuculidæ	80
Curlew, Long-billed	87
Cyanospiza amœna	78, 91
Cyanurus cristatus	79
stelleri macrolophus	79, 92
Cyathophylloid coral	110, 121
Cygnus buccinator	88, 92
Cynomys ludovicianus	67
Cystiphyllum	121

D.

Dafila acuta	88, 92
Daisy Dean Creek	15
Dana, E. S.	9, 97
Dawson, G. M., report of	136
Deep Creek	15, 114
Deer, Black-tailed	70
Mule	70
Red	70
White-tailed	70
Deer Creek, White-tailed	73, 115
Dendrœca œstiva	74
audubonii	74, 91
Deposits, alluvial	97
Descriptions of new fossils	141
Desert, Idaho	21
Destruction of geyser craters	26
Devil's Slide	18
Workshop	23
Dinosaurs	135
Dipper	72, 89
Distances on Missouri River from Bismarck to Benton	53
Distribution of the formations	132
Diver, Great Northern	90

	Page.
Dog River	55
Dolichonyx oryzivorus	78
Dove, Common	83
Turtle	83
Downy Woodpecker	81
Drift near Missouri River	101, 135
Duck, Gray	88
Pin-tail	88
White-winged Surf	89
Duck Creek	57
route	15
Duck Hawk	82
Dusky Grouse	86

E.

Eagle, Golden	83
White-headed	83
Eastern Montana	89
East Gallatin Range	118
Ectopistes migratoria	83
Elephant's Back	20
Elk	69
Creek, Big	57
Little	57
Range	113
Ellis, Fort	16, 130
Elotherium	116
Emigrant Peak	17, 82
Empidonax pusillus	92
Eporeodon	116
Eremophila alpestris leucolæma	74
Erithizon epixanthus	69, 91
Euomphalus	121
Euspiza americana	78

F.

Falco columbarius (?) richardsonii	82
communis anatum	82, 92
laniarius polyagrus	82
sparverius	82, 92
Falcon, American Launer	82
Richardson's	82
Falconidæ	81
Falls of the Yellowstone	26
Lower	21, 72
Upper	22, 73
Fan Geyser	29
Feldspar	105
Felidæ	63
Felis concolor	63
Ferruginous Hawk	83
Fiber zibethicus	68
Finch, Cassin's Purple	76
Grass	77
Lark	78
Lazuli	78
Pine	76
Firehole River	25
Valley	66
Fish-hawk	83
Flathead Creek	118, 123, 134
Pass	134
Fleshman's Creek	57

	Page.
Flicker	81
Flycatcher, Arkansas	80
Say's	80
Forks of the Musselshell	83
Fort Benton	9
Berthold	11
Buford	11, 81
Ellis	16, 130
Peck	11, 13, 80
Shaw	11
Stevenson	11, 65
Pierre Group	99
fossils of	101
Union Group	135
"Fossil Ferns"	102
Fish"	102
Fossils, invertebrate	96
vertebrate	96
Fox Hills Group	103, 104, 134
Fox, Kit	64
Prairie	64
Swift	64
Freeman, Maj. H	15, 76
Fringillidæ	76
Fulica americana	88
Fuligula affinis	89
Fusus Galpinianus	103

G.

	Page.
Gadwall	88
Galeocerdo	112
Gallatin River, Middle Fork	58
Valley	15, 120
Gallinago wilsonii	86
Game, destruction of	59
Gap, Judith	64, 111
Gardiner's Falls	19
River	18, 68
Springs	17, 83, 86
General conclusions	132
report	9
Geological report	95
Geothlypis philadelphia macgillivrayi	75
trichas	74, 91
Gervillia erecta	121
sparsalirata	121, 142
Geyser Basin, Lower	25, 80, 86, 130
Upper	12, 16, 25, 131
Geysers of Yellowstone Park	130
Giant	26, 132
Giantess	26, 131
Giant's Thumb	18
Glauconome	129
Golden-crowned Thrush	74
Golden Eagle	83
Golden-winged Woodpecker	81, 95
Goniaphea melanocephala	91
Goosander	89
Goose, Canada	88
Common Wild	88
Snow	88
Gopher	68
Grakle, Blue-headed	78
Grand Cañon of Yellowstone	22

	Page.
Grand Geyser	26, 131
Granitic rocks	132
Grass Finch	77
Gray Duck	88
Jay	79
Wolf	63
Great Blue Heron	87
Horned Owl	81
Northern Diver	90
Yellowshanks	87
Grebe, Horned	90
Pied-billed	90
Greene, F. V	9
Green-winged Teal	89
Grinnell, George Bird	9, 62, 97
Grizzly Bear	66
Gros Ventres of the Prairie	64
Grotto Geyser	25, 132
Ground Squirrel, Missouri	67
Richardson's	67
Grouse, Blue	84
Dusky	84
Rocky Mountain Ruffed	85
Sage	85
Sharp-tailed	85
Gruidæ	87
Grus canadensis	87, 92
Gryphæa	112, 122
planoconvexa	121, 142
Gulch, Emigrant	45
Gull, Ring-billed	90
Gulo luscus	90

H.

	Page.
Hadrosaurus	125, 135
Haliaëtus leucocephalus	83
Hancock, Mount	20
Hare, Prairie	66
Harporhynchus rufus	73
Harris's Woodpecker	80
Hawk, Cooper's	82
Duck	82
Ferruginous	83
Fish	83
Marsh	81
Red-tailed	82
Rough-legged	83
Sharp-shinned	82
Sparrow	82
Swainson's	82
Western Red-tailed	82
Hayden, Dr. F. V	9, 18
Haymaker's Creek	15, 111
Height of Lower Falls	22
plateau at Carroll	100
Upper Falls	21
Helena, Mont	13, 15
Helena road	100
Heron, Great Blue	87
Hesperomys	67
leucopus sonoriensis	68, 91
Hills, Sweet Grass	71
Hirundinidæ	75
Hirundo horreorum	75, 91
thalassina	75, 91

INDEX. 151

	Page.
Hooded Merganser	89
Hopley's Hole	15, 111
Hornblende	105
Horned doe-antelopes barren	70
Grebe	90
Owl, Great	81
Lark	74
Hot Spring Creek	57
House Mouse	68
Wren, Western	73
Humphreys, Mount	14, 20
Hystricidæ	69

I.

Icteria virens	75
Icteridæ	78
Icterus bullockii	91
Idaho Desert	21
Inoceramus	101, 103, 122
tenuilineatus	101

J.

Jamestown, Dak	76
Jay, Gray	79
Long-crested	79
Jay Creek	29
Jones, Captain	9, 18
Judith Bad Lands	55, 124
Basin	9, 14
Gap	14, 64, 111
Mountains	14, 70, 87, 103
River	14, 64
Jumping Mouse	68
Junco oregonus	77, 91
Jurassic	119, 133

K.

Killdeer Plover	85
Kingbird	80
Kingfisher	80
Kit Fox	64

L.

Lagomys princeps	91
Lake, Yellowstone	24
Lamna	112
Laniidæ	76
Lanner Falcon, American	82
Laridæ	90
Lark Finch	78
Lark, Horned	74
Shore	74
Western Meadow	78
Larus delawarensis	90, 92
Lazuli Finch	78
Least Sandpiper	86
Leporidæ	69
Lepus artemisia	69
bairdi	91
campestris	69
Lesser Blackhead	89
Yellowlegs	87
Letters of transmittal	9, 62, 96
Lewis, Camp	14, 107

	Page.
Lewis' Woodpecker	81
Liberty Cap	18
Lion, Mountain	63
Liopistha (Cymella) undata	103, 126
List of Mammals and Birds	63
Little Belt Mountains	14, 84, 111
Crooked Creek	13, 72, 80, 101
Missouri	65
Rocky Mountains	33, 127
Rocky Creek	34, 128
Timber Creek	57
Trout Creek	109
Lobipes hyperboreus	86
Long-billed Curlew	87
Marsh Wren	74
Long-crested Jay	79
Longspur, Chestnut-collared	76
Maccown's	77
Long-tailed Chicadee	73
Loon	90
Louisiana Tanager	75
Lower Falls	73
Loxia curvirostra americana	76, 91
Lucina occidentalis	101
ventricosa	101
Ludlow, Edwin	10
Col. Wm	8, 62, 96
Lunatia concinna	103, 126
Lutra canadensis	65
Lynx, Bay	63
Canada	63
Lynx canadensis	63, 90
rufus	63, 90

M.

Maccown's Longspur	77
Mackinac boat	9, 33, 35
Mactra sp	101
maia	103, 144
Warreniana	103, 126
Madison River, East Fork of	25
Magpie	79
Mallard	88
Mammals, list of	63
Mammoth Hot Springs	17
Mandans	11
Mareca americana	88
Marsh, O. C	96
Marsh Hawk	81
Marsh-Wren, Long-billed	74
Marten	65
Martin, Purple	75
Sand	75
Maryland Yellowthroat	74
Meadow Brook	20
Meadow Lark, Western	78
Medicine Peak	57
Meeting of the Three Waters	120
Melanerpes erythrocephalus	81, 92
torquatus	81, 92
Melospiza melodia fallax	77
Mephitis bicolor	90
mephitica	65, 90

INDEX.

	Page.
Merganser, Hooded	89
Mergus cucullatus	89
merganser	89, 92
Merriam, C. H.	61, 88, 90
Merychyus	116
Mimus carolinensis	72, 91
Mink	65
Miocene Tertiary	115
Missouri Ground Squirrel	66
River, alluvial deposits of	97
Sky-lark	74
Molothrus pecoris	78, 91
Moose	69
Moss Agate Springs	116, 117
Motacillidæ	74
Mount Hancock	20
Humphreys	20
Sheridan	20
Washburne	20
Mountain Buffalo	71
Chickadee	73
Lion	63
Mocking-bird	72
Plover	86
Sheep	70
Mountain-elevation, period of	137
Mountains, Bear's Paw	13, 55
Big Belt	115
Bitter Root	120
Crazy Woman's	57, 120
Judith	14, 70, 103
Little Belt	14, 84, 110
Rocky	33, 127
Snowy	15, 109
Sweet Grass	71, 79
Yellowstone	57
Mourning Warbler, Western	74
Mouse, House	68
Jumping	68
Meadow	68
Western White-footed	68
Mud-geysers	23
Mud-hen	88
Mud-puffs	131
Mule Deer	70
Muridæ	68
Mus decumanus	68
musculus	68
Muskrat	68
Musselshell River, cañon of	84, 111
forks of	83, 112
north fork of	112
Mustela americana	65, 90
Mustelidæ	65
Myacites (Pleuromya) subcompressa	121, 142
Myalina (Gervillia) perplana	121, 143
Myiodioctes pusillus	91

N.

Narica crassa	126
National Park	69
Neocorys spraguei	74
Newland Creek	114
Nisus cooperi	81
fuscus	81, 92

	Page.
Northern California	84
Northern Diver, Great	90
Phalarope	86
North Fork of the Musselshell	112
Norton's Creek	123
Numenius longirostris	87
Nycticejus crepuscularis	90

O.

Obolella	117
Œdemia fusca	89, 92
Old Faithful	26, 131
Olive-backed Thrush	72
Oregon	84
snow-bird	77
Oreodon	112
Oreoscoptes montanus	72, 91
Orthoceras	107
Orthoclase	105
Ostrea	112
congesta	103, 110, 113, 121
Otter	65, 68
Otus palustris	81
Otus vulgaris wilsonianus	92
Ovidæ	70
Ovis montana	70, 91
Owl, Burrowing	81
Great Horned	81
Short-eared	81

P.

Paint Pots	25, 131
Pandion haliaëtus	83, 92
Panopæa occidentalis	122
Paridæ	73
Park, National	63
Partial list of Mammals and Birds	90
Parus atricapillus septentrionalis	73, 91
montanus	73, 91
Pass, Bridger	82
Passenger Pigeon	83
Peck, Fort	80
Pediœcetes phasianellus columbianus	85
Pelican Creek	24
Pelican, White	89
Pelicanidæ	89
Pelicanus trachyrhynchus	89, 92
Period of mountain-elevation	137
Perisoreus canadensis capitalis	79, 92
Petrochelidon lunifrons	75, 91
Phalarope, Northern	86
Phalaropodidæ	86
Pholadomya	122
subventricosa	126
Pica melanoleuca hudsonica	79, 91
Picicorvus columbianus	79, 91
Picidæ	80
Picoides arcticus	92
americanus dorsalis	92
Picus pubescens	81, 92
villosus harrisii	80, 92
Pied-billed Grebe	90
Pigeon, Passenger	83
Pigeon Hawk	82
Pine Finch	76

	Page.
Pinna Ludlovi	113, 143
Pintail Duck	88
Pipilo chlorurus	91
maculatus arctica	78
Platycrinus	121
Plectrophanes maccowni	76
ornatus	77
Pliocene Tertiary	115
Plover, Killdeer	85
Mountain	86
Upland	87
Podiceps cornutus	90, 92
Podicipidæ	90
Podilymbus podiceps	90
Point, Wolf	80, 85
Porcupine, Yellow-haired	69
Potsdam	132
limestone	114
Prairie Dog	67
Fox	64
Hare	69
Squirrel, Striped	67
Wolf	64
Presilurian rocks	132
Primordial series	132
Procyon lotor	66
Productus	129, 133
cora	121
costatus	121
multistriata	110, 113
muricatus	113
Nebrascensis	121
Prattenanus	113, 121
punctatus	113, 121
semireticulatus	113
Wortheni	110
Profile-section from Carroll to Cone Butte	102
Little Rocky Mountains	127
Progne subis	75
Prong-horned Antelope	70
Punch Bowl	26
Purple Finch, Cassin's	76
Martin	75
Putorius pusillus	90
vison	65
Pyramid	26
Pyranga ludoviciana	75, 91

Q.

Quadersandstein	107
Quartz	105, 113
Quaternary	135
Querquedula carolinensis	89
discors	89

R.

Raccoon	66
Rallidæ	88
Rat, Brown	68
Raven	79
Recommendations relative to National Park	36
Recurvirostra americana	86, 92
Recurvirostridæ	86
Red clays	107

	Page.
Red Crossbill	76
Deer	70
Squirrel	66
Red-headed Woodpecker	81
Red-shafted Woodpecker	81
Redstart	75
Red-tailed Hawk	82
Western	82
Red-winged Blackbird	78
Rees	11
Regulus calendulus	91
Remarks on alluvial deposits	97
Indian forays	32
Report, general	9
geological	97
of a reconnaissance to Judith River	55
zoological	59
Reynolds, Charles	10, 70
Rhinoceros	116
Rhynchonella	133
osagensis	121
Ricebird	78
Richardson's Falcon	82
Ring-Billed Gull	90
Riverside Geyser	29
Robin	72
Rock Wren	73
Rocky Cañon Creek	17
Rocky Mountain Ruffed Grouse	85
Roe, Lieut. C. F	96
Ross's Cut-off	106
Fork	14, 109
Rough-legged Hawk	83
Ruffed Grouse, Rocky Mountain	85

S.

Saccomyidæ	68
Sage Grouse	85
Rabbit	69
Salpinctes obsoletus	73
Sandhill Crane	87
Sand Martin	75
Sandpiper, Baird's	86
Bartramian	87
Least	86
Solitary	87
Spotted	87
Sanguinolaria oblata	103, 144
Savannah Sparrow	77
Sawmill Geyser	132
Saxicolidæ	73
Sayornis sayus	80
Say's Flycatcher	80
Scaphites larvæformis	122
nodosus	101
Schizodus	110
Rossicus	110
Sciuridæ	66
Sciurus hudsonius	66, 90
Scolecophagus cyanocephalus	78
Section across Hopley's Hole	111
from Carroll to Cone Butte	102
Little Rocky Mountains	127
of cañon below Lower Falls	23
Seiurus aurocapillus	74

INDEX.

	Page.
Selenite crystals	99
Sentinel Geyser	29
Setophaga ruticilla	75
Sharp-shinned Hawk	80, 92
Sharp-tailed Grouse	85
Shaw, Fort	9, 13
Shields River	16, 57, 118, 121
Shore Lark	74
Short-eared Owl	81
Shoveler	89
Shrike, White-rumped	76
Sialia arctica	73, 91
Silurian	113
rocks, primordial series	132
Sioux	14, 103
Sitta carolinensis aculeata	73, 91
Sittidæ	73
Sitting Bull	11
Sixteen-mile Creek	16, 118
Skunk	65
Skunk-bear	65
Sky-lark, Missouri	74
Slaughter of game	61
Slender-billed Nuthatch	73
Smith's River	15
Snipe, Wilson's	86
Snowbird, Oregon	77
Snow Goose	88
Mountains	109
Soda Mountain	23
Solitary Sandpiper	87
Song Sparrow, Western	77
Sparrow, Clay-colored	77
Savannah	77
Tree	77
Western Song	77
White-crowned	77
Yellow-winged	77
Sparrow Hawk	82
Spatula clypeata	80
Spermophilus Richardsonii	67
13-*lineatus*	67
Townsendi	91
Sphæriola moreauensis	126
Spheotyto cunicularia hypogæa	81
Sphyrapicus thyroideus	81, 92
Spirifera	133
centronata	107, 108, 110, 121, 129
(*Martinia*) *lineata*	107
Spiriferina Kentuckensis	110, 121
Spizella monticola	77
pallida	77
socialis arizonæ	77, 91
Spotted Sandpiper	87
Square Butte	55
Squirrel, Missouri Ground	66
Pine	66
Red	66
Richardson's	67
Striped Prairie	67
Steamboat Point	24
Stevenson, Fort	65
Stictopora	108, 110
Storm on Mount Washburne	30

	Page.
Streptorhynchus	133
crassus	121
Keokuk	110
Strigidæ	81
Sturnella magna neglecta	78
Suggestion relative to National Park	36
Sulphur Springs	23
Summer Yellowbird	74
Summit Creek	57
Surf Duck, White-winged	89
Surface-drift in Judith Gap	111
Surnia ulula hudsonia	92
Swallow, Bank	75
Barn	75
Cliff	75
Violet-green	75
Swan, Trumpeter	88
Sweet Grass Creek	57
Hills	71, 79
Swift Fox	64
Sylvicolidæ	74
Syringopora mult-attenuata	108, 121

T.

Tamias quadrivittatus	66, 90
Tanager, Louisiana	75
Tanagridæ	75
Tapes montanensis	103, 143
Taxidea americana	66
Teal, Blue-winged	89
Green-winged	89
Tellina (*Arcopagia*) *subulata*	126
Utahensis	126
Tellina scitula	103, 126
Telltale	87
Terebratula	107
Tertiary	115, 135
fossils	116
Tetons	20
Tetrao obscurus	84, 92
Tetraonidæ	84
Thistlebird	76
Thomomys talpoidis	68, 91
Thompson, Lieut. R. E	9, 55
Thomson, Prof. James	98
Thracia (*Corimya*) *Grinnellii*	126, 144
Thrasher	72
Three Forks	116
Peaks	31
Thrush, Brown	72
Golden-crowned	74
Olive-backed	72
Thymallus	114
Timber Wolf	63
Titlark	74
Totanus flavipes	87, 92
melanoleucus	87, 92
semipalmatus	86, 92
solitarius	87, 92
Tower Creek	20, 81
Falls	20
Trachyte	105, 108
Trail Creek	17, 84
Tree Sparrow	77

INDEX.

	Page.
Trilobites	117
Tringa bairdii	86, 92
minutilla	86
Tringoides macularius	87
Trionyx	125
Troglodytes aëdon parkmanni	73, 91
Troglodytidæ	73
Trout	20
Trout Creek	107
Trumpeter Swan	88
Turban	27
Turdidæ	72
Turdus migratorius	72
swainsoni	72, 91
Turkey Buzzard	83
Turk's Head	27
Turtle Dove	83
Turtles	116
Twining, Capt. Wm. J	9
Tyrannidæ	80
Tyrannus carolinensis	80, 92
verticalis	80

U.

United States Boundary Commission	9
Union Pass	134
Unios	135
Upland Plover	87
Upper Falls of the Yellowstone	72
Geyser Basin	87, 131
Ursidæ	66
Ursus americanus	66, 90
horribilis	66, 90

V.

Vandalism of visitors to National Park	26
Vanikoropsis Toumeyana	145
Vespertilio lucifugus	90
yumanensis	90
Violet-green Swallow	75
Vulpes alopex macrurus	64
velox	64

W.

Warbler, Audubon's	74
Western Mourning	75
Yellow	74
Wanton destruction of curiosities in Geyser Basins	36
Warm Spring Creek	33
Washburne Mountain	21
Washings at Emigrant Gulch	31
Water Ouzel	72
Waxwing, Bohemian	76
Western Bluebird	73
Chippy	77
House Wren	73
Meadow Lark	78
Mourning Warbler	75
Night Hawk	80
Red-tail Hawk	82
Song Sparrow	77
White-footed Mouse	68

	Page.
Western Woodchuck	67
Wood Pewee	80
Whistling of Elk	69
White Pelican	89
White-crowned Sparrow	77
White-footed Mouse, Western	68
White-headed Eagle	83
White-rumped Shrike	76
White-tailed Deer	70
Creek	115
White-winged Blackbird	78
Surf Duck	89
Whitfield, R. P	8, 96
Wild Cat	63
Widgeon	88
Wild Goose	88
Willet	86
Wilson's Snipe	86
Wolf, Gray	63
Prairie	64
Timber	63
Wolfing	64
Wolf Point	12, 80, 85
Wolverene	65
Wood, W. H	10
Woodchuck, Western	67
Woodpecker, Black-breasted	81
Downy	81
Golden-winged	81
Harris's	80
Lewis's	81
Red-headed	81
Red-shafted	81
Wren, Long-billed Marsh	74
Rock	73
Western House	73
Wyoming	61

Y.

Yellow slates underlying Tertiary	116
Lake	24
Yellow Warbler	74
Yellowbird	76
Yellowbird, Summer	74
Yellow-breasted Chat	75
Yellow-haired Porcupine	69
Yellowlegs, Lesser	87
Yellowshanks, Greater	87
Yellowstone Mountains	57
Park	9, 63, 66, 79, 84, 87
River	11, 79, 82, 86
Yellowthroat, Maryland	74
Yellow-winged Sparrow	77

Z.

Zaphrentis	133
centralis	108, 110, 113
Zapus hudsonius	68, 91
Zenædura carolinensis	83
Zonotrichia leucophrys	77, 91
intermedia	91
Zoological report	60

Printed in Dunstable, United Kingdom